MARADONA

MARADONA

THE AUTOBIOGRAPHY OF SOCCER'S GREATEST AND MOST CONTROVERSIAL STAR

Diego Armando Maradona

With Daniel Arcucci and Ernesto Cherquis Bialo

Translated by Marcela Mora Y Araujo

SKYHORSE PUBLISHING

2758417

www.skyhorsepublishing.com

10 9 8 7 6 5 4 3 2 1

ISBN-13: 978-1-60239-027-0
ISBN-10: 1-60239-027-4

The Library of Congress Cataloging-in-Publication data is available on file.

Printed in the United States of America

To Dalma Nerea and Gianinna Dinorah Maradona
To my parents, Don Diego and La Tota
To my wife, La Claudia
To my brothers, Lalo and Turco
To my sisters, Ana, Kity, Lili, Mary and Caly
To my friend, Guillermo Cóppola
And to all the footballers of the world

To Fidel Castro and, through him, all the Cuban people
To Rodrigo
To Carlos Menem

To all my nephews and nieces

To all Los Cebollitas
To all of Fiorito
To the Neapolitans
To all the fans of Boca
To the people of La Quiaca
To Francis Cornejo

To Caniggia and his sons
To Marito Kempes
To Claudio Husain, Turu Flores, Turco Asad and Rifle
    Pandolfi
To the memory of Juan Funes
To Julio Grondona

To Ciro Ferrara
To Salvatore Bagni
To Rivelinho

To Agustín Pichot
To the volleyball team

To Emiliano Díaz, Ramón's son
To the lawyers who got my friend out of prison
To Carlos
To Salvatore Carmando
To Quique and to Gabriel

To Los Piojos
To Charly and to Calamaro
To Gabriel
To Omar
To Leo
To Fede Ribero and Andrea Burstein
To all the kids from Tortugas
To Cristian from Las Cañitas

To Dr Oliva
To Dr Lentini
To Ciego Signorini
To Renegado Vilamitjana

To Negro Avila
To Costy Vigil
To Shaquille O'Neal, Michael Jordan and the twin towers of San
    Antonio

Finally, to my heart and to God

Contents

Introduction

In the autumn of 1996 I was among dozens of journalists waiting for Diego Maradona to give a press conference. He was in London for a Puma promotion and when he entered the room the usual flurry of activity ensued. Suddenly I heard someone call my name and before I realised what was happening an arm was guiding me to the table where Maradona sat; I was to be his interpreter.

I handled it quite well until someone asked a question in Spanish. Without thinking, as if on automatic pilot, I turned to Diego and repeated the question in English. He laughed, patted my head, and said with the slightest raise of an eyebrow: 'I can understand Spanish.'

I have been writing about Argentina and its football and footballers for an English audience for almost fifteen years. Trying to explain *us* to *you* has been my objective – from the cultural significance of the game to the interpretation of the rules both on and off the pitch, from the codes of hooliganism in each country to the subtleties influencing the elite players' game, always working on the premise that despite the many differences in tactics, technical style and speed it is actually the similarities between both countries in their love and respect for the game that are the most interesting. As Jorge Valdano so aptly puts it, England vs. Argentina is the one game where the Mexican wave doesn't stand a chance. For us both, it is too serious a matter.

Naturally, Diego Maradona has been the focus of my attention time and time again. That press conference was neither the first nor the last time we have been face to face. I first met him while he was still playing, although his glory years were over by then. However, I belong to the generation that grew up watching him on the pitch. We weren't told he was the best in the world; we actually saw him in action. A lifelong Boca Juniors fan – like my father and my grandfather before me – I was a teenager experiencing the buzz of the terraces the season Diego helped us pick up the cup. Getting up at ungodly hours with my school friends in order to watch the 1979 Youth World Cup is one of my earliest memories of adolescence. I saw every minute of every subsequent World Cup match he played. By the time I finally met him personally, almost ten years ago, I had accumulated a debt of countless moments of joy and national pride, like my fellow countrymen.

Professionally too I am indebted to him. Hanging out with him for a couple of days in Paris, in 1995, resulted in my first cover story for a national glossy. Subsequently, being a Maradona 'expert' has awakened the interest of publications as far afield as Japan, Mexico, Israel and Holland. Once, a Dutchman told me he thought *that* second goal in 1986 was the only miracle of the twentieth century. He was dead serious. I remember researching a story while working for the BBC World Service when he was kicked out of the 1994 World Cup: several hundred people in Bangladesh had attempted mass suicide as a result.

It is impossible to overestimate the scope and intensity of Maradona's popularity, and the range of sometimes contradictory emotions he evokes. Nowhere more so than in Argentina, where his place in the collective national psyche is worthy of lengthy volumes of analysis. From god to political manoeuvrer, from saint to machiavellian drug abuser, from villain to victim and back, every possible interpretation has been covered somewhere along the line. Even in England Maradona stirs extreme reactions. Despite the bitter aftertaste left behind by his hand-ball in 1986, the general public continues to vote the second goal in the same match the best ever scored in a World Cup. When FIFA recently decided to name the best footballer ever they had to hand out two awards; one for officialdom's choice: Pelé. The other went to the people's choice: Maradona.

Diego Maradona, the genius who would blow a million-dollar meeting if he felt like it, the rebel from the slums who travels without a tie, the archetypal hero from a millennium fairytale, has never been afraid of speaking his *feelings*, let alone his mind. He's a crazy little giant who dices with death and toboggans into hell on a daily basis, since for him *any* compromise is just too painful. But the years have gone by, and taken their toll on his body; his resilience has diminished.

In April 2004, just as this translation was coming to an end, Maradona collapsed with arterial hypertension. He was admitted to an intensive care unit in a Buenos Aires hospital. Fans mounted an impromptu vigil outside the hospital while the world's news wires went into overdrive; the people of southern Italy lit candles in makeshift shrines and offered prayers for their hero. His condition was broadcast to the world in the form of daily medical reports. Reportedly, when it was rumoured he might need a heart transplant there were offers of donations . . .

He did not die and his own heart is still beating inside him. A few years ago, during another of Maradona's scandalous outbursts, it was once again Jorge Valdano who found the words to convey his ordeal. 'Poor old Diego,' wrote Valdano. 'For so many years we have told him repeatedly, "You're a God", "You're a star", "You're our salvation", that we forgot to tell him the most important thing: "You're a man".'

In this autobiography it is the man who finally speaks.

The complexity of translating Maradona is manifold. On the one hand, as befits one of the greatest geniuses of our time,

Maradona has a unique use of language. Born and raised in poverty, he has never abandoned the jargon of the streets. His narrative is peppered with the dialect known in Argentina as *lunfardo*, a repertoire of terms brought into the country mostly by Italian immigrants before the First World War, fused with words of peasant origin, and some indigenous terminology. Adopted at first by the working classes and to a large extent by prisoners, so that the guards wouldn't understand what they were saying, *lunfardo* typically inverts syllables. It became the language of the tango par excellence but nowadays it is as commonplace among the literati and the jet set as it is among the slum dwellers. Translating these words posed the first of many dilemmas. One option would be to pick similar slang terms in English but there came a point where Maradona's discourse started to read more like a cross between *My Fair Lady* and *Lock, Stock & Two Smoking Barrels* . . . a strangely foreign cockney rhyming slang. It was decided that, to retain the sense of Maradona's voice, some of these might best be served by being left in the original Spanish.

'*Bronca*' is a case in point. *Bronca*, probably derived from inverting the Spanish '*cabrón*', is a very Argentinian word to denote anger, fury, hatred, resentment, bitter discontent . . . For Diego Maradona it is the most familiar of emotions, and he is constantly referring to it as his motivator, his fuel, his driving force.

Argentinian expressions such as '*chau*' and '*viejo*' have also been left in the original Spanish form. *Chau*, from the Italian '*ciao*', is frequently used in the same way as 'end of story' or 'that's all'. *Viejo* means 'old man' but its colloquial usage is equivalent to 'mate'. It is a very Argentinian way of speaking, and so it seemed right to preserve the original term throughout.

I have done the opposite with several curious expressions which have been entirely made up by Maradona himself. Although they are not common usage in Argentina, people tend to understand what he's saying when he's saying them. (That said, when I've quoted them in isolation professional translators and football fans alike have reacted with puzzled blankness.) I have translated these literally in the hope of getting across a certain style which is peculiar to Maradona's way of speech, believing they will have the same effect on English-speaking readers as they do on their Spanish-speaking counterparts. The first use startles, but by the end of the book it is so obvious what he's saying – there is no other way to say it:

Vaccinate – literally meaning to inject or jab, Maradona uses it in the same way as 'fuck', both literally and figuratively. Thus, if he vaccinates a woman he has had sex with her and if he vaccinates an opponent he has scored a goal;
Thermos-head – someone who is stupid or slow;
Take the cat's milk – this is generally used in a sense similar to 'take the piss', or 'be out of order'. It also suggests stealing, doing something illegal;
Let the tortoise get away – this suggests someone who has reacted slowly, been not with it, not on the ball;
Give the dog its face back – someone who is dog-faced, disqualified from or lacking in authority to pass comment.

Above all else, Diego Maradona is the greatest footballer who has ever lived. His reading of the game is amazing – unique – and his ability to see everything that is going on on the pitch as if from above is uncanny. His descriptions of every move, every detail of every passage of play he has been involved in, or seen, are expert, accurate, and concise. Translating these has been the greatest challenge and I have tried to avoid leaving words in the original Spanish. However, there are times when the descriptive richness of Argentinian football terminology has no English equivalent. I have drawn on the help of many fellow football lovers in the hope of conveying as precisely as possible what Maradona tells us. I have asked footballers to physically show me the action described, then demonstrated the same move to English writers. Sometimes the reply has been, 'We don't have an English word for that, probably because no player here can do it.'

Translating Maradona has been a strange journey into the language of football and, in so far as language reflects thought, into the mind of the greatest talent I have known.

The Argentinian writer Juan Sasturain says Maradona is an artist, because he didn't interpret but rather, like all great poets and painters, he created something where there was nothing. His rags-to-riches-to-hell story is as full of drama, suspense and excitement as the greatest works of fiction. His storytelling is informal, hilarious, and almost poetic. I have tried to remain as faithful to that voice as possible in the hope of conveying its uniqueness. Alas, it may be well the case, as Robert Frost claims, that poetry is what's lost in translation.

I am indebted to Klaus Gallo, Alejandro 'El Huevo' Figueroa, Julia Napier, Pedro Arnt, Laurence Allan, Nick Hornby, Alex Aberg-Cobo, Esteban Nofal, Facundo Sava, Juan Sebastian 'La Brujita' Verón, Daniel Arcucci, Ariel Scher, Robert 'El Chango' Newman, Mercedes Guiraldes, Georgia Garrett, Rachel Cugnoni and Beth Coates for their part. And to Giles and Sebastian for everything.

Marcela Mora Y Araujo
London, July 2004

Reader's Note

The names of the main football tournaments in each country have been kept in their original languages. Hence, Serie A and *scudetto* in Italy, La Liga and Copa del Rey in Spain, and so on.

Argentinian Football

In Argentina, when Maradona started playing, the main local tournament was the Metropolitano, which was played among the Buenos Aires clubs plus a cluster of the main clubs from other provinces. The season started around February and ended in August. In the second half of the year the Nacional was played, a nationwide competition which finished in December. In the mid-'80s the Nacional was abolished, and the Metropolitano included more teams from round the country.

From 1991, and by the time Maradona ended his career playing for Boca Juniors, the main league was divided into two halves, the Apertura and the Clausura. The Clausura is played in the first half of the year and the Apertura in the latter part of the year. Both winners qualify for the Copa Libertadores, South America's answer to the Champions League.

During the summer break, usually between early December

and late February, what's known as 'summer tournaments' are played. They usually take place in beach resorts and other cities away from the capital, and they are quasi-friendlies. But they serve as pre-season training for the teams and are an important source of revenue for the clubs.

Argentinian club football has nine youth divisions: ninth, eighth, seventh, sixth, fifth, fourth, third, reserves – there is no second – and then first. Roughly, British equivalents would be under-15s (ninth), Under-17s (reserves), etc. Children under the age of fourteen may be attached to a club, but they cannot play in the ninth division until their fourteenth birthday.

The Copa América is the South American equivalent of the European Championships. Until the late 1980s it took place every four years. Since then it has been held every two years.

Footballing Terminology

Barra brava: Organised gangs of violent fans. Literally, 'tough gangs'.

Bicho: a term used to denote an Argentinos fan. Means insect.

Bombonera: Boca's stadium. '*Bombonera*' means chocolate box, and the name derives from the shape of the stadium. The pitch is enclosed by steep, high terraces which are very close to the playing field.

Bostero: a pejorative term used to denote a Boca fan. Relates to manure.

Cebollitas: the name given to a pre-Ninth Division group attached to Argentinos Juniors. All the tournaments in which the Cebollitas participated are amateur tournaments (the Evita tournament, for example) played by pre-Ninth Division kids from various clubs. Argentinos Juniors' biggest claim to fame is the number of top flight players who have emerged from their lower divisions.

Concentración: both at club and international level, players are required to gather on the eve of every game and spend the night either at the training ground or at a hotel. This is known as 'concentrating', hence, *'concentración'*, which denotes the place where they are gathered. It also applies to the hotel or training ground where players stay during international tournaments.

Hen: a pejorative term used to denote a River fan. In Spanish, '*gallina*'.

Monumental: River's Stadium. Since 1978, when it was renovated to host the World Cup Finals, it has been the ground most frequently used to stage international games.

Superclásico: Boca Juniors vs. River Plate – the Buenos Aires derby, contested by Argentina's two biggest clubs.

For an explanation of the language Maradona uses, see the Introduction.

The Beginning

Villa Fiorito, Los Cebollitas, Argentinos Juniors,
the National Side

Sometimes I think that my whole life is on film, that my whole life is in print. But it's not like that, it's not like that at all, there are things which are only in my heart – that no one knows. At last I have decided to tell everything. Even though I've already said so much, I don't think I've ever told the important stuff, the most important stuff.

Here in the Havana night, while I learn to savour Cuban cigars, I begin to remember. It's good to look back, when you feel well, when, in spite of your mistakes, you have nothing to regret. When you've come from the very bottom and you know that everything you've ever been, are, or will be is entirely due to your own struggles.

Do you know where I come from? Do you know how all this started?

I always wanted to play football, but I didn't know where or how I wanted to play. I had no idea. I started out as a defender. I always was and I still am seduced by playing as a *libero*, even now that I'm hardly allowed to touch a ball for fear of my heart exploding. As a *libero* you see everything from the back, the whole pitch is in front of you, you get hold of the ball and you say *pim* let's go that way, *pim*, let's look from another perspective. You're the owner of the team. But back in the beginning, *libero* schmibero. All I wanted was to run after the ball, to get hold of it, to play. Playing football gave me a unique peace. And that same sensation has been with me always, even today: give me a ball and I'll have fun, I'll stand my ground, I'll tussle. I'll want to win and I'll want to play well. Give me a ball and let me do what I know best, anywhere. True, people are important and people motivate you but people are not on the pitch. And that's where the fun is: on the pitch with the ball. That's what I've always done, whether at Wembley or the Maracana, with a hundred thousand people watching. And that's what we did in Fiorito.

Villa Fiorito is the poor neighbourhood on the outskirts of Buenos Aires where I was born and grew up. I was born there on 30 October 1960, my parent's fifth child and their first son. I was covered in fluffy baby hair – *pelusa* – so that, or 'Pelu', became my nickname. My parents were humble working folk, and when I was christened my mother's request to God was simply that I 'grow healthy, and be a good person'. That was her ambition for me.

The first challenge in Fiorito was the sun. My old girl, La Tota, who was always spoiling me, used to say: 'Pelu, if you're going to play . . . play after five o'clock, when the sun's going down.' And I would answer: 'Yes, Ma, yes, Ma. Don't worry.' And I'd leave the house at two o'clock with my friend El Negro or my cousin Beto or whoever, and at quarter past two we'd be playing, on and on, under the most intense heat of the sun. We didn't care about anything, we were killing ourselves. At around seven o'clock we'd stop for a bit, ask for some water in a nearby house, and then carry on. We played in the dark as well. Sometimes now when I hear someone going on about how in such and such a stadium there's no light, I think: I played in the dark, you son of a bitch! I don't know if we were street children: I guess we were 'potrero' (waste ground) children more than anything. If our parents were looking for us, they knew where to find us. We would always be there in the potrero, running after the ball.

Saturdays and Sundays were spent like that all day long. Weekdays too, but only from five o'clock, because during the day I had to go to school. I went to the Remedios de Escalada de San Martin, opposite Fiorito train station. I went to school because I had to, because I didn't want to let my old man, Don Diego, and La Tota down, and because I suspected that there I might get an opportunity to go to a club or to play football. Everything I did, every step I took, was because of the ball. If La Tota sent me on an errand I would take with me anything that resembled a ball: it could be an orange, or scrumpled-up paper, or cloths. And I would go up the steps on to the bridge that crossed the railway, hopping on one foot, the right one, and taking whatever it was on the left, *tac, tac, tac* . . . That's how I walked to school as well. People on the street passed me and stared, but those who knew me weren't surprised. They were my friends, the kids with whom I shared everything, even a slice of pizza. Four or five of us would go to La Blanqueada, next to the Alsina Bridge, which to me felt like the gateway to the big city, to the centre of Buenos Aires. We would buy a single slice between us – we couldn't stretch to more – and we ate it together, one bite each.

I have happy memories of my childhood, although if I had to define Fiorito with just one word, it would be 'struggle'. In Fiorito, if it was possible to eat, people ate, and if it wasn't, they didn't. I remember the winters were very cold and the summers very hot. Our house had three rooms. It was made of solid materials, a real luxury: you went through the wire gate at the entrance and there was a patio, of earth; then the house. There was a dining room, where we cooked, ate, did our homework, everything, and then two bedrooms. On the right was my parents'; on the left, measuring no more than two metres square, was ours, all eight of us kids. When it rained we walked around dodging the leaks; you got wetter inside than out. Forget about a sink: we didn't even have running water. That's how I started weight training. We would use empty twenty-litre cans of oil to fetch water from the only tap in the street, so my mum could wash, cook, everything. That's how we bathed, too: we would take water from the can with our hand and pass it over our face, our armpits, our balls, between our fingers. Washing our hair was more complicated, and in winter it was best avoided.

The truth is we didn't have much to do for fun, but sometimes I made and sold kites with El Negro. And I had the ball, of course. The first ball I had was the best present I've ever received in my life: my cousin Beto gave it me. It was a leather number one; I was three years old and I slept with it hugged to my chest all night.

I was a professional footballer from the start, I would play for the team that picked me first. Of course, I wasn't allowed to play whenever I wanted, and sometimes at home they wouldn't let me go. I would cry like mad, but five minutes before kick off La Tota always gave in. Don Diego was harder to convince.

I understood my old man. He was breaking his back to enable us to eat and study, and that's what he wanted, for me to study. In 1955 he had come to Fiorito from Corrientes, a province north of Buenos Aires, because one of my aunts, Sara, who already lived in Fiorito, had said that they would be better off in the capital. La Tota had come first, with my sister Ana strapped to her back. My dad had stayed waiting for news in Esquina, the small town where they lived, with my other sister Kity and my gran, Mamma Dora, who was a phenomenon. Don Diego was a boat man, he worked for Don Lupo, a man who owned some animals, mostly cows. My dad would carry them over to the islands of the Paraná Delta, to graze. He rowed the cows out in little boats when the river was low and sailed to pick them up again when the tide was coming in. His life was on the river and he knew all its secrets. He still knows them. He had a lot of the things he liked there, things we still share today: fishing, *asados* or barbecues, and football. Even today one of my favourite things to do is go out fishing. No one will ever make a tastier *asado* than my old man. And, according to what I've been told, he was really good at football, he hit the ball like a mule. But when La Tota called for him, he set off for Buenos Aires to get a job, and he got one. Job is a loose description, he worked in the Tritumol mill pounding cattle bones from four in the morning to three in the afternoon.

They settled in Buenos Aires as best they could. It wasn't easy, not at all. First they rented a shed. Then they moved to another one, a little bit better. And finally they managed to move into a house with a lot of corrugated iron and wood and some bricks, near the corner of Azamor and Mario Bravo, in Fiorito. It still stands there today, that little house, practically the same. That's where the rest of us were all born: Elsa, María (La Mary), then me, Raul (El Lalo), Hugo (El Turco) and Claudia (La Caly).

It was hard work feeding all those mouths, and my old man nearly killed himself doing so. That's why I tried not to fuck up too much, but it was hard. Sometimes, after dad picked up his paycheck, he'd buy me a pair of trainers which I would ruin immediately because I played football all day long. It could make you weep! And in fact I would weep because not only would my trainers be wrecked but on top of that the old man would thrash me. But I don't hold it against him. They were different times and different customs. My dad didn't have the time to talk to me, so he had to smack me. He didn't have the time to say, like I can now to my daughters Dalma and Gianinna, 'Come over here, I want to explain this to you.' My old man had to catch up on at least a little sleep so he could get over to the factory at 4 a.m. If he didn't, the whole household would fall apart and we wouldn't have enough to eat. It wasn't unusual: many families were and still are forced to live this way. In fact, it was a very valuable experience for me. My skin got thicker because of what I lived through in Fiorito and elsewhere, but my feelings never changed.

Don Diego is the kindest person I've ever met in my life. The truth is that thanks to him I never lacked a meal. That's why I had strong legs, even though I was thin. Perhaps, in other houses, the kids didn't eat every day, so they got tired before me. That's what made me different from the others: I had good legs and I ate. I never ever thought that I had been born to play football, that everything that later happened to me would happen to me. I had my dreams, sure, like the one that got recorded on TV, when I said that my dream was to play in a World Cup and be a champion with Argentina, but it was the same dream every child had. I did feel, however, that with the ball I was different from all the others. Any *picado* or kickaround that I was chosen for, I always won it. The same way you make choices in life, you make choices in *picados*; the two eldest kids chose and that's how the whole thing got started. *Pelusa* always got chosen first in the *picados*.

We always played round the corner from my house, in the Siete Canchitas, the Seven Little Pitches. They were enormous patches of waste ground; some pitches had goals and some didn't. The Siete Canchitas! It sounds like one of those sports complexes you get now, with synthetic turf and all the rest. There was no grass, synthetic or otherwise, but to us it was wonderful. The pitches were made of earth, really hard earth. When we started running we stirred up so much dust that we felt as if we were playing at Wembley in the fog.

One of those little pitches was Estrella Roja's, Red Star, my dad's team, where I played come what may. Another pitch belonged to Tres Banderas, the Three Flags, my mate Goyo's dad's team. Red Star against Three Flags was like Boca Juniors *v.* River Plate. That was very common, in those days, and I think maybe also now: fathers who were really into football built teams and made their kids play – sometimes even for money. And we were the neighbourhood derby. But everything was fine between me and Goyo. So fine that one day, in mid-1969, when we were nine-year-old classmates, he ran up to me, very excited.

'Diego, Diego, on Saturday I went to train at Argentinos Juniors and they told me to bring more kids over for a trial. Do you want to come?'

'I don't know, I have to ask my dad. I don't know . . .'

I wanted to go more than anything in the world, but the truth was that I knew if I asked my dad to take me it meant he would have to spend money on two bus fares and the trip would eat into his rest time. So that held me back. But of course, I did what I always did when I needed something from Don Diego: I told La Tota that I really wanted to go and she did right by me, as ever. My old man decided in the end that we ought to find out everything about it and that he would take me . . . I ran off to Goyo's house faster than Ben Johnson. It was about three kilometres away, I had to go through the Siete Canchitas, and I got there, breathless: 'Goyo, I'm coming, I'm allowed to come with you!'

A few days later my dad and I picked up Goyo and Montañita, another kid from the neighbourhood who played well. The trip itself was an adventure. I had never travelled that far from Fiorito. For the first time I took the route that I would eventually repeat thousands of times. We left Fiorito on the green bus, which is what we called the number 28. When we got to Pompeya we took the number 44 bus to Las Malvinas, where Argentinos trained, on the corner of Tronador and Bauness. The trip had taken almost two hours. I swear that crossing the Alsina Bridge felt to me like crossing Brooklyn Bridge. I swear.

When we arrived at Las Malvinas, it had been raining so much that they told us we wouldn't be able to play in case we ruined the pitch. We were so disappointed. I think if we had all burst into tears we really would have flooded the place and it would have been impossible for anyone to play on it ever again. Then Francis, who ran the show there, said: 'Don't worry, let's take

Don Yayo's truck and go to Parque Saavedra, we'll be able to play there.'

Francis Cornejo was the manager of Los Cebollitas (the little onions), a group of kids born in 1960 whom he would train and enter for every single tournament possible before we reached fourteen years of age. At this point Argentinos could register us with the AFA, the Argentine Football Association, to take part in the ninth-division tournament, the lowest of the official youth divisions. He knew then that when the time came, we would be ready. Don Yayo (José Emilio Trotta) was Cornejo's assistant, a man more or less the same age as Francis and who owned the pick-up truck in which they drove us everywhere.

At Parque Saavedra they picked two teams. Goyo and I played on the same team and we went on in the second round. On the Siete Canchitas we were always rivals, but we understood each other perfectly and we wiped the floor with the others. I did nutmegs, back-heel flicks and *sombreros* (where I chipped the ball over the opponent's head and recovered it on the other side). I scored a few goals; I can't remember how many. What I do remember is that Francis told Goyo that I should keep coming, that he wanted to see me again. But he didn't believe that I was nine years old. He confronted me with a serious expression on his face, saying:

'Kid, are you sure you were born in 1960?'

'Yes, Don Francis . . .'

'Let's see your ID.'

'I haven't got it, I left it at home . . .'

It was true, but he didn't believe me. Much later, once he had become friends with my dad, he confessed that at first he'd thought I was a midget.

My dad trusted Francis Cornejo and Don Yayo as if they were family. It's because of that trust that I ended up with Argentinos rather than another team. Living where we did, I could have gone to Independiente or Lanus, possibly River Plate. If I could choose now I would always choose Boca, Boca. But in those days, while I was developing as a player, I was in love with Ricardo 'El Bocha' Bochini, the best player in Independiente's history. I fell madly in love and I confess that I supported Independiente in the Libertadores cup of the early 70s, when I was about to go up from the Cebollitas to the ninth division, because Bochini seduced me so. Bochini . . . and his legendary team-mate Daniel Bertoni. The one-twos between Bochini and Bertoni are so imprinted on my mind that I would put them among the greatest playmaking in the history of football. I also really liked Beto Alonso because he was left-footed and I think us left-footed players are easier on the eye. As is the case with Rivelinho, the best example. I think that's the only thing that let El Bocha Bochini down, he didn't have a left foot. But he dummied with his foot over the ball, and defenders fell over themselves. I used to think: It can't be, it's inexplicable. I cut back to get past a guy, face him, and I have to move the ball to pass him. Bochini didn't move it, he simply leant over a little, and the ball stayed where it was, and the defenders fell on their arses anyway. In those days my dream was to play with Bochini. I got over it later.

I watched them all and I learnt. In the meantime, Los Cebollitas were beating everyone we played against. We won 136 matches in a row; I've got the details written down in a notebook Francis and Don Yayo gave me. My wife Claudia still keeps it like a treasure. If the goals I scored back then counted, I'd have more than Pelé under my belt! Sure, it can't be proved, but I know I scored them. We travelled all over the place to play. We were such a great team. That's when I started becoming a true footballer. In Fiorito all I'd really done was run after the ball.

I always played for Los Cebollitas, no matter what state I was in: even once with seven stitches in my hand, which was wrapped in a huge bandage. I had been about to sit down to eat at my house with Goyo, and La Tota asked me to go and buy a bottle of water. I ran to the shop with Goyo, and on the way back, as we turned the corner, I fell badly. The bottle smashed and I got a huge cut. I was in pain, not just because of the cut but because I knew what lay in store: La Tota's fright, my dad's thrashing and above all the next day's match. We were to play away at Banfield, another Buenos Aires club. They took me to a hospital and I got stitches and the huge bandage. I looked like a mummy.

The next day I went with the other kids in Don Yayo's truck. I was afraid that Francis wouldn't let me play, and that he might give me a telling-off. The respect we had for him resembled fear. In the dressing room Francis called me over and said:

'What happened to your hand, Maradona?'

'I fell and cut it, Don Francis, but I can play . . .'

'What? No way! You can't play like that.'

I turned round and went back to the bench, biting my lip so as not to cry. Goyo saw me and went to Francis.

'Go on, Francis, let him play, at least for a little while. Don Diego said he could.'

Francis frowned and groaned something like, alright, but just for a bit. My soul returned to my body. I didn't just play for a little while. I played all ninety minutes. We beat them 7–1 and I scored five goals.

Mono Claudio Rodriguez played in our team, and he was an exceptional number eight. Goyo wore the number nine shirt, I was the ten, and Polvora Delgado the eleven. But Rodriguez's dad was very linked to another Buenos Aires club, Chacarita, and when we became old enough to go into the ninth division he took his son there and dismantled our team. Francis had to play Osvaldo Dalla Buona, who was one of my best friends but a terrible troublemaker. So the derby of the inferiors was born: our Argentinos against the Chacarita of Pichi Escudero and Mono Rodriguez. We would win because we made the difference on the left. A typical formation was: Ojeda; Trotta, Chaile, Chammah, Montaña; Lucero, Dalla Buona, Maradona; Duré, Carrizo and Delgado.

Those days of the Cebollitas marked me for ever. Nowadays there's always such a fuss about age, like when the Brazilians field older players in their youth teams, but I have to admit the same happened to me, only the other way round: I was twelve years old, three years younger than the rest of them, and Francis would sit me on the bench anyway. If things weren't working out, he sent me on. The first time was against Racing, on their own turf: there was half an hour left, we were drawing 0–0 and nothing was happening; he sent me on, I scored two goals and we won. Palomino, the rival coach, knew Francis very well and he asked him: 'How can you have that kid on the bench? Look after him, he's going to be a genius.' Francis showed him my ID and Palomino couldn't believe it. Another time, against Boca, Francis did the same thing but this time, because by then I was fairly well known in the youth circles, he wrote my name down as Montanya. We were 3–0 down, I came on, scored a goal, then we started pressing them and we drew. But my team-mates grassed me up: Nice one, Diego! they shouted until the Boca manager cottoned on. He confronted Francis: 'You played Maradona ... I'll let it go this time, I'm not going to report you. You really are lucky. That kid is wonderful.'

There were times when I didn't make it into the team for reasons other than my age. In 1971 we went to a championship in Uruguay. It was the first time I had left my country. I couldn't play because I had forgotten my documents. I wanted to die! I had my picture taken with the team, wearing long trousers and a grimace on my face that said it all. That year was the first time my name appeared in a newspaper: On Tuesday 28 September *Clarin* published a little insert saying a boy had appeared 'with the demeanour and class of a star'. According to them I was called Caradona. Incredible, the first time my name is published and it's a typo. I was also invited to do tricks with the ball on *Sabados Cirlculares*, a TV programme everyone in Argentina watched.

The people who went to see Argentinos knew me well – not by name, but because one day, when I was ballboy in a first-division match, Francis had the bright idea of throwing me the ball at half-time, so that I could show off my skills. I got the ball and began to play with it, as always: bouncing it from instep to thigh to back heel to head to shoulder, and back again, on and on. Francis started leading me to the centre of the pitch. I was getting embarrassed because the other kids couldn't follow me and I realised people were staring. They started clapping and it turned into a classic event. But the best time was during an Argentinos–Boca match, in 1970, at the Vélez stadium. Us kids played all week with a broken ball, a disaster, so come Sunday when we saw the official Pintier ball from the first-division matches our little eyes went all shiny . . . we always had a kick-about at half-time and one time I shot from outside the area and the ball bounced and hit Don Yayo on the head – he was standing on the other side of the goal. People in the crowd noticed and began to laugh, so I started with my skills, *tac-tac-tac-tac*, and the crowd started clapping along and the first team players returned, the ref came back, but the crowd started shouting: *¡Que-se-que-de, que-se-que-de!* (let him stay, let him stay!) It was the whole crowd shouting: not only the Argentinos fans, but the Boca fans too, even louder. The Boca fans, that's one of my happiest memories of them. I think that's when I started feeling what I still feel for them now: I knew then we would come together one day.

Los Cebollitas lost the final of the Nacional championship in Rio Tercero, Córdoba. We were beaten by a team from Pinto, from the poor northern province of Santiago del Estero, managed by a man called Elías Ganem. When his son, César, saw how upset

I was he came up to me and said: 'Don't cry, brother, you're going to be the best in the world.' People still believe he gave me his medal but no way: he kept his medal and he deserved it too.

There's a well-known photograph of me from that tournament. I'm kneeling down, comforting an older boy who is weeping. The boy was Alberto Pacheco, he played for Corrientes, and they'd lost a match against Entre Ríos. We'd become good mates because Don Diego, like a good Correntino, went to watch all their games. Even in those days I loved playing against River and beating them. I remember three matches: a 3–2, in a four-way in which Huracán and All Boys also played. A 7–1! And the best of all, a 5–4 in the final of the Evita championship 1973. If I was to seek a precedent for the goal I scored against England I find it there: I dribbled past seven and scored; I vaccinated them.

I scored a forerunner of the other goal, the hand of God, while I was at Los Cebollitas. I scored a goal with my hand; the opponents saw and launched themselves on top of the ref. In the end he allowed the goal to stand and it was mayhem. I knew it wasn't right at the time, but it's one thing to say so in the cold light of day and quite another to take a decision in the heat of the match: you're trying to reach the ball and the hand moves independently. I always remember a referee who ruled out a handball I scored against Vélez, many years after Los Cebollitas and many years before Mexico '86. He advised me not to do it again. I thanked him, but I also told him I couldn't promise anything. I don't know whether he cheered our victory over England or not.

A week after that match against River the president of the club, William Kent, asked my dad to name my price, he wanted to buy me. Don Diego turned him down in no uncertain terms: Dieguito is very happy playing for Argentinos, he answered. But it wouldn't be the last time River sought me out.

※   ※   ※

By the time I was fourteen years old and playing in the ninth division for Argentinos I had met Jorge Cyterszpiler, who would come to play a crucial role in my life. He'd always followed Argentinos' lower divisions because of his brother, Juan Eduardo, who was apparently a genius with the ball. But he died of some terrible disease, and Jorge was very shaken. He never came back to the club. He stayed away until someone, a friend, I don't know who, told him that there was a kid in the Cebollitas who was something else. That kid was me, and Jorge came out of his hibernation. He became something of a coordinator of the lower divisions. Whenever we had important matches he would take us to his house to make sure we rested properly, ate well. He lived in San Blas Street, in La Paternal, close to Argentinos' stadium, and many Fridays I would sleep over at his place. We played Scrabble, Monopoly, and that's how our friendship started . . . I used to sleep in Juan Eduardo's bed, I became like another family member. It wouldn't be long before Jorge became my manager.

I see now it all happened very fast for me. In 1974 Los Cebollitas won the ninth-division championship. I was fourteen years old. The following year I went up to the eighth division with the same team, and once we had a lead of about ten points I got promoted to the seventh. In the seventh I played two matches and moved up to the fifth; four matches there and immediately on to the third. I had my debut against Los Andes, in their stadium, with one goal. Two more matches and *pum*, first team just before my sixteenth birthday in 1976. All that in two and a half years.

A lot of people claim that they were there on 20 October 1976 when we played Talleres de Córdoba at home. The truth is, if everyone who says they were there for that match – my debut in the first team – had actually been there it would have had to be played at the Maracana, not La Paternal. By then I had already started training with the first team on the Comunicaciones pitch. One Tuesday during practice the manager, Juan Carlos Montes, came up to me and said: 'Listen, tomorrow you're going on the bench with the first team, OK?' I was speechless; all I managed to mutter was: 'What? How?' And he repeated: 'Yes, you'll be on the bench ... and please be well prepared because you will be played.' I ran all the way home with my heart in my mouth to tell my old man, my mum. And of course, two seconds after I had told La Tota the whole of Fiorito knew that I was playing with the first team against Talleres the next day.

By then Argentinos had started renting an apartment for me in Villa del Parque, at 2746 Argerich Street. But I still kept some of my stuff in Fiorito, and my grandmother Mamma Dora continued to live there, refusing to move. So that was where everyone went, my cousin Beto, my cousin Raúl, they all went by the house to find out if there was a game, and if I was playing. They always did that because they always tried to go and watch me play, even in the lower divisions. If they had money for the bus fare they would come, and if they didn't, they didn't. Same with me really. Sometimes I wouldn't have enough to go training and my married sisters, Ana and Kity, would steal the bus fare from their husbands. That was until Argentinos started to pay for my travel expenses, which was the case by the time of my first-division debut.

When my cousin Beto, the one I loved the most, heard I would be playing in the first team he burst into tears and we couldn't stop him. At that moment the penny dropped that the next day was going to be huge for me. And I realised too that because the next day was a Wednesday, my old man would be working. He was going to miss that day we had dreamt of together so much. I prepared to go to the game alone.

Wednesday 20 October 1976 was hot. Or at least it felt that way to me. I put on my white shirt and the turquoise corduroy trousers with the big turn-ups; the only pair I had! There'd been so much talk about the prize money and I thought: Well, in such a game there'll be a bit for the sub, and if I come on, a bit more even . . . And I'd do my sums: Maybe I could buy myself another pair of trousers, or something else. To me, my debut in the first division meant the possibility of buying a second pair of trousers.

La Tota walked me to the door. 'I will pray for you son,' she said. And the cherry on the cake was when she told me that my old man had asked permission to leave work early – he could come to watch me play after all. I can't remember the exact time of the match, if it was 3 or 4, but I do remember that before I went on the pitch I was told that Don Diego had arrived in time.

The first thing that made an impact on me was seeing the Talleres fans. There were Cordobese folk everywhere! The Argentinos players had got together for lunch before the game, across the road from the stadium. We had the classic steak and mash with our manager Montes's technical chat for pudding. Then we crossed the street and walked to the stadium with the crowds, among all the people. Nobody knew who we were! They were all from Córdoba. *I'm Taaaaaaaeere, Taaaaaaeeeeeeeeeeeerre I am!!* they'd sing to that unmistakeable tune. They had a great team: Luis 'El Hacha' Ludueña, Ocaño, Luis Galván, Miguel Angel Oviedo, Jose Daniel Valencia, Umberto Bravo. We didn't have that many stars. In truth they should have scored eighteen goals against us. I remember our squad by heart: Munutti; Rona, Pellerano, Gette, Minutti; Fren, Giacobetti, Di Donato; Jorge López, Alvarez and Ovelar.

The Cordobese lot were really leading us a merry dance and in the twenty-seventh minute El Hacha Ludueña scored for them. Just before the end of the first half, Montes, who was at the other end of the bench, turned towards me and fixed me with a stare, as if he was asking me, *Do you dare?* I held his stare and that was my answer. I started the warm-up immediately and I came on for Giacobetti in the second half, with a number 16 on my back, on the red shirt crossed by a white stripe. I used to love that shirt! It was like River's but the other way round. On the touchline, Montes had said to me: 'Go on, Diego, play like you know how . . . and if you can, nutmeg someone.' I did as I was told: I received the ball with my back to my marker, Juan Domingo Patricio Cabrera. I dummied and kicked the ball between his legs. It went clean through and I immediately heard the *Ooooolé* . . . of the crowd, like a welcome. Not everyone who says they were there was there on my debut, but still, the stands were packed out, you couldn't see the tiniest section of terrace. I remember the thing that struck me the most was the lack of space: the stadium seemed small compared to the youth team's. But the knocks were big. I was used to getting the shit kicked out of me when I played with the kids, but here I would soon learn that I had to jump in time; you had to dribble round a player, jump over his kick and continue with the ball. If you don't learn that, after the third kick you can't go on. I was a fast learner.

We lost that first match, yes, but I was fifteen years old, and I had started a long and beautiful history with Argentinos, an unforgettable history. I always say, in football terms that day I touched the sky with my hands. I knew something very important was starting in my life. I played another ten matches in the Nacional tournament, eleven in total, and I scored two goals, both against San Lorenzo of Mar del Plata, at the San Martin stadium, on 14 November 1976.

I began to be noticed, newspapers interviewed me, journalists wrote about me. I remember one headline in particular, because it summed up everything that was happening to me at the time: *At the age most kids hear stories, he hears ovations*, it said. In only three years I had gone from Fiorito to the magazines, the TV, the media. It was all too fast. I used to get nervous in interviews. I didn't buy my own hype, I didn't feel I was anybody special, and I always ended up repeating the same things: where I was born, how I lived, and who my favourite players were. I had to grow up too fast. I got to know other people's envy, I didn't understand it, I'd lock myself in my room and weep. I had to grow up quickly. I started to watch what I said but it wasn't easy. Nobody could have imagined then what I'm going through today. Too much was happening to me, it was a different world and it came very suddenly. I realised I had left behind a time of enormous effort and sacrifice, not just on my part, but my family's too. The days when my father and I shared our dreams on the bus were over. Now I had the possibility of parking my car at my own front door. Even my oldest dream, the dream of playing for my country, came true immediately, when I had played just eleven games in the first division.

Like everything in my life, things were unfolding too fast. It was early 1977, hardly three months after my debut with Argentinos. I was with the national youth team, training against the first team. I'd been called up by Don Ernesto Duchini, who was a master, a true master, and we played against the first team, against the great names: Daniel Passarella, René Houseman, Mario Kempes, monsters the lot of them! Which is how César Luis 'El Flaco' Menotti, who was already the manager of the national squad's first team, got to see me play.

In one of those training sessions apparently I excelled, because El Flaco singled me out to speak to. Each one of his words echoed inside me; it was almost a religious experience. El Flaco was a god – and there he was, talking just to me. He told me that I would play in the friendly against Hungary, that I would make my debut in the national first team.

He called me to one side and said: 'Maradona, when you leave here today I want you to go straight to the hotel with the rest of the squad. The only thing I ask of you is that you don't tell anybody. If you want to, you can let your parents know, but don't let the press get hold of it. I wouldn't want you to get nervous.'

I went to the *concentración* where the squad were gathered

in preparation for the next day's match. I stayed calm. The following morning Menotti spoke to me again: 'I want you to know that if the game goes well, and if our team scores, it's possible you'll come on.'

Still, I stayed calm. I don't know why, but I did. After all, everything depended on how the team played. On Sunday 27 February, the day of the match, I didn't have any breakfast. I wanted to rest as much as possible, so I got up at eleven. I had a bath and watched TV in my hotel room until twelve. Then I went downstairs and chatted with the lads until lunchtime. I went back to my room and stayed a bit longer watching TV. We left for the Bombonera, the Boca Juniors stadium where Argentina played most of its home games at the time, at 3.30 p.m.

It was only when the coach parked at the Bombonera that I began to realise where I was, what was happening to me. So many people were coming up to us, patting our backs, shouting advice that I started to feel my legs trembling . . . it's amazing how scared people can make you feel.

First the players in the starting line-up got changed. Then us, the subs. When I stepped out on to the sidelines and heard the crowd's roar, I thought that they were all cheering for me, that they were all shouting Maradona. The truth is probably no one noticed me, but that's what I felt.

The game started and bang! Penalty! So I thought: This is the goal, get ready, Diego. But the goalie saved it and I realised that it was going to be hard for me to go on. Then Bertoni scored a great goal, and then came a second and a third, and with every goal we scored I felt a shiver run down my spine. If we carried on like this I would come on, no doubt about it.

I sat on the bench with my team-mate Roberto Mouzo; Ricardo Pizzarotti, our physical trainer; Doctor Fort and Menotti himself. We were twenty minutes into the second half when El Flaco called me over. I got up and walked to where he sat. I knew I was going to play. 'You'll go on for Luque,' Menotti told me. 'Do what you know, stay calm, and move about all over the pitch, OK?' That gave me courage. I started warming up and I heard the stands chanting my name. *Maradoooó, Maradoooó!* I don't know what came over me. My legs and hands were shaking. The crowd's roar was so loud. Menotti's words were echoing in my head, and my team-mate Perez was egging me on, 'Come on, Diego, give it everything!' It was all mixed up in my head. I'm not kidding, I was shitting myself.

I got my first touch immediately. Hugo Orlando Gatti, the goalkeeper, kicked it out to Américo 'El Tolo' Gallego who passed it swiftly on to me. He did it on purpose, I could tell; it was a sign of great camaraderie. I put Houseman into space with a pass between two Hungarians. And then I began to calm down. Ricardo Villa was cheering me on, Gallego was looking after me, Carrascosa was shouting, 'Well played! Well played!' Even if it wasn't.

When the match finished the first to hug me was Gallego. 'That's how I want to see you always, Diego! Like this!' I couldn't believe it. It was all over. I went home with dad and Jorge Cyterszpiler. I had dinner and turned the TV on to watch the match. I realised I'd made several mistakes: I passed it to Bertoni on the right while it was in fact Felman who was free, on the other side; I tried to dribble around a Hungarian but my cut-back was too short. I remembered that on the pitch I'd thought about playing it longer and then changed my mind. I also saw the kick a Hungarian had given me, but it hurt less watching it on TV. Then I went to bed. I didn't dream at all. I slept like never before.

By now my family and I had settled into the house on Argerich Street. It was a typical Argentinian neighbourhood house, one of those old ones with an apartment at the back and one at the front. We lived at the back and at the front was the Villafane family: Don Coco, a taxi driver and avid Argentinos supporter, Doña Pochi, a housewife, and their daughter, La Claudia. I think we started eyeing each other up on the very first day I moved in, back in October 1976. She used to watch me through the window every time I left the house and I clocked her all right although I played dumb. I only dared ask her out eight months later. On 28 June 1977 I went to a neighbourhood dance: the Social y Deportivo Parque. This was the local sports and youth club and some great parties took place right there, on the same pitches where all the little monsters who would end up playing for Argentinos trained. After two in the morning, the slow dancing started, and that would be the great moment. I parked my red Fiat 125 outside the front door and headed straight for her . . . she was already inside, with her school friends. She was in her last year of high school. We both knew we had been watching each other so I barely had to nod my head and she accepted. Without a word we started dancing, and straight away the song 'I propose' by Roberto Carlos came on, thank God! It saved me from having to think of the right words to say, which wasn't exactly my forte. From that very moment on, we were El Diego and La Claudia. And we don't know how to live without each other. She had to get used to some things, and I don't just mean the *concentraciones*.

One time I came home very late, it was morning, in fact. I didn't sleep: I showered and straight away left for training. Don Diego heard me but kept quiet and then, at lunchtime, when I came back, I saw him talking to Claudia, almost shouting: 'You can't keep my boy up so late, you have to look after him a bit more, he has to train, you know?!' I wanted the earth to swallow me; I hadn't been out with La Claudia that night.

2

The Explosion

Argentinos Juniors, Argentina '78, Japan '79

I think I could have played in the 1978 World Cup: I was up for it, I was readier than I'd ever been. When I found out I hadn't been selected, I cried a lot, I cried so much. Not even at USA '94, with the drug test, did I cry so much. I see both events as terrible injustices. They're different, but they're both injustices. I have never forgiven Menotti for it, nor will I ever – I still feel he let the tortoise get away from him – but I've never hated him. Hating is not the same as not forgiving. In spite of everything, I'll never forget the wisdom El Flaco Menotti showed in guiding me over the years.

It was raining on 19 May in the town of José C. Paz, at our *concentración* on Natalio Salvatori's estate. El Flaco Menotti called all twenty-five of us to the centre of the practice pitch. I could see it coming, I could see it coming. The squad had five players competing for the number-ten position: Villa, Alonso, Valencia, Bochini and me. I think El Flaco liked Valencia the most because he had discovered him; and then Villa; Alonso was included in the team because there was a tremendous campaign by the press and I don't know who, and El Bocha Bochini got the nod before anyone. As for me, well, my time had come.

The day before, Francis had been to visit me at the *concentración* and he'd found me crying in my room – as I said, I saw it coming. When the news broke that Humberto Bravo, Lito Bottaniz and me were left out, only a couple of the players came over to comfort me: Leopoldo Luque, a great guy, and El Tolo Gallego. No one else. At the time they were too important to waste a word on a kid. I'm not saying they were wrong in anything they did; everyone wanted to play their first World Cup and everyone was looking after their own interests. Someone had to be El Flaco's snitch. That's how it works with the stars in football. What happened to me was something that could happen to any new kid on the block. That's how it was, I was just another kid. Now, with hindsight, it's a different matter. I didn't stay another minute when I heard the news: I no longer felt a part of that group. If you're in, you all pull forward together. If you're out, best to get out.

It was terrible when I got home. It was like a funeral. My mum was crying, my dad was crying, my brothers and sisters were crying. They kept telling me that I was the best, that I shouldn't worry because I would play five World Cups. But they were all crying. That was the worst thing. On that day, the saddest of my career, I swore I would get my revenge. It was the biggest disappointment of my life, it marked me for ever, it defined me. I felt in my legs and in my heart and in my mind that I would show them all. I would play in many World Cups. That's exactly what Menotti had told me, but at the time I wasn't able to listen to reason. I lived through Argentina '78 like any other Argentinian – I even went to a couple of matches: against Italy and the final against Holland. When Argentina were crowned World Champions, I went out in Claudia's father's van to celebrate all over Buenos Aires. But I kept thinking that I could have been a part of that squad. I was sure I could have made a contribution.

At that point, when I was left out of the final squad of twenty-two I realised that *bronca*, or anger, was a fuel for me. It really got me revved up. I played best when I was after revenge. Two days after El Flaco broke the awful news to me, I put on the Argentinos strip and went out on to the pitch: we beat Chacarita

5–0; I scored two goals and made two assists. I remember that, after scoring one, Huguito Pena, a great guy, may he rest in peace, came up to me, put his arm round my shoulder and whispered in my ear, 'Dieguito, if I wasn't wearing a different strip I'd celebrate with you . . . Don't worry, kid, you're going to play in many World Cups and you're going to shut everyone up.'

There, at Argentinos, I learnt what it means to fight your way up from the bottom, to challenge the big guys when you're small. To leave aside the word relegation in order to dream of a championship title. Our form picked up, against everyone and against everything. We came fifth in the Metropolitano championship of '78, and I was top scorer with twenty-two goals. I hardly played in that year's Nacional but I made the most of it: I played four games and scored four goals.

By then I had formalised my relationship with Cyterszpiler. From my time with Los Cebollitas until 1977 we had handled everything on the basis of friendship, not a single piece of paper was signed. But the story had changed too much and the time had come to turn the friendship into something professional. I wanted someone I could trust, and I trusted him. We had offers from everywhere, from brands wanting me to represent them, as well as football clubs. There had even been an offer from England: one million and forty thousand dollars for me and Carlitos Fren. One million and forty thousand dollars! So one day, walking out of my house in Argerich, when I was sixteen and he was eighteen, I said to Jorge: 'I want you to handle my affairs.' And that's how it all started. He had dropped out of college where he was studying economics – after the second year I think – and came with me when I played for Argentina's youth squad in the South American Youth Championships in Caracas, Venezuela, in 1977. It was a complete disaster: no one supported that team, everyone was thinking about the 1978 World Cup and only that. We weren't a bad team, but we were lonelier than Adam on Mother's Day.

It wasn't until after Argentina '78 that they remembered us. Argentina had won its first World Cup and Menotti turned his attention to the national youth team as soon as the victory lap was finished. His idea was to coach us for the first Youth World Cup which was to be played in Japan in 1979, thereby grooming a whole new generation of players ready for the 1982 World Cup. Our youth squad was a spectacular team, chosen by the master Duchini: Sergio García was the goalkeeper, from Tigre; Abelardo Carabelli, who had played against the Cebollitas with Huracán, now with Argentinos; Juanchi Simón and El Gringo Sperandío, from Newell's; Rubén Juan Rossi, from Colón; Huguito Alves and Bachino, from Boca; Juancito Barbas and Gaby Calderón, from Racing; Osvaldito Rinaldi, from San Lorenzo; Pichi Escudero, from Chacarita; Ramón Díaz, from River; Jorge Piaggio and Alfredito Torres, from Atlanta; El Flaco Lanao, from Vélez; Tucu Meza; Barrera . . . We went all over the country playing against the biggest teams, we scored non-stop, the stadiums were full. We were the business.

In November 1978 we beat the famous US Cosmos 2–1 in Tucuman, in a packed stadium. I scored one goal and Barrera the other. At the end of the match I swapped shirts with Franz Beckenbauer.

El Flaco had promised us that he would always be with our youth team. And he kept his word. He came with us to a tournament in Montevideo, which was really tough. That's where we qualified for the Youth World Cup. I was incredibly proud to be a part of Menotti's team. He was the architect of the team, responsible for getting it into our heads that all that stuff about being moral champions was useless. When I went to register myself at the AFA at the age of twelve I didn't see a single World Cup trophy there – all the cabinets were empty . . . Now, thank God, we have a couple and El Flaco had something to do with that.

We were really up for it in Montevideo. We thrashed Peru, we drew against Uruguay, and we drew against Brazil. That Brazil side was constantly passing the ball, they never lost possession. At half-time Menotti gathered us in the centre of the pitch and said, 'Do what they do!' And it was a great match. The little black guys played, *taca taca*, reached the box and had some great shots which shaved the post; then we'd get the ball, *taca taca*, and we would light up their penalty area. We drew o–o but we knocked them out, eventually qualifying along with Uruguay and Paraguay.

At the end of that championship I turned another dream into reality, maybe the most important one: I took my whole family to see the sea for the first time. We spent a few days in Atlántida, in Uruguay, and there and then, on the beach, when we were all together, I asked my old man for a very big favour: I pleaded with him to stop working. He was fifty, he had done enough for us. Now it was my turn.

El Flaco started fielding some of us youth team players in the national squad first-team games. He was getting us ready to reach the Youth World Cup in tiptop form. He played me and Barbas against Bulgaria, at the River stadium, in the first match after the World Cup. We won 2–1. Then he took us to Berna, to play a game against Holland, for a FIFA party or something. I went out on to the pitch to play against Neeskens, against Krol, against that incredible team. We drew o–o and then we won on penalties: I took one of them, and Barbitas took one too. We were kids, sure, but we felt important.

Around this time, Argentinos declared me non-transferable. The problem was how they would manage to pay me and keep hold of me, given the offers that were coming in from abroad. So a deal was struck with Austral, a domestic airline now gone bust: they put their logo on the Argentinos strip and that's how I managed to stay. Otherwise I might have played in Argentina even less than I eventually did. By then I was already the face of Puma, of Coca-Cola, of Agfa, of a whole bunch of brands that two years previously I hadn't even heard of. Soon after I played another match with the national first team, against Italy, in Rome. By then I was ready to dive head first towards my objective.

When we arrived in Japan we knew we couldn't lose. I was adamant; I had decided to take revenge for the 1978 World Cup. That team in Japan was, by a long way, the best team I have been a part of in my career. I've never had so much fun on the pitch. At the time it was the greatest joy of my life and the truth is, with the exception of my daughters, I can't think of anything quite like it, we played such beautiful football. And everyone followed us. Ask any Argentinian what they remember about that team and I bet they'll say: 'It was amazing. We'd get up at 4 a.m. to watch them on the telly . . .' And that's what it was like: for a fortnight we got the whole country out of bed in the middle of the night.

Argentina was under a military dictatorship at the time, a junta headed by Lieutenant General Jorge Rafael Videla, and still high on the 1978 World Cup victory, people were really clinging on to the joy football can bring.

I don't know if the military who were in power at the time used us, I just don't know. Some people seem to think the fact that the military government relished our success belittles what we achieved. I'm sure the military did try to turn our popularity to their advantage because that's what they did with everything. But one thing shouldn't take away from the other: it's not right that our triumph should get dirtied because of the military. There should be no doubt as to what I think about them, though. Videla and his cronies, who made thirty thousand people disappear, don't deserve anything, least of all to tarnish the memory of the success of a group of kids. People complain about me, they say I'm contradictory, but what about Argentina? In our country there are still people who defend Videla but far fewer who defend Che Guevara. Far fewer! They've not even heard of him. Videla dirtied Argentina's reputation abroad; Che is someone we should all be proud of. But in those days Videla was in charge. And if there is a picture of me shaking hands with him all I can say is: I didn't have a choice.

In terms of the relationship with the military dictatorship I will always remember the attitude of the Argentina and River Plate goalkeeper Ubaldo 'Pato' Fillol towards Admiral Lacoste. Lacoste was a member of the military government who liked to pull his weight in Argentinian football. And particularly so with River Plate. The story was that Pato had got stubborn about signing – he was a tough cookie when it came to money! – and Lacoste tried to get involved and put pressure on him to sign. Pato wouldn't budge. Once, just before kick-off, when we were all lined up ready for the national anthems, this guy Lacoste came before us to shake hands, one by one. When he reached Fillol, Pato stayed still, completely stiff, refused to shake his hand. Unbelievable! I thought he was phenomenally brave – it was the best way to make his feelings clear.

In the summer of 1979 the Japanese adopted us immediately, they warmed to us. In our opening match on 26 August, we scored five against Indonesia, 5–0, in Omiya, where we headed our group. From then on we were unstoppable: 1–0 against Yugoslavia, on the 28th, and 4–1 against Poland, on the 30th. We won our group easily. We played so well, with such style. I was the captain and I loved it: every time I spoke on the phone to Claudia she said that when I wore the captain's band I carried my right arm higher, lifted it up. She called me *'El Gran Capitan'*. I did feel more responsible, although there were things that I couldn't control, things to do with my personality. I was so fixated on revenge that I had resolved to play every single match of the Youth World Cup, all ninety minutes of every match, I didn't want to miss a thing. When we played against Algeria in the quarter-final, El Flaco substituted me. I was so pissed off. At first, I sat on the bench sulking. Then I stormed into the dressing room. And it was there I really lost it, I wept like a baby. When the match was over and the others came in with another 5–0 under their belts they realised something was up, that I wasn't well.

They asked me what was wrong and I confessed – I was devastated by my substitution. They were all trying to comfort me, especially El Flaco. He said: 'But Diego, you always want to play. I was thinking of taking you off against Poland. Don't you realise I want to rest you?' Rest me my arse! I wanted to play, I wanted to play every match. That evening I nearly didn't go down for supper but I thought about the captaincy, about the responsibility. My *bronca* didn't disappear until two days later, when we faced Uruguay in the semi-final, on 4 September. That's what I was like, even in those days.

That match against Uruguay was like any match against Uruguay. It had all the ingredients of a classic River Plate derby. They kicked the shit out of me and if we won it's because we outsmarted them with the ball: we didn't abandon our style and it ended 2–0, with a goal from Ramón 'El Pelado' Díaz and one from me, a header. When El Pelado scored the first I ran out celebrating like a madman and suddenly I realised I was right in front of the Uruguay bench. It looked like I was taking the piss and I apologised after the match. But I was crazy with joy. It was my team and we were in the final, against the USSR. I was obsessed with the idea of returning to Argentina with the cup. I imagined walking down the airplane steps with the cup in my hands, it was like a film going round my head all the time. But I knew it might not come true. Not because we could lose in the final against the Russians – I was sure we would beat them – but because El Flaco had already told me I would be playing on tour with the first team, which meant I might have to go straight from Japan to join them, not giving me enough time to fly home ... I wanted to die: I didn't dare refuse to play with the first team but I also didn't want to miss out on my dream of returning to Argentina holding the cup. You know what saved me? Military service. That's right. I was a conscript in those days and me and Juan Barbas, who was in the same boat, had an expiry date on our military licences . . . so we had to fly back come what may! I heard the news the day before the final, so everything was perfect.

I shared a room with Barbas, a guy I love very much. The final was to take place on 7 September, at 7 p.m. Tokyo time. Juan and I tried to take a siesta but we couldn't sleep: our eyes were fixed on the clock. Bastard, it was for ever 3 p.m.! We were so anxious. Those waits always killed me. I preferred to play in the afternoon because I liked to sleep until midday so I didn't have time to get anxious, but playing in the evening meant you couldn't avoid it. The only consolation was that back in Argentina the fans didn't have to get up so early. The final would be shown at 7 a.m.

We took the coach to the National Stadium, in central Tokyo, and there we began to enact each and every one of our unnecessary rituals. Before the game against Uruguay, César had been about to start the technical chat and I had got delayed. Rogelio Poncini, the assistant, called me: Diego, the only one missing is you. So, before the game against USSR, I played the fool and hung around, holding myself back on purpose so as to repeat history, until Poncini realised what was going on and called me over. And then there was this mania Menotti had: he used to tap the wall with his fingers and it sounded like he was making music. On the last match he seemed not to be doing it so I asked him: 'César, aren't you playing today?' And El Flaco started beating his fingers, on and on. I had another ritual, more intimate: I would go into the last shower and pray; I would ask God for my mum's help, and for Him to play with me, and for La Claudia to pray for me, and finally that we win.

We won of course. We won the final of the first FIFA

Coca-Cola Youth World Cup against the Soviet Union by three goals to one, on that unforgettable 7 September 1979, and I wrote it all down in a travel diary I kept.

At no point in the first half did I think they could score against us. And even though we didn't get into their area much, when we did so we were better than them. In the second half, when they scored their goal, we had five or six minutes of uncertainty. I started thinking about the match against Uruguay, when we seemed unable to find the net however hard we tried: we'd shoot from inside the six-yard box and it would hit the goalie's knees. Unbelievable! But the main thing was that we didn't despair. When Tucu Meza came on, he managed to lead us all, give us all direction. He played the best match of his life. The atmosphere was less tense than against Uruguay. It was a much less physical game, mainly because the Russians have absolute confidence in their strength. When they go after the ball they do so firmly, but always fairly.

We continued without losing our heads, without kicking long balls; we tried to impose our skill and that helped us; we didn't play rough. We did everything with clarity, simply. And we equalised with a goal from Alves, a penalty kick. That's when I knew we were going to win. I was convinced. Even when we were down 1–0 we never lost faith in ourselves. With the equaliser I knew that if we continued like this, the cup was ours.

Everything happened within the space of a few minutes. First El Pelado Díaz scored, and then I took a free kick. I sized it up, saw the gap, and then . . . goal. There we were at last. I couldn't believe it, we were World Champions!

Calderón was the first to cross my path. Then I hugged my dad, then Jorge, the other lads, and immediately after I looked upwards to give this championship to La Tota. I thought back to being left out of the 1978 World Cup and I savoured my revenge. I got ready to go and lift the trophy. I saw the president of FIFA, João Havelange, stretching his hand out to me. I asked him if I could lift the cup, I couldn't hold myself back any longer. I took it from him. I took a step back and made a reverential bow, Japanese style, and we looked for Menotti, who at that point was not with us. We ran towards him with the cup, we gave it to him, we lifted him in the air and we started our victory lap. All around us we could hear the Japanese joining us and shouting *Ar-gen-tina! Ar-gen-tina!!*

Suddenly the lights went off and a beam lit us all the way round the pitch. At that point we burst into tears, like children. It was madness, people were asking us to raise the cup and show it to them as if they were Argentinian.

When I returned to the dressing room, there was dancing and partying. We didn't want to leave the stadium, but the celebrations were continuing back at our hotel, so we had to go. And there I had a very special moment: El Flaco Menotti tying the knot on my tie and saying very quietly, as if he didn't want the others to hear: 'Diego, you've been chosen as best player of the tournament. You will be awarded the Balon d'Or.' It was all too much for me.

We finished in the early hours, all of us in Poncini's room, drinking *mate*, the traditional Argentinian tea, a very strong brew which is passed round the group like a ritual. As if we were in Argentina, as if nothing had happened. Then I remembered a phrase of Francis Cornejo's, a phrase he had used to define me, when my name started to become known the world over. Francis always said that I could be at a gala dinner, with a white dinner jacket on, but if I saw a muddy ball coming my way I would stop it with my chest. And what's more: if it was coming towards my head, I would knock it with my forehead, and if it fell near my left foot, I would start playing keepy-uppy among the dinner tables. And that's it: that's how I felt playing with that beautiful team in Japan – we were just kids, drinking *mate* in our room. That's how football was for me. I had wanted, at all costs, to return to Argentina, to step down from the plane, with the cup in my hands. I managed it, and it was one of the most beautiful moments of my life.

And I managed to shake off the military service to boot: all of us who were doing it, Escudero, Simón, Barbas, the lot of them, they all asked me to get them out of it. So I became the spokesman. When I met with the officers in charge of conscription I saluted and said to them: 'We've given you the title, would you give us an honorary discharge?' Incredibly, I pulled it off. Another triumph. It wouldn't have been right to leave shouting and punching the air, but I wanted to.

Almost as soon as I stepped off the plane, I put myself at El Flaco's disposal once again. How could I not? All my dreams were coming true, one after the other. I went on tour with the Argentinian first team. In Glasgow at Hampden Park on 2 June 1979, I celebrated my first goal in the blue and white of the first team. We beat Scotland 3–1 and I felt I could beat the world. During that tour poor Negro Ortiz had to return to Argentina because he had some sort of attack that left him half-paralysed. He acted as a generous postman for me, and took Claudia all the letters I'd been writing to her, every day. On 25 June, a year after the 1978 World Cup final between Holland and Argentina, the final that I should have been a part of, a celebration match was played: us against the Rest of the World. I made myself noticed, yes: I scored one of the finest goals I can remember against Brazil's Emerson Leão. I curled it with my left, from outside the box, and nailed it in at an angle . . . Fucking motherfucker, why wasn't I on the pitch a year earlier, just a year earlier, was I that much younger, for fuck's sake?

I swore I would never ever again miss an Argentina game, wherever I was, whatever happened. I didn't care who my opponents were. England at Wembley weren't any old rivals, though, and that's where we were heading next. We lost 3–1 but I nearly scored what would have been a great goal against them. In fact, what happened in London in May 1980 helped me, six years later, to score the best goal of my life. I dribbled past all of the England defenders at Wembley, but instead of dribbling past the goalie I tried to finish too soon . . . and it just missed the post. My little brother, El Turco, who was only seven years old, told me I'd made a mistake. In the World Cup in Mexico I remembered his advice.

In the meantime I was still struggling with Argentinos Juniors. During the Metropolitano championship of 1979 I scored twenty-two goals along with Sergio Elio Fortunato, and we finished joint second with Vélez. We had to go on to play a decider for second spot. I'd been suspended after a referee took a dislike to me in a friendly I'd played a couple of weeks earlier. It was the first time I had to watch an Argentinos decider from the outside and sadly it wouldn't be the last. We lost, 4–0.

I was top scorer in the Nacional of '79, with twelve goals, and in the Metropolitano '80 also, with twenty-five, but once again I missed the crucial match: this time I was ill for the final against Tigre and went to the stadium wearing jeans and a sweater rather than the club strip. Although we lost we celebrated coming second. It must be the only runners'-up title I've ever celebrated in my whole career. For Argentinos, in those days, coming second was like becoming champions.

In the Nacional '80, the last one with Argentinos, a couple of unforgettable things happened to me. On 14 September, at the age of nineteen, I scored my hundredth goal, against San Lorenzo in Mar del Plata. Then I had a famous falling out with Boca goalkeeper Hugo 'El Loco' Gatti.

It was towards the end of October, the Nacional championship was coming to its conclusion. Hugo Gatti had been interviewed in a Santa Fé newspaper, and *La Razón*, a national newspaper which had a very wide circulation in those days, picked up the interview. They published it on the Saturday, the night before the match we were due to play against Boca. Gatti had said that I was quite a good player but that the press were hyping me up

... and that I was a fatty, or I was going to be a fatty. I was furious because I'd at last got my chance to play in a deciding match and he came out with that. We'd played on the Wednesday against Union, in Santa Fé; and the very next day, we played a friendly in San Justo, nearby. Now we had the possibility of qualifying for the finals of the Nacional if we beat Boca on Sunday. I answered Gatti with everything I had: I said to the press that it was a question of jealousy, that in my view he had been a great goalie but now he was a nobody, that he let in stupid goals and that was why he was picking on me and on El Pato Fillol (he had also said El Pato only saved goals because he was lucky). In reality, I was surprised at Gatti's comments because I thought there was a good vibe between us. During another Argentinos–Boca game we were asked for a picture together and it was cool, no problem. But Gatti pissed me off. And since Cyterszpiler had already noticed that the angrier I was the better I played, he started winding me up.

'OK, today you score two goals against him and that's the end of the matter.'

'No, Jorge, not two; I'm going to put four past him!'

Before the match Hugo came up to me and said that he hadn't said what had been reported, that he thought I was a phenomenon. But by then I didn't care, I just wanted to keep my promise to Jorge. In the end, I vaccinated him four times.

The first time I received the ball from the left, got it to the centre of the box with a left-footed back-heel flick and it hit Hugo Alves on the arm. I took the penalty gently, towards Gatti's right; he dived towards the left.

The second time, I started off down the right, four or five metres away from the corner flag, and took the ball in diagonally towards the centre of the pitch. Ruggeri fouled me and their defenders lost a little bit of concentration. I took my opportunity and shot immediately. The ball went high and inside the far post.

For the third goal, Pasculli took the ball out wide. I ran down the middle and he placed a perfect pass to me on the edge of the box, beating Abel Alves. I brought it down with my chest and then I moved a little towards the right. When Gatti came out I swept it gently into the far post with the inside of my foot.

For the final goal I played a one-two with Pasculli. I went down the middle and Abel Alves fouled me from behind. I thought I was already inside the box but the ref called it outside; just right of centre. Vidal stood in front of Gatti, taking advantage of the fact that they had Hugo Alves on the post playing him onside. I kicked it hard, towards the post where Gatti was standing, and the ball went in over him.

I answered Gatti in the best possible way, and I also achieved something valuable for Argentinos: qualification for the quarter-finals of the championship. Also, the Boca terraces shouted my name for the first time: *Maradoó, Maradoó!* It was enormously emotional: those were the same fans who had sung to me a few years back, *¡Que-se-que-de que-se-que-de!* Something very special was beginning to happen between us . . . Love, they call it. After the game, I took my whole family to the USA, to Disneyworld. From Fiorito to Disneyworld in four years.

Many thought that this was the best spell I'd had with Argentinos Juniors since I'd started playing in the first division. It's possible. For me, the most important thing was that the fans loved me, probably because Argentinos was a small club. But the national squad also wanted me and once again I was left unable to play important games with Argentinos. Uruguay was soon to host El Mundialito: a FIFA-organised tournament between the six World Champions to that date (Uruguay, Brazil, Argentina, Italy, England, Germany) and Argentina had a long way to go to prepare. In Montevideo we beat Germany, we drew with Brazil and were knocked out . . . It was 1981 and I would not play another championship with the strip that had launched me into my world, the world of football. Argentinos Juniors was over for me.

3

The Passion

Boca Juniors '81

I always knew Boca Juniors would be special, always. In my home everyone supported Boca. They had been the first fans to cheer me on a pitch: *¡Que-se-que-de, que-se-que-de!* The same fans who gave me an ovation when I scored four goals against Gatti. I always knew I would have a future with Boca, but they took their time in calling me. In reality, I orchestrated the whole thing: yours truly set it all up.

River Plate, Boca's main rivals, had made Cyterszpiler an offer that was more than interesting. Club president Aragón Cabrera told Jorge I would earn as much as the top-paid player in the club, who at that point was Pato Fillol. When I heard this I said: 'I hope El Pato is on 50,000' – I don't know, some amount of money which to me sounded ridiculously large, because unless it was for a lot of money I wouldn't go. River's offer was interesting, but where I came from our hearts belonged to Boca. I remember walking around with my father one afternoon, he told me about a dream of his ... this was unusual for him, it surprised me. It's not like him to tell me about what's going on inside him, so when he does I listen. He said: 'Dieguito, you know what I was thinking last night? It would be great to see you playing in the Boca strip some day, you at the Bombonera, your family cheering your goals.' That's part of the reason why Boca had a real pull for me. But they were broke, they didn't have a penny.

Over at River, Aragón was beginning to realise that I wasn't convinced. He sent me a message through Jorge: 'Tell Diego to settle for the same money as Fillol or he will have trouble.' It sounded like a threat to me and I liked the whole deal even less. Jorge managed to find out how much Fillol was earning, and it was a good package but I had already made up my mind. If I had joined that River squad it would have been the death of competitive football in Argentina – it was already an amazing squad. With me on board nobody would have been able to touch us. River had Passarella, Gallego, Merlo, Alonso, Jota Jota Lopez. Boca, meanwhile, was bleeding to death, in the worst campaign of its entire history, with Osvaldo Rattin as manager. Whenever I think of that disastrous season, when Boca picked up just three points, I think: Fuck you, Rattin, you were given Boca and you managed three points!

We were to-ing and fro-ing when I got a call from Franconieri, a journalist with *Crónica*, asking if River was a done deal. I saw where he was coming from immediately. He wanted to get me to spill the beans so I let him talk for a bit and then I took a gamble: 'No, I'm not going to sign with River because Boca have called me.' I came up with it on the spot, it was inspiration, one of those ideas you get now and again. Of course, Franconieri was delighted with this nonexistent news and he took the bait. That afternoon, *Crónica* came out with a headline that read: 'Maradona to Boca'. The operation was underway, we just needed the Boca directors to take the bait as well. They did.

First, they asked me if I really wanted to go to the club or if I'd only made the claim to put pressure on River. It was an odd situation: River, who had all the money but none of my heart; Boca, with no money and all of my passion. We began to negotiate with club directors Carlos Bello and Domingo Corigliano. In the middle of the mess I went to Mar del Plata with Argentinos Juniors, to play in the Gold Cup against River. By then everyone knew I would die for Boca and they didn't stop insulting me the whole match, chanting: *Maradona/son of a whore/the whore that/gave birth to you!* But after the match, even though we lost, I was the happiest guy in the world. I'd got what I wanted: I was able to drive the message home to River that I didn't want them at all. Up until then, aside from the *Crónica* headline, I hadn't made any comments, but that night as soon as I walked out of the dressing room I said, practically shouting, 'After all those insults I have no doubt in my mind: I want to go to Boca and not River.' They all fell upon me: Martín Noel, the Boca president; and the old man, Próspero Cónsoli, the president of Argentinos. Cónsoli adored me but at that point he wanted to kill me! He'd asked River for thirteen million dollars he knew he would get, but with Boca? Not a chance. What to do? How to do it? Then negotiations started in earnest.

One more incident made me certain I would go to Boca. One Tuesday in February '81 I invited Claudia and a bunch of relatives to watch the final of the Children's World Cup – Inter Milan against the Tahuichi Academy of Bolivia – at the Monumental, River's stadium. Claudia hesitated: she didn't understand why I was willing to expose myself to such a situation, but off we went anyway. The atmosphere was tense. When we got to the VIP box a man said: 'You and your girlfriend can go in, but there's no room for the rest. If you like, they can go to the seats in the stands.' I didn't like it at all but I accepted, I didn't want to make too much of a fuss. Claudia and I settled down in the VIP area, but after a few minutes a couple of the club directors started shouting behind me: 'What are you doing here, *bostero*!?' I turned round. I wanted to kill them. We got into a fist fight and Claudia and I were kicked out. The last thing I shouted at them, before joining the others in the seats, was something I already knew: 'I'm never coming back to this club! I swear: never again!' Never again.

But now I had to find a way to turn the Boca dream into a

reality. By Thursday 12 February Argentinos and Boca had come to an agreement, but the following day Aragón carried out the threat he had made to me through Jorge: Boca received a surprise visit from the Inland Revenue and the money they had set aside for my transfer disappeared. A horrible tug of war started which went on until Friday the 20th. Eventually, I was transferred to Boca on loan, with Boca gaining the option to buy me. For that loan Boca would have to pay four million dollars, and give Argentinos a load of players: Santos, Rotondi, Salinas, Zanabria, Bordón and Randazzo . . . they were all represented by the same agent, a man called Guillermo Cóppola whom I didn't know at the time but who would later play a key role in my life. Randazzo must have thought he was Uwe Seeler because he wasn't interested in leaving Boca and he made quite a fuss. Now that I look back on it, I realise that because of Guillermo my transfer to Boca practically fell through. He was insisting that Randazzo didn't want to move to Argentinos and the Boca directors were saying to him: 'Guillermo, it's a lack of respect, the people will kill us if we don't close Diego's transfer', but Guillermo would answer: 'Lack of respect? It's a lack of respect to Randazzo.' It endangered my own transfer but I was impressed: he really looked after his players.

I was due a lot of money from the deal but it was as if I had signed for nothing. My percentage from the transfer alone should have been 600,000 dollars but in the end I was paid in kind. Boca gave me some apartments constructed by businessman Tito Hurovich which might as well have been made out of cardboard. We couldn't get the deeds written up for the apartments, there were no papers for them, nothing. One was in Correa and Libertador in Núñez, and for quite a few years I ended up living there just opposite the ESMA (Escuela Mecánica de la Armada), the Navy training school, which had become notorious because of the dictatorship, because of the disappeared. Another of the flats was in Republica de la India, the street opposite the Botanical Gardens. They were a disaster, we couldn't sell them to anybody.

I had rejected an offer from River, who were very wealthy, to accept one from Boca, who didn't have a penny. It was madness, I lost money. Or at least, I lost out on earning money. By now I knew, however, that Europe would be my destination eventually. Barcelona had already expressed their interest in me very emphatically while I was still at Argentinos, and it was obvious that Argentinian football would not be able to afford me for ever – partly because of the economic situation the country was in at the time and partly because Europe has always been where our top players end up.

With that transfer to Boca I went from one life to another. I was already famous, but I had never imagined that wearing the Boca strip would signify such a huge change. I couldn't go to dinner at a restaurant without something getting smashed up or two hundred thousand people scrambling around me, asking for autographs. I'd moved away from the little house on Argerich Street to a bigger one. I had outgrown my Fiat 125 and was driving a Mercedes Benz. It was another story, another life.

I signed my contract on Friday 20 February 1981 at the Bombonera in front of Channel 13's cameras; they had the exclusive rights. That same night I stepped out on to the pitch to play in a friendly against Argentinos. It was part of the deal. I played one half for each team. The shirt I wore in the first half, the Argentinos one, I gave to Francis Cornejo. Then, on the steps of the away changing rooms, I changed and wore Boca's colours for the first time. I walked out on to the pitch, crossed myself, stepped on to the turf right foot first. I knew it was the start of a great story, but right from the beginning it would be turbulent, starting with the penalty I scored in that match against my former club, the club I loved.

At my last training session with Argentinos, I had strained something in my right thigh during a sprint. I spent the rest of the afternoon with an ice pack but it didn't go away. I really looked after myself, I rested, I thought I was going to be OK, but as soon as I stepped out for Boca the following Friday and started to run, *zas*, I felt it strain again. I arrived at Boca injured and I couldn't immediately give the people what they expected from me. But my official debut took place only two days later, on Sunday the 22nd, against Talleres de Córdoba at the Bombonera.

I gave my all, as always, but I knew better than anyone that the Boca fans expected more, much more. I knew it because I myself expected more. But I simply couldn't sprint or move too much. What saved me was that I scored goals; I vaccinated them from the start. (The penalty I had scored against Argentinos, at my presentation match, hardly counted; it even hurt me to think about that.)

When I stepped on to the pitch I crossed myself, as always. I was very nervous. The Bombonera was stuffed to the rafters! It seemed as if the ground was moving. And I was thinking about that bastard strain, but I couldn't let them down, least of all that day. Boca's *concentración* was at La Candela in San Justo, and on the eve of the match they did everything they could think of to ensure I could play. Doctor Luis Pintos had given me an injection of painkillers but I was still hurting. They even gave me sleeping pills. I was running at 60 per cent, more or less. I gritted my teeth through the frustration of being unable to run, I felt my leg pulling me backwards, but I pressed forwards anyway.

El Negro Baley, the Talleres goalkeeper, fouled me and gave away a penalty. I took it and scored. Then another. I remember both those goals with enormous warmth; they were my first for Boca and contributed to us beating Talleres 4–1. When I took penalties in those days there was no mystery to it: I relied on my sharp vision, and my ability to predict which way the goalkeeper would go. I still remember the first time I touched the ball in a Boca shirt. Mouzo got the ball passed back to him and I went looking for it the way I always did at Argentinos: because we hardly knew each other Mouzo wasn't expecting me; he kicked it incredibly hard and smashed me in the back. But it was only to be expected. Only five days earlier I had been training with Argentinos. On the pitch we shouted instructions at each other. I would say to Miguelito Brindisi 'Move back' and Marcelito Trobbiani would shout at me to close in on Talleres's central defenders. Each player made their own contribution and the fans sang: *They wanted him at Barcelona/ they wanted him at River Plei/ Maradona IS OF Boca/ because he is not a hen!*

I'd been through so much in such a short space of time that I had started to wonder if this moment would ever arrive: to be at the Bombonera, to win, to score. My parents had come down from Esquina to see me and so had my brother Lalo. The only one who missed it was my brother El Turco because he was performing in a *comparsa*, singing and dancing in a street parade.

I was settling into my new role but I was upset by the fact that all those boys had had to leave because of my arrival. I was almost embarrassed to show up at the *concentración* at La Candela. I was worried about making my entrance. I even left the car quite far away. Out on the patio were Mouzo, El Colorado Suárez, Perotti. I missed Galíndez, the masseur from Argentinos who'd gone everywhere with me. It was a very sudden change. I'd left behind a squad I knew very well. I had real friends, from way back: I was godfather to Negro Carrizo's son. At Argentinos, we all knew each other's strengths and weaknesses. Zurdo Miguel Angel Lopez, who was the manager, understood us like no one else. Suddenly I was at Boca, and within ten minutes of setting foot at La Candela, Silvio Marzolini, the Boca manager at the time, called me over and told me this club was different from Argentinos Juniors. He said that if over there I enjoyed some privileges, that wasn't going to be the case here, and that if I was used to travelling to matches with my family, that wouldn't be possible at Boca.

Silvio didn't know me and he made a mistake speaking to me like that in our first meeting. He let the tortoise get away, truth be told. By contrast, Yiyo Carniglia, who was a senior member of the technical staff at the club, told me I shouldn't feel I was expected to be anyone's saviour. Yiyo was older, he understood me better. Silvio was less patient with me: I think he was afraid I would get out of control. Perhaps I gave the wrong impression of myself, but honestly I needed – and I still do need – to feel love and warmth from others. Yiyo gave me that. Silvio didn't.

Looking back, though, I have fantastic memories of that Boca squad. I had known Pichi Escudero and Huguito Alves from the 1979 Youth Squad: we had shared a lot of time together during the South American Cup in Montevideo and the World Cup in Japan. Pichi looked like a quiet kind of guy, but he was one of those who after a match, in Uruguay, would run to the beach and dance around like a madman. Hugo on the other hand was more serious, and when I got to Boca I immediately got on with Ramoa, Ruggieri and Abel Alves, Hugo's brother. It wasn't that I wasn't paying attention to the older ones, but we simply didn't have much in common. Nobody actually told me, but I sensed that my team-mates as well as the fans expected a lot more from me.

And then there was the problem of money. During the first game, against Talleres, the box office takings had been a million dollars. In the second game I don't think it reached a thousand. We'd been caught by devaluation, Martinez de Hoz's infamous little 'Tablita' had gone to hell.*

My injuries worsened over those first two games with Boca.

---

* Translator's note: Martinez de Hoz, Jorge Rafael Videla's Economics Minister, introduced a schedule of gradual devaluation to slow down Argentina's inflationary tendencies, known as 'La Tablita'. For several years the currency was artificially strong until eventually a huge run on the peso in 1981 led to a massive devaluation almost overnight.

I was crawling on the pitch. But I still managed to score: again at the Bombonera, this time against another club from Córdoba, Instituto. I scored two: one from a penalty kick and the other a little gem. I faced the penalty area, chipped the ball over El Negro Nieto, ran round him, recovered it again before it landed – a *sombrerito* – and stuck it into the net first touch with my left foot. The ball even went through Munutti's legs. A *golazo*!

But with the mid-week friendlies – necessary to pay for my transfer – and a particularly trying match against Huracán on 8 March, I was beginning to feel I'd had enough. Every time I ran it felt as if I was being stabbed in the back of my right thigh. So I stopped.

I was out for four matches but Boca won them all anyway. The boys wanted to prove that they could win without Maradona.

In those early days, my relations with Marzolini and with the Prof, Gustavo Habbegger, who was the physical trainer, were not the best. They were very rigid about the *concentración*, the training, and too many stupid demands which I couldn't stand. With time and success we began to understand each other more. At the time I made a statement about Silvio: 'He's an honest man who works all day trying to improve the team and although he doesn't have much experience you can tell he knows something.' But at the beginning I was really sulky with him and the Prof. Things weren't simple.

I was back for the game against Newell's on 29 March, and scored from a penalty kick. We drew 2–2. The following Sunday we were to play a derby against Independiente, about which I felt strongly. I had to fight Marzolini so he would play Oscar 'El Cabezón' Ruggeri. Ruggeri already had an incredibly strong personality; he was a defender who was always willing to move up front if necessary. Since Marzolini didn't pay any attention to me I got together the older guys, Brindisi, Mouzo, Pernía, and asked them: 'Tell me the truth, don't you guys feel safer when this kid plays?' They replied: 'Yes, yes, Diego, you're right, this kid really has got balls.' So we went and squeezed Marzolini. Ruggeri played against Independiente in Avellaneda, and we won 2–0, with a volley from me from outside the box and a goal from Ruggeri. I knew he was going to be brilliant, and he was never out of the team again, unless he was injured or sent off.

People always say that forwards shouldn't complain, but I also felt that I wasn't getting the ball as much at Boca as I had at Argentinos, and I wasn't afraid to make my feelings known. I told my team-mates that we needed to work together, that we needed to play off each other more.

That's what I was like. I kept quiet about nothing. If I was sure of what I felt, I said it. So what? Why shouldn't I? How had I got out of Fiorito? With balls.

Finally it was time to repay what I felt was a debt towards the fans. One night in April, when it was raining as if it were the end of the world, I played my first *superclásico* derby, Boca Juniors against River Plate at the Bombonera. It was better than I could have imagined even in my wildest dreams. Don Diego was watching comfortably from Sector E, the seated area of the stadium, and I was thinking about him as the minutes went by and things unfolded as if it was my own private party. The old man had only seen one *superclásico* in his whole life before that one: a Boca defeat at the Monumental which he had watched standing in the terraces, sad and squashed among the away fans.

I really wanted to win that match. Firstly, for my family, Boca fans through and through. And then for the club and my team-mates: in Argentina people are always going on about River being Boca's father. I hadn't made much of a contribution until then. I wanted to prove everybody wrong. So I felt ecstatic, as happy as you can get – especially if you score a goal like the one I hammered past El Pato Fillol. That one, that's one I will never forget. It was my first in a *superclásico*. Córdoba made a superb move. When I saw he was going diagonally, I went for the far post. I received his cross, brought it down with my left foot and almost hit it as Fillol came out. But instead I cut inside and left Pato crawling . . . I was going to walk the ball into the net when I saw Conejo Tarantini – the tiger! – closing me down. I decided I'd better get a move on. My shot squeezed inside the post. That's when I finally felt the warmth from the terraces, warmth I hadn't noticed when I first stepped on to the pitch. It was madness, it was happiness. Brindisi had scored two goals before my one, so we finished 3–0. Then we went to eat at Los Años Locos, classic steak and chips, San Felipe white wine . . . just as I liked it . . . and autographs. Autographs here, autographs there. I was on a cloud. I was the happiest man in the world.

At the time it seemed that that win against River Plate was enough, that we were already touching the sky with our hands. But there were players at Boca – me among them – who didn't have a very clear idea of what we wanted, of what we were aiming for. We didn't realise the magnitude of what was involved if we were to win the title. We managed to grasp it half way through the championship, but it wasn't easy.

We had no consistency. We went up, we went down, we won, we drew, we lost. On a Wednesday night just after the *super-clásico* we drew with Vélez in Liniers. I thought it would do us good, wake us up, but not at all: we were all over the place. Against a Ferro team managed by the old master Carlos Griguol – Ferro were our closest rivals in the struggle for the title and the most complete team of all – we drew 0–0 in Caballito: I've rarely had the shit kicked out of me as badly as I did on that day at the beginning of May. There's an incredible picture: I'm flying about two metres in the air, like Michael Jordan, because of a terrible kick Carlitos Arregui gave me. But they didn't need to kick us; they were the better team.

That match began our worst run of the whole tournament,

in total contrast to Ferro. After a good win over Central at the
Bombonera, we drew with Racing, lost against Talleres and drew
with Instituto. It was the midway point of the tournament, and
we had a five-point lead. But we were convincing nobody. It was
a struggle.

The basis of the team was there. It just needed a few little
adjustments. Pantera Rodriguez was in goal because Gatti was
injured. At the back, we had Tano Pernía or Colorado Suarez
on the right; Mouzo and Ruggeri as central defenders – Ruggeri
was by now one of the first names on the team sheet – and the
phenomenal Cachito Córdoba on the left. In the midfield Chino
Benitez, so experienced he was going grey; the Uruguayan
Karsouski, even pronouncing his name hurt; and me, although
sometimes I liked playing more up front. The alternative to any
of us was Marcelo Trobbiani, who stood out from all the others
in one particular respect: he was just as good as a man-to-man
marker as he was on the ball. Up front we had Pichi Escudero,
who could dribble around anything, Miguelito Brindisi who with
all his experience had an unerring eye for goal, and El Loco
Perotti, who when his neurons were in the right place could kill
you. Then there was Pancho Sá, who was captain until I was
given the armband; the brothers Alves, Abel and Hugo; Pascucci,
who had started off as a central defender and went out when
Ruggeri came in; El Puma Morete, who scored only three goals
but important ones; Rigante, who was the substitute goalkeeper
while Gatti was out although he never played. And there were
a load of kids as well: Acevedo, Cecchi, Ramoa, Sánchez,
Quieroz. It was a good squad, we just needed to get going.

After that run of bad luck, we had a couple of great games:
first we beat Huracán 3–2 on 31 May, and immediately after, in
the Vélez stadium, we gave Platense a thrashing: 4–0. I scored
twice, but the loveliest goal was scored by El Loco Perotti: he
dribbled past half the Platense team and he left Biasutto, their
goalie, spreadeagled. He nailed it. We were off again, or so it

seemed, until we crashed against Union in Santa Fé, losing 2–0. We were still on that seesaw because we then beat San Lorenzo 4–0 at the Bombonera. I put a great goal past Cousillas from a free kick, around the outside of the wall. I saw the young Argentinian Riquelme do a similar thing against River while he was still at Boca, just before he went to Barcelona (I'll never understand why he wasn't picked for the 2002 national squad). I've always said this: with a free kick near the box, the only option is a curler round the outside. If it goes over the wall then it will certainly go over the bar as well.

And the story continued: another victory, against Newell's, and then four draws one after the other, including River at the Monumental, with another goal from me, once again shaving Pato Fillol's arse, and Conejo Tarantini's. But for Boca, four draws were too much. That's when the *barra brava*, the organised gangs of the terraces, took over the *concentración* at La Candela.

There was a little room where the phone was, near the entrance to the *concentración*. I had been waiting to use it to call Claudia. And Mono Perotti wouldn't get off the phone.

'Come on Mono, you motherfucker, you've been on the phone for two hours,' I was saying to him. And Mono, with his feet up, was giving me: 'Hang on, Maradona, hang on!'

And then I saw this guy force Mono's legs down with a thump . . .

'Stop, you'll hurt him!' I shouted, and when I looked up I saw a huge thug who said to me, 'You can shut up too!' But I wasn't afraid. 'What's wrong with you?' I said, and the guy eased off.

'No, no, Dieguito, the problem isn't with you . . . stay cool.'

I looked around and saw that there were about two thousand people in the ping-pong room. It was the *barra*, the hardcore fans, and they were going into the bedrooms. Their leader at the time was José Barritta, known as 'El Abuelo' (the

Grandfather), and he was there – they were all there. I saw guns, real guns. I looked out of the window and saw about ten cars in the car park, all theirs. They wanted to hit Tano Pernía, Ruso Ribolzi, Pancho Sá. I couldn't believe it. They were saying, 'Boys, don't take it the wrong way, but the fans are getting pissed off and we've come to warn you. If you don't win the tournament, there will be no end to their *bronca*. We've just come to warn you, that's all . . .'

So I said to them, 'Hang on lads . . .'

And El Abuelo says to me, 'Don't you get involved because this isn't about you . . .'

But I refused to let him finish. I couldn't stand the situation. 'This may not be about me but it's not helping anyone . . . coming in here to squeeze us like this, why? Tomorrow no one's going to play . . . at least, I'm not playing.'

And El Abuelo insisted . . .

'Listen Diego, the papers are saying some of these guys don't want to pass the ball to you, that they're not willing to run for you, so we're aiming at the ones who are messing things up for you. We'll take care of it . . . if they won't run, we'll make mincemeat of them all.'

It was madness! OK, I'd arrived as a big star, the people loved me, whatever you like, but this was really crazy! And Silvio Marzolini wasn't showing his face, he was hiding. When he finally appeared I confronted him and said, 'Our team can't play like this.'

El Abuelo spoke again: 'OK. Alright. Play. But you lot had better give it your all because otherwise we'll sort you all out.'

'What do you mean? You'll kill us all, mate? Listen to me . . .'

'Not you, kid, you're going to be the captain, you're our representative, you wanted to come to Boca.'

I was twenty years old and I confronted Boca's *barra brava*. I faced up to El Abuelo. That day, I earned the respect of the entire squad, the older ones, all of them . . . because they didn't know me. They knew me as Maradona the footballer, but that night they realised I could also stand up for them off the pitch.

The following day, with me as the team captain, we beat Estudiantes 1–0, with another of Perotti's goals. The commando group that took over La Candela ended up helping to build us as a team, because after that night we were something else. We'd drawn four consecutive games; Ferro were gaining on us, and things were getting grim. But we just managed to pull through.

I'll never forget what happened that day at La Candela. Any player from that '81 Boca squad could tell you about it. Pantera Rodriguez was pale; little Quieroz burst into tears and said to me: 'I thought they were going to kill all of us, Diego, thank you.' Thank you? I don't think so. I was shitting myself. I had such a big turd, I couldn't believe it! But I had to say something to the *barra*. They had wanted to fob me off with all that 'You're going to be the captain, you're our representative, you wanted to come to Boca' stuff. El Abuelo realised they'd gone too far: if the police had arrived at that moment they would have opened fire and it would have been a bloodbath. The only one who was joking was Loco Gatti: 'All this fuss just because I'm coming back to the first team.'

He returned to the first team against Estudiantes: that day he came out from his goal to the middle of the pitch and made the pass for Perotti to score. Then came Colón, an incredible game. It was on 26 July. They kicked the shit out of us and then ended up pulling out of the tournament because they claimed the ref had been biased against them. As a result they were relegated and we were on course for the title. We still had to face Ferro, the best team. They were more organised than we were. But Ferro's will to win was not the same as Boca's.

Ferro led us a merry dance at the Bombonera, but we fought back hard. I gave Perotti the pass for the goal and I saw the terraces celebrate like never in my life: it was a sea of heads, a

wave coming on to the pitch . . . stunning. Ferro had us cornered,
but Gatti made some unbelievable saves: he was the man of the
match. We beat Griguol's team 1–0. We were on the verge of
victory. No one and nothing could stop us.

At least that's what we thought when we travelled to Rosario
to play Central. We were sure that the title was ours, and with
a game to spare. With a draw we would be sorted. On that fatal
Sunday in August I had triumph almost in my grasp, but I let
it slip away. I missed the penalty that would have crowned us
champions. To this day I cannot forgive myself – the sadness in
the faces of the Boca fans on the road back home, from Rosario
to Buenos Aires, would stay with me for a long time.

We lost 1–0 in Rosario but we were still way on top, with the
chance of winning the title against Racing at the Bombonera. A
draw would get us the point we needed to win. A week later,
we were 1–0 down when we were awarded a penalty. I stood up
to take my revenge. The dollars that had been paid for me weighed
me down but I managed to forget everything. Thank God, my
mind was clear when the penalty came, I was calm when I
slammed the ball home. In the morning I had prayed a lot. I
had asked God to look after Boca, and Argentinos (who were
on the verge of being relegated) as well.

I heard the final whistle and I went crazy. Suddenly there's a
kid hanging on my shoulders, climbing on my back, it was my
brother Turquito . . . my legs crumbled, I hugged him so hard I
don't know how I didn't break a bone. Then I took him round
the pitch with me, and immediately my brother-in-law Indio
came up to me and said: 'Pelusa, Argentinos are saved, too.' It
was too much for me, I felt like I was drowning, but I didn't
want to stop running. I was a champion . . . a champion with
Boca. At last, I kept telling myself, after all I'd suffered in
Rosario on Sunday. It meant so much. And the oddest thing
came to my mind: a couple of months before that match my
grandmother was hospitalised at the Güemes Sanatorium. I went

to see her with Claudia and when the little old man at the car park realised Maradona was driving he started shaking ... he wept ... he thanked me for all the happiness that we, the Boca players, brought to him, and he told me that he never missed a single match on the radio. As I celebrated on the pitch I remembered that man; I think he sums up the true Boca fan. I owed the fans, even if everyone said that missing a penalty could happen to anybody. Thank God I was able to repay the debt in the best possible way – bringing home the Metropolitano Cup with Boca.

We celebrated at La Candela, which had been our home throughout the year. It's sad Boca has now lost it, but it's true that it was in a rather uncomfortable, out-of-the-way location. It was unsafe, too: you wouldn't believe the gunfire that could be heard at nighttime. But I loved it, it was Boca's home. Of course, I would sleep more than anyone. And even if I got up at eleven, I liked to drink my coffee with milk in the kitchen, in my pyjamas: it was just like being at home.

By now River, still pissed off about my transfer, were looking to buy someone else, to calm the fans down. They chose well, repatriating my friend Mario Kempes who had been playing in Valencia since the mid-'70s. I was proud of that. I had always admired Kempes, and the fact that they made the effort to bring him back to Argentina on my account, to compete against me, made me feel important. In the first duel between us, in the Metropolitano championship, I came off best, but in the second, in the Nacional championship, he took the laurels.

I had the opportunity and the pleasure of inviting him to my weekend house in the Buenos Aires suburb of Moreno. I remember the way my folks, my brothers and my friends stared at Marito. Just three years earlier, he had been the best of all, during the World Cup. He was the great Kempes, great. I always liked to use him as the best argument against Passarella when, as manager of the national squad, he decided you couldn't play with long hair. If he'd stuck to this rule, in 1978 we would have had no Kempes!

Unlike the Metropolitano, the Nacional championship ended in the worst possible way for me. I think it was exhaustion: it seemed as if we played a thousand matches a week. From the moment the Metropolitano finished, in August, the only thing everyone was talking about was my transfer to Barcelona and Boca's efforts to hold on to me. The club only had one way to make money: to schedule friendlies with me on the pitch. That's why, less than fifteen days after our lap of honour, we were travelling to Mexico to play against Neza, without having had a break at all. From there to Spain, against Zaragoza. And immediately after that, to Paris. It was my first time in the city I had heard so much about and I loved it. Especially one night we spent at the Lido: I was allowed in even though I wasn't wearing a tie . . . I didn't know you couldn't go into a cabaret without a tie. They sat me at a table right next to the stage. At the Parc des Princes, we beat Paris Saint-Germain 3–1. But no one was talking about football, everyone was talking about my transfer.

In the end Boca held on to me, but the climate at the club wasn't the best. We started off badly in the Nacional and poor old Marzolini's heart wasn't up to it. He had to walk wrapped up in cotton wool because any minute his heart was going to explode. In that atmosphere, we managed to lose three games in a row. After being defeated by Instituto at the Bombonera – 1–0 to a goal by Tucu Meza – Pablo Abbatángelo appeared in the dressing room. He was a very influential director and he insinuated we were not giving our all. I was outraged, so I went on a really famous TV programme, 60 *Minutos*, and said that only someone very stupid could talk like that. In the wake of my interview, you could have cut the air with a knife at the club. And in the meantime, we travelled, we travelled, we travelled. I got to know the world. And I realised that the world knew me.

In mid-October 1981 we landed at Abidjan airport, in the Ivory Coast, after a stopover in Dakar. I'd never seen anything like it before and I don't think I ever lived through it again in my whole career: a crowd of locals stepped over the machete-wielding police and hung round my neck, saying to me: *Die-gó, Die-gó!* They moved me, they really moved me. Afterwards, when we were having lunch at the hotel, about twenty fans came up to me, and one said: *Pelusa . . .* He said 'Pelusa' to me! A little black kid in the Ivory Coast knew my childhood nickname. We played two matches there, against two first-class teams: ASEC Nimosa and Africa Sport. Boca made good money, as did my team-mates, not to mention me: 18,000 dollars just for going out on the pitch. My team-mates never made a fuss about those things; I guess it was simply because if I hadn't been in the squad they would never have got paid at all for playing a friendly in Africa.

There were 25,000 people in the Félix Houphouet-Boigny stadium and everyone compared Boca's presence there with an earlier visit by Pelé's Santos. That was way off the mark, we were something else. The way the Africans greeted me had made me think. I was treated like a king abroad. Whereas in Argentina . . .

During that trip the idea of leaving football first entered my mind. That same month I would turn twenty-one years old. And I seriously thought about quitting. I discussed it with Don Diego, with Jorge, with my friends. In Argentina the press was full of reports that I was going to jail because I wasn't paying the Inland Revenue. People said all I thought about was money. My dream, in those days, was quite crazy: I wanted to play a match with kids, against kids, with kids on the terraces, with kids as stewards, kids for police – just kids. Innocents. The pressure was too much. I didn't want to know any more. I watched Escudero, Pascucci, any of my other team-mates, wandering calmly about, without anybody bothering them, and I felt envy. In my heart I knew there was no going back: that was the way my life was going to be. I felt I was a prisoner of fame. But I thought about the little African kid calling me Pelusa and I thanked God. They had greeted me like never before in my life. They had shown me that they loved me.

We flew from Africa and, after twenty-seven hours in the air, arrived back in Argentina just in time to play another fixture in the championship. We thrashed San Lorenzo of Mar del Plata all the same and got ready to continue in the Nacional. In total, I played twelve matches, scored eleven goals, we reached the quarter-finals against Vélez, and there it all ended . . . on the night of 2 December 1981, in the Bombonera. Referee Carlos Espósito sent me off with ten minutes to go, in a very heated game. Moralejo had been all over me, marking me however he could: even he was embarrassed by what he was doing. He didn't pass the ball once, all he did was hack at me throughout the match. Until I reacted. The Italian in me came out and to hell with it. When they sent me off, we were still 0–0; in those final minutes, Vélez took the lead. Cabezón Ruggeri equalised, and immediately Mono Perotti scored the winning goal for Boca. We won 2–1. I never imagined that was going to be my last match in the championship proper, with Boca . . . Never. And I ended up being sent off. In the second leg, the lads arrived shattered and Vélez killed them. That was the end of the story. Marzolini was no longer the manager: Vladislao 'El Polaco' Cap had arrived.

Between that forgettable Nacional and the preparations for the 1982 World Cup in Spain, Boca had another incredible tour, in the US, Hong Kong, Malaysia, Japan, Mexico and Guatemala. Eight matches, between Wednesday 6 and Wednesday 27 of January, in exchange for 760,000 dollars. Eight matches in twenty-one days. I made my folks travel with me, my three younger siblings (Hugo, Raul and Caly) and of course Claudia and Jorge. And I already had a cameraman, Juan Carlos Laburu, who followed me everywhere. I remember after the first match, against

El Salvador, in Los Angeles, a Brazilian gentleman came up to me in the dressing room and said: 'I want to say hello because some years back Carlos Alberto, world champion in 1970, played against you for Cosmos and said to me, "I have just seen an Argentinian boy who's going to be a world sensation." And what do you know, he was right.' It was Rildo, who had been number 3 for Santos and for the Brazilian squad.

As for the trip, well, Raúl Madero, who was Boca's doctor at the time, said of it: 'I've been in this business many years, I'm sure there are teams who have played four matches in one week. I myself experienced it in Estudiantes, in Zubeldía's day. But this Boca thing must be a world record, without a doubt. We started last Sunday in Tokyo. We played and flew to Los Angeles. Changed plane and flew to Mexico. The match against America was on Tuesday night. We finished supper and nobody slept because at 6 a.m. on Wednesday we went to Guatemala. That same day we played against Comunicaciones. That same day! On Thursday we started our way back, via Miami. We took a flight that connected in Rio and arrived in Buenos Aires on Friday lunchtime. And Saturday, another plane, to appear in Mar del Plata to play . . . I think it was a miracle. Take a map and have a look: it was a world record.'

On Saturday 30 January 1982, in front of a full stadium, I began my farewell to Boca. We beat Racing 4–1 in the Copa de Oro, the summer tournament held in the beach resort of Mar del Plata. I scored. In the same tournament I played against Independiente and at the end, in the last match, against River. We lost 1–0, on Saturday 6 February, to a goal scored by Pelado Díaz. Afterwards, Polaco Cap, the new manager, gave me permission to return to Buenos Aires, to spend some time with my family and rest a little. I couldn't even go to the beach in Mar del Plata. People loved me too much. I locked myself in my Moreno house and waited.

At this stage the discussion was whether or not I stayed at

Boca. The economic situation in Argentina at the time was disastrous and the offers from abroad exerted an enormous pressure. A lot of money was being talked about, a lot, although not as much as in the '90s. Clubs were offering eight million dollars for me, which in those days was an incalculable fortune, impossible to turn down. Nowadays clubs pay that for any old defender. I missed out! In that respect I let the tortoise get away from me. At a press conference, during Boca's epic tour, Domingo Corigliano had been asked about what was going to happen and he answered: 'We're going to do everything possible to make him stay.' So I stood up on my chair and started shouting: 'Co-ri-gliano, Co-ri-gliano!' But I knew it was very difficult, very difficult. And it gave me *bronca*, because I wanted to play in the Copa Libertadores, the South American version of the Champions League, to this day my great regret in Argentinian football. I wanted to win a title outside Argentina for once. But my relationship with Argentina, with my country, was beginning to suffer. I had begun to think that they loved me more abroad than in my own country. The matches I played with the national squad, in the run-up to the World Cup '82, at the River stadium, against Yugoslavia, against Czechoslovakia, against Germany, left me with a strange sensation. There was bitterness. For the first time the fans whistled at me, they shouted that I should get my head down, start training and stop fucking about. I couldn't believe it. I hadn't even had a holiday: I went from Boca to the national squad non-stop. I hadn't played well, it was true, but didn't Maradona have the right to be average, once in a while? I thought about the World Cup and I didn't give a shit if I was average in the way I maybe had been in those international matches: I would swap anything for Argentina becoming champion of the world.

When that series of games ended, I went to Esquina in Corrientes, the land of my parents, seeking out my roots. I went up the River Corrientes, the Paraná Miní, through those places that only my old man and his mates were capable of wandering into without getting lost. I took comfort in the company of La Claudia, my brothers and my friends. They were my lifelong friends, from Esquina, and together we travelled the river, sailing and fishing. I spent a lot of time thinking. I thought about everything that had happened to me in just a couple of years. And a phrase stayed in my soul: 'People have to understand that Maradona isn't a happiness-making machine.' It was time to think about myself, and Spain was calling.

4

The Frustration

Spain '82, Barcelona FC

After that summer tournament in Mar del Plata, which turned out to be my goodbye to Boca, I spent four months training with the national side for the World Cup '82 in Spain. By the time the tournament started we believed we had already won the cup. We forgot one detail: in order to win you have to play first. Maybe because things had gone so well in 1978, and better still in 1979, we believed that we were already there, that it would be easy. But there was something else, something crucial: our physical preparation was terrible. I can say this now for the first time: that was the biggest mistake. You can't evaluate a kid like me coming straight out of playing a whole championship. You can't do that! It wore me out, and I'm sure it did the others too. So that no one could say I wasn't working hard, I responded with everything I had. But with the work that Prof Ricardo Pizzarotti made us do I reached the '82 World Cup tired, over-trained. Dead. Without that sparkle, without the spring in my step that had become my trademark.

It was a shame, because I really wanted to be there. I knew it would be four months of preparation, a huge amount of time to spend in a *concentración*, but I didn't give a shit. It was my first World Cup. I was really excited. I dreamt of sharing a room with my mate Juan Barbas, of the training sessions with all those monsters, of Menotti talking to me, telling me off.

I had promised La Tota and La Claudia that I would only kick the ball with my right foot during the four months of the *concentración*, to preserve my magical left one for the actual tournament. But in spite of all the dreams and promises everything got fucked up.

In those days it was hard at the *concentración*. It was hard just being there. Don't get me wrong ... it was hard. I'm not saying that I was the only one who did things right and the others didn't, no. I think all of us, every single one of us, lost concentration. In football spirit is contagious: if the team is in good form, then even the biggest donkey in the team can pick up on it. And boredom, mediocrity is also contagious. And within a closed group in training, all that is magnified. We were in Villajoyosa, in Alicante, a beautiful place. We thought we were the best and we hadn't even played a game.

We were to play the first match of the World Cup tournament against Belgium, on 13 June. I knew the spotlight was on me because my transfer to Barcelona was a done deal and I had to be the star no matter what. Just before the start of the championship Barcelona had secured my transfer for an unprecedented amount, a fortune. The Catalans had paid over eight million dollars for me. Before the World Cup they made me pose holding up the *blaugrana* strip – that's what they called it, the blue and red. If I didn't win they'd kill me. As it turned out we lost: Belgium beat us 1–0, but we were robbed of a blatant penalty for a foul committed against me. After that we wiped the floor with Hungary, on 17 June. We scored four goals, and won 4–1. I scored twice in that match, my first two World Cup goals; the first one a diving header and the second with the outside of my foot, my left of course. Six days later I had the shit kicked out of me against El Salvador. We still beat them 2–0 but I could already imagine what was coming. I'm not complaining, I'm not going to paint myself as a victim, but I was kicked a lot. Everyone remembers how Claudio Gentile marked me when we played against Italy in the second round, on 29 June in Barcelona. We lost 2–1 and he only got booked for it. But, of course, people only remember the result. In Italy, many years later, Gentile admitted to me that his game had been to stop me from playing: every time I tried to receive the ball he'd be snapping at my ankles. I could hardly move or turn around and he didn't even get sent off. It wasn't Gentile's fault, that's his job; it was the ref's.

Then Brazil did us in. On 2 July they beat us 3–1. But every time I watch that match on video I become more convinced that we weren't the lesser team. And again we should have been awarded a penalty for a foul against me. It ended badly, I lashed out, kicking Batista in the balls. But it was meant for Falçao. Falçao masterminded a midfield move; they went *tac tac tac* and left me for dead. As I ran past them I turned round and hit out at the first guy I saw, I was so pissed off ... poor guy, it was Batista. I was sent off. Even today I can see myself walking off, leaving the pitch, and Tarantini's pat as we pass each other. Everyone thought it was going to be my World Cup, and so did I, but it was over. I left the World Cup in a bad way, and Argentina didn't make it to the semi-finals.

In my first interview after the tournament I said that I hadn't failed in the 1982 World Cup; I'd done what I could. A player never fails alone; he can do better or worse, but he doesn't lose alone. One player can't make champions of a team. What I do know is that I was the one that lost the most; nobody had risked so much, nobody wanted more than me for things to work out well. The whole thing had been really hyped up; there weren't that many stars for the publicists to focus on, and it was my first World Cup. Before I'd left Argentina I'd said to those who wept over my transfer to Barcelona: 'Come on, who are you trying to kid; in our country there are more important things than Maradona ...'

And then there was Barcelona. I truly believed Barcelona was the club for me, the best club in the world, even better than

Juventus. But I didn't anticipate the idiosyncracies of the Catalans. I didn't imagine, either, that I was going to come across as an imbecile like the President, José Luis Nuñez. He was such a publicity seeker. He would do anything to appear in the media. When we lost he would come weeping into the dressing room to offer us more money, as if playing better or worse depended on the cash. He would organise press campaigns against me because he had a huge influence at a particular newspaper. In reality, that whole time was very complicated: it caught me at a dark, difficult moment. I found it hard to adapt from the calmer football of the Argentinian league to a very different game, rougher, faster. At the beginning I couldn't get the ball from any direction; in the training sessions you could end up getting kicked in the mouth. That wasn't football. We had the best players in Spain. I'm not turning against the lads at Barcelona, because they did what they could, but I found the transition from technique to fury very hard: all they did was run whereas I relied on my touch. And I couldn't get used to that: to run, run, run . . . In Copper's test – that test which gauges the aerobic capacity of a player by measuring in metres the distance he could run in twelve minutes – I would score 2,700 while the others made it to 5,000, 6,000. They'd go off the scale! And I started to realise: of course, this means that they're already running before they get a touch.

Víctor was a runner, Periko Alonso was a runner . . . The German player Bernd Schuster and I understood each other well enough but when I arrived he was just coming back from an injury. Lobo Carrasco also helped me a lot. The thing was either to go along with this style of play or quit. So I got stronger. But it was very difficult for me, and it wasn't my team-mates' fault. Without entering wholeheartedly into the frenetic pace, I would do my thing with the ball. And they started to understand me; I would set the rhythm, the tempo, impose my technique without taking away their more furious, physical game.

But just when it had all come together, when we had started
to communicate properly, when we hadn't lost since the first
fixture, when I had already played fifteen matches and scored
six goals, I came down with hepatitis. It was diagnosed in
December 1982. My ankle had been bothering me for a few days
and I wanted Doctor Oliva, the osteopath with the Argentinian
squad, to come and see me but he couldn't. Barcelona sent me
to a clinic for standard treatment; I went straight from the
training ground. But when I walked into the clinic the doctor,
instead of looking at my ankle, started looking at my eyes ...

'Come on brother, what do you want with my eyes, I came
about my ankle.'

'No, *hombre*, let me take a blood sample, I don't like the
colour of your eyes at all.'

I went home shitting myself, I didn't know what to think.
The following day, one of the Barcelona doctors, Doctor Bestit,
came round.

'What's wrong with me, Doc, what's wrong with me?' I asked
him.

I realised he didn't dare answer me when he started beating
about the bush.

'Well, it could happen to anybody . . .' he kept saying and I
was getting more and more scared.

'Come on, *viejo*, out with it!'

'You have hepatitis, Diego,' he finally said. That killed me.
Killed me. Because an injury, well, we footballers are used to
that. But hepatitis? I locked myself away. I didn't even want to
watch football on TV. It was banned in my house. Thank God
La Tota came over for Christmas. And when it came to the
toast, Nuñez gave me the only joy in all my time in Barcelona:
he sacked Lattek and brought Menotti.

When I arrived in Spain in August 1982 the German Udo
Lattek was the manager. Then, when he was fired and Nuñez
suggested Menotti's name to me I said yes, I thought he was

the best man for the job. But it was he who asked me, I didn't suggest Menotti's name to him. With Menotti at the helm we won a Copa del Rey and a La Liga cup, the two main tournaments in Spanish domestic football. That was the best Barcelona team I was a part of, tactically and technically. Very different from the first. Very different.

The differences started in the way we worked. Lattek made you slog from goal to goal with medicine balls that weighed eight kilos each. One day I kicked one into him and said, 'Look here, *Mister*, why don't you do this once and see how you feel tomorrow?'

I wasn't being spoilt, but all my life I had been used to a different routine. At Argentinos, at Boca, I would sleep until two hours before the match, wake up for the technical chat, then we would eat and go off to the stadium. But in Barcelona, before one of the first games of the championship, on the Sunday of the match itself, there was a knock on my door:

'Yes?' I said, half-asleep, on my own, because Schuster and me had our own rooms.

'Yes?' What time is it? I wondered, and looked at the clock: eight-thirty. 'What's up?' By now I shouted a little bit, and I was told, 'The boss says you have to get up to go walking.'

'Tell him I don't walk.'

A few seconds later, almost immediately, Lattek arrives.

'You do as I say.'

'I want to rest . . . I'm the one who's got to run around later . . . this is what I'm used to. If that's OK with you, fine. And if not . . .'

'There will be a sanction.'

'No, there will not be a sanction,' I heard Migueli saying; the defender didn't even want to give me time to answer.

'It gets to me too, this walking at eight thirty in the morning.' Schuster added his voice.

I put a stop to that practice and others – like the medicine balls.

Before the important games, against Real Madrid, for example, Lattek would up the weight of the medicine balls to twenty kilos. Eight-kilo balls were bad enough! Just because the match is going to be tough doesn't mean you have to train with more weight. He was a German. A German who said he was revolutionising football. I respected him as far as I could and no more.

With Menotti it was something else. All the lads fell in love with him because of the way he treated them. They weren't used to it. Today, with anyone I see from that group the first thing they do is ask after El Flaco. It was a different Barcelona, a terrific Barcelona!

I remember a great match from those days: 2–2 against Real Madrid, at the Bernabéu. I scored a great goal: we started a counter-attack from the middle of the pitch, I ran with the ball. The goalkeeper came out, I passed him and ran through on my own to the goal. I could see that behind me Juan José was chasing me. He was a short defender, bearded, blond, with very long hair. I dummied to walk the ball into the net; I waited for him and, when he caught up, I touched the ball inside almost on the line. He carried on past and I rolled the ball slowly into the goal.

With El Flaco Menotti in charge we finished fourth in La Liga, and I was able to play the last seven matches. I returned on 12 March 1983 against Betis, in Menotti's very first game as our manager. We drew 1–1 and I left the pitch really heated, very pissed off: I felt I'd been drowning, I didn't get one shot on target and the crowd were pissed off with us. In the penultimate match I scored three against Las Palmas but even that didn't calm me down. And to top it all off, my confrontations with Nuñez were about to reach their climax: the final of the Copa del Rey was looming, I wanted to win it as much as he did but as always Nuñez had to go that little bit further. He made Jordi Pujol, the president of Catalunya, come to training to tell me, very clearly: 'Young man, we really trust you and need you. All of Catalunya will be thinking of this match, we have to win.' Motherfucker!

Nuñez knew that, along with Schuster, I had an invitation to play at Paul Breitner's testimonial just before the final of the Copa del Rey. He was dead against letting us go. And now he was even using local politicians to put the pressure on us ... 'If Madrid isn't letting Santillana go, then we will not let you two go either!' he kept shouting hysterically.

Things spiralled out of control when he confiscated my passport. I was full of pride that Paul Breitner, the great Paul Breitner, had invited me to his testimonial. I really wanted to go and he was sending a private plane for me and Schuster. I'd called him and told him yes, I was coming. Until Schuster asked me with his German voice: 'Do you have ze passport?' And I answered: 'Yes, of course. Jorge, go get it.' And then I saw Cyterszpiler's face transform. The thermos-head had handed it to the club, for European Cup trips and so on ... I wanted to kill him! That's when I got an inkling that Nuñez wasn't going to make it easy for us. On the contrary, he was going to bust my balls. It was Monday: I had him called at the club to get the passport sent to me but no, they weren't going to send it over. Another day, and nothing. So I went over and asked to speak to Nuñez. 'He's not here,' they told me at first. But I'd seen his car and chauffeur. 'He can't see you right now,' they said, changing tactics. Another director came over, Nicolas Causus, a guy I was very fond of who had been born in Mendoza. He was on the verge of tears: 'No, Dieguito, we can't give it to you, the president doesn't want to ...' We were in the room where the trophies are kept, at the Camp Nou. So I said: 'So the president won't come and face me? I'm going to wait for five minutes ... If I don't get my passport, all these trophies here, these lovely trophies, made of crystal, I'm going to smash them one by one.' Casaus was begging me: 'Dieguito, you can't ...' And Schuster added his voice to mine once again: 'Let me know when we can start.' I picked up a Teresa Herrera, a beauty, and gave Casaus one last chance ...

'You won't give me my passport?'

'No, the president says no . . .'

'OK, he denies me and won't give me my passport . . .'

'He's just saying he can't give it to you!'

I picked the trophy up as high as I could and threw it . . . *Craaaaashhh!* . . . It made such a noise . . . 'You are crazy,' Schuster said to me. 'Yes, I'm mad. They can't confiscate my passport! The more seconds that go by, the more minutes, the more trophies I'm going to smash,' I replied. They gave me my passport back, but they didn't let us go to Breitner's testimonial. I don't know what the fuck it was all about, some Spanish Federation clause. But I smashed a Teresa Herrera and I got my passport back; it was unconstitutional for them to confiscate it.

We won the Copa del Rey anyway, even though I was bursting with anger. The final was in Zaragoza, on 4 June 1983, against a Real Madrid managed by a great man, Don Alfredo Di Stéfano. It was an enormous rivalry, beautiful: Barcelona against Madrid, Menotti against Di Stéfano, Maradona against Stielike. We started off with the advantage, with a goal by Víctor laid on by me. Santillana equalised for Madrid (ironically the other guy who hadn't been allowed to go to Breitner's testimonial). Marcos scored the winner, with ten seconds to go before the final whistle. We showed Spain – and Nuñez – what we were capable of.

Claudia and I had settled into life in Spain. We had decorated the house in Pedralbes – a smart suburb of Barcelona – the way we liked it. It had a tennis court, a little football pitch, a huge swimming pool and a barbecue which was never wanting for meat. I'd made a lot of friends and they loved coming round to eat in the Argentine way, *asado* or whatever. My team-mates Quini, Esteban and Marquitos always used to come round. They loved it. And I felt the time to celebrate had finally come.

We wanted to go into La Liga '83/'84 with everything we had, but we kicked off our campaign with a loss: 3–1 against Sevilla on 4 September. That was a bad omen, I think. But we immediately started to pick up: we beat Osasuna and Mallorca. For our fourth fixture we were expecting Athletic de Bilbao at the Camp Nou . . . it was 24 September 1983. That morning a strange thing happened to me. I went to a hospital to visit a little boy who was in a bad way after he'd been run over by a car. His legs were in a state, poor little thing! When he saw me his face lit up. I said hello, kissed him, and hurried to leave because I was playing later that night. When I got to the door, he made a huge effort and almost shouted at me from his bed: 'Diego, please be careful because they're going after you now!' That's what he said to me: they're going after you now.

We were beating Athletic 3–0 when the Basque Antoni Goikoetxea fractured my ankle. I was able to see the move on the telly, three days later while I was lying in a bed in the hospital in Barcelona. I hadn't seen him coming on the pitch or I would have dodged him as I had on so many other occasions with so many other kicks. But I just felt the impact, heard the sound, like a piece of wood cracking, and realised immediately what had happened. When Migueli came and asked me what was up, how I was, I said, weeping: 'I'm broken, I'm broken.'

It seems incredible but just before that happened Schuster had gone into Goikoetxea very hard because the Basque had recently injured the German. And the stadium was roaring *Schuster, Schuster,* shouting as if they applauded his revenge. The Basque was flying. 'I'm going to kill this guy,' he was saying. Of course, I had him next to me all the while, because he was my marker. So I said to him: 'Calm down, Goiko, stay cool, you're 3–0 down and you might get yourself a yellow for nothing . . .'

I swear I meant it from the heart, because I saw that he was on edge. I wasn't trying to wind him up or anything like that. And immediately, the move. They had broken up one of our attacks and they launched the ball back. I ran back towards our goal to pick up the ball around the halfway line. I ran because

I thought Goiko would anticipate what I was going to do. Offside rules applied and I could see him in our area already, so I sprinted with him, won the ball, kicked it with the tip of my toes, and when I went to step, *crack*, I felt the axe's blow from behind, I felt my leg seize up, and I knew that everything was destroyed.

Afterwards, all I wanted to know was when I could return to playing. El Flaco Menotti came into my room and said: 'You're a star, Diego, and you'll come through this one.' They all decided between themselves to operate on my leg. Nobody wanted to tell me until a hospital cleaner came in and made a comment, as if he needed to comfort me: 'Don't worry, Diego, the operation only lasts two hours.' Only two hours! Very frightened, I told Doctor González Adrio, who was in charge: 'I want to come back soon, doctor.' Crazy as I was I thought I would be able to play against Real Madrid, a month later. Absurd, impossible . . . and it hurt, how it hurt! It was the first time in my life I had been in an operating theatre and when I came to the first thing I did was ask after my dad, because I'd seen that he was very worried, even more than me.

With time I forgave Goikoetxea. Back then my brothers and the Barcelona fans said he was a murderer and I never disagreed with them. But I'll never forgive Clemente, the Athletic manager at the time. He declared, just after the match, that he was very proud of his players, and that he would wait a week to see if my injury was really so bad. The best response came from *Marca* newspaper, which came out with the perfect headline: 'Forbidden to be an artist'. It was a good summary because at the time there was a big fight between those of us who played and the ones who . . . ran. And I was something like the standard-bearer for those who loved having fun with the ball, right there in the country where they hit hardest. Because the Italians knew how to mark but the Spanish *murdered* you on the pitch.

The injury was so serious that it forced me into a tremendously lengthy recovery programme. I did it with a genius,

Doctor Ruben Darío Oliva, and in Buenos Aires, which is where I wanted to be.

I kept El Loco Oliva – which is what I call him, but respectfully, he knows that – at my bedside table. For my money there isn't a doctor in the world who knows more than him about sports medicine. Given that I used to call him at least seventy times over any old cramp, with the fracture I needed him more than ever. He lived in Milan (and still does). Every time I phoned him he took a flight and an hour and a half later he would land in Barcelona. Sometimes he came at night, stayed over in Spain, saw me in the morning and left in a hurry to get back to Italy in time to see his other patients. But when I got injured Doctor Oliva arrived at dawn the next day. He had a meeting with Doctor González Adrio and asked how everything was going. They struck a deal between them. Oliva told him: 'If in a fortnight we take some X-rays and we can already see the first evidence of the bone healing, I'll take over the rehab treatment using my own methods. If not, you stay in charge.' But Oliva cheated, he didn't wait a fortnight: a week later he took the cast off, took some X-rays, saw what it all looked like and said:

'Take a step . . .'

'What? Are you crazy? I call you Loco but it's just a nickname . . .'

'Trust me. Have I ever let you down? Step, step gently.'

And I stepped, shitting myself, but I did it.

A week later, when we all had the meeting to assess my progress, Oliva and I practically gave Gonzáles Adrio a heart attack. I arrived walking on crutches, with my left leg raised . . . 'This way, Diego, carefully,' the Barcelona doc said to me and he pointed to some steps I needed to go down in order to get the X-rays done. So I said to him: 'Can you hold these for me please, Doctor?' I gave him the crutches and walked down very calmly. González Adrio dropped his glasses.

I remained in Oliva's care. We worked for a little while in

Barcelona and then put the idea of travelling to Buenos Aires to the club. Of course the thermos-head Nuñez didn't want to know anything about it but Cyterszpiler had a great idea. He told the dwarf, 'If you let Diego travel to Argentina we promise he'll be back on the pitch in January. If not we won't demand a single peseta of the contract until he does come back.'

That bastard Nuñez, his eyes sparkled with delight of course, the general feeling was that I wouldn't be able to play for a minimum of six months. So he figured he'd save money.

Thanks to the wisdom and ideas of Doctor Oliva, which contradicted what the majority of the doctors suggested, they removed my cast seven days after the operation and I was back on the pitch 106 days after the fracture. What Doctor Oliva managed to make everyone understand was that one of the key things about my game was the mobility of my ankles. I have an above-average ability to rotate my ankles, and he was the first to recognise this.

I played in the rain against Sevilla on 8 January 1984. We beat them 3–1. I scored two goals, the second and the third. When we were 2–0 up people began to ask El Flaco to take me off so they could applaud me. It was then that Sevilla pulled one back and everyone shut up. I scored the third and they started again until Menotti took me off. The stadium went wild, they were all shouting and clapping, it was more than the classic: 'Maradoó, Maradoó!' I don't know . . . it was like a shriek: it's one of the ovations I remember most clearly of my whole career. No one could believe it.

In the following match I scored two goals against Osasuna but they meant nothing because we let four in. Straight afterwards we drew with Mallorca, and then we faced Athletic again on 29 January. We won 2–1 and I scored both goals. We were neck and neck with Real Madrid in the title race but when we played against them on 25 February 1984 we fell behind. We were 1–0 down, I equalised and with five minutes to go we scored an own goal which ended up costing us the championship. We finished third.

The problem wasn't on the pitch but off it. One of the many confrontations I had with Nuñez was because he wouldn't let me speak. He wouldn't let me talk to one journalist in particular, José María García, who was very critical of Nuñez. I spoke out anyway. I talked to García, and to any Tom, Dick or Harry. I spoke for the people . . . So one day Nuñez called me and said: 'I forbid you to give interviews to García.' I said no, he couldn't forbid me to do anything. As long as I trained and played, which is what I had signed a contract to do, he couldn't forbid me to do anything. I told him he hadn't bought my life. He went ballistic . . .

But I knew I was fucked. Nuñez had already told me that he was boss. 'OK. I think that's terrific that you're the boss,' I answered, but from then on we started a terrible fight through the press. When we played well nothing happened. But as soon as we drew he would start off with insinuations about why I'd come down with hepatitis, that I went out at night, that I went with women, that this, that and the other . . . He controlled the club's dealings with the media very tightly. So one day I decided to cut my losses and said to him:

'I want you to sell me!'

'No!'

'In that case, I'm not playing any more.'

My time at Barcelona was always ill-fated. Because of the hepatitis, because of the fracture, because of the city as well, because I'm more . . . more Madrid. Because of my bad relationship with Nuñez and because there, in Barcelona, my relationship with drugs began. I have to admit that that's when I got going and in the worst possible way: when you go into it, in fact you're wanting to say 'no' and end up hearing yourself say 'yes'. Because you believe you're going to control it, you're going to be OK . . . and then it gets more complicated. But the drugs thing, in Barcelona, had no effect on my football life. None whatsoever. Nuñez has said he sold me because he knew

I was taking cocaine . . . Bollocks! If that were true I wouldn't have achieved everything I achieved in Italy, because cocaine, instead of motivating you, discourages you, it dulls you . . . it's no use for football and it's no use, either – I've only just learnt this – for life. It started like another little bit of fun. And what at the time seemed like fun turned into drama. Today I regret it. But I'm in this dance now and I have to make it through somehow. For my daughters, for all the people who love me and who I've made, or am still making, suffer. But it's inevitable, it's the way it is. I didn't invent it; it rules the world today. I want to be clear on this issue: governments do nothing to stop this. Why? Because it's to their advantage to have addicts.

In those days people spoke of the 'Maradona clan' and it made me so angry. What was the 'clan'? It was my people, my family, my friends, employees . . . I had a house in the nicest area of Barcelona. Three floors, ten bedrooms, tennis court, swimming pool. Why shouldn't I open my doors to the people I loved? I am happy when I am surrounded by people I love. For me they – Osvaldo Dalla Buona, Galíndez, Néstor 'Ladilla' Barrone among others – were Argentines in need of someone to protect them, and that someone was me. So that all the Catalans would hear me I stated on television: 'I want to tell the people of Barcelona that not all Argentines are bad, that us Argentines don't bulldoze anybody, that we know how to live. We are not responsible for all those who came to damage the city, and now you want to make us pay for what they did.' I never tired of repeating it, so they would understand: there were things my Argentinian friends could do, like drink, smoke or fight, without it meaning that people had to talk about the 'Maradona clan'. I could approve or disapprove of whatever my friends did, but that wouldn't stop them being my friends, and it didn't mean that I was implicated in everything they did. I was sick to death of hearing talk of the Maradona clan; there was no clan in Barcelona! I helped those whom I thought needed it and many didn't thank me. In fact, a lot of them turned against me. So I decided, never again. From that point on I would focus on my family, my true friends and no one else. But no clan, no entourage, no one led me to do what I did, to make the mistakes I made. If one doesn't want to do it, one doesn't do it. That goes for the drugs, too.

Nuñez stayed at Barcelona until quite recently. The funny thing is, he's not even Catalan, he was born in the Basque country. He doesn't know what a ball is, and never will. He will never be more important than a football player. He continued to persecute Schuster in the same way he had me and later he had it in for Rivaldo. He feels forced to make things up in order to keep people: if Barcelona doesn't win with a two- or three-point lead, like it used to, then he gets paid more attention than the players who step out on the pitch. If they don't win La Liga, they'll make up a story about Rivaldo. Romario was sacked by him, Stoichkov was sacked by him . . . all stars.

There's something very perverse going on with many football directors. They're not grateful: we the players give them power, we give them fame . . . while they are just the money-men. Nuñez may have become famous for being the president of Barcelona but 'Nuñez y Navarro' is his bread and butter: that's the construction company he owns with his wife, the company that built many of the sites for the Olympic games. That's what most of them are like.

I could no longer stand it at Barcelona. My last match, on 5 May 1984, in Madrid, was symbolic of everything that happened to me there. The Copa del Rey final, against our arch-rivals, Athletic de Bilbao, turned into a battlefield and we lost 1–0. The Basques would remind me of that goal by Endika many years later, when I returned to play in Spain with Sevilla. I ended up lashing out at everybody, because they were beating us and teasing us, until one of the Bilbao players gave me the two fingers and the shit really hit the fan.

We beat the shit out of each other in the middle of the pitch ... Thank goodness Migueli and the lads came out to defend me because otherwise they would have killed me. I don't know, I think Goikoetxea wanted to finish the job he'd started a few months earlier. Off the pitch all my people wanted to jump in, all those friends they called the clan wanted to defend me but couldn't. They were hanging on to the wire fences, as if they were caged, and the police were hitting their knuckles to get them down. Madness! Later, I was very embarrassed because of the King. Of course, King Juan Carlos was there, in the Royal Box, it was his cup, and we were beating the shit out of each other. I felt sad because of him, because I was very fond of him, he made a good impression on me. I'd read in magazines what he said and I thought he was a good guy. That was why once, before this scandal, I'd asked for an audience with him, officially. And two months later, *ping*, I got my reply, he expected me at the Palace, at the Zarzuela. He was terrific, Juan Carlos, he gave everyone twenty minutes but with me he stayed for an hour and a half. We spoke about football, about Argentina, about *asados* – Argentinian barbecues – even about boats! He loves to sail. I imagined the King of Spain on the rivers of Corrientes. Anyway, the thing is, there we were, chatting away, and suddenly a door opens and who comes through? Felipe Gonzalez! The *president* of Spain. They both asked me for an Argentina strip for their kids.

But the Barcelona chapter of my story was coming to an end. A bad end, but an end nevertheless.

After the Copa del Rey scandal I made my mind up once and for all and I slammed the door shut. I'd left behind a blank contract offered to me by Joan Gaspart, the vice-president: 'Just name your price,' he was saying to me, and behind me Jorge was whispering, 'Go on, go on, name your price and let's stay.' I said thank you very much and left. I had no idea where I would go.

5

The Resurrection

Napoli '84–'91

Napoli had come looking for me as early as 1979, while I was still at Argentinos. They had even sent their club strip to the hotel where I was staying during training, with a letter saying they were waiting for the borders to open up to foreigners so they could buy me. They invited me to spend ten days in Naples, all expenses paid. They wanted to shower me with gifts. I didn't understand what was going on! In those days there was also talk of Barcelona, Sheffield United even. Back then to me they were all the same as Fiorito's Estrella Roja. Napoli meant no more than something Italian, like pizza. Nothing more.

And when they came looking for me in Barcelona years later I still didn't know much about them. I just wanted to leave Spain, Catalunya, Núñez, and the rest – I didn't care where I went. Everyone asks me now: why not Juventus, why not Milan, why not Inter? Well, because the only one who bothered to offer me something was Napoli. And also because Giampero Boniperti, who had been a player and was the president of Juve, had said that someone with a physique like mine wouldn't get anywhere. Well, I got somewhere didn't I? Football is so beautiful, so unlike anything else, that it finds a way to fit everyone in. Even dwarves like me.

I wanted a change of air, and I wanted to play. I'm not saying play well, I'm saying play … I wanted to play a whole championship. And there were other reasons why I ended up at Napoli. On the one hand, when Barcelona sold me they knew very well who they were selling me to. It's not easy to pull one over the Catalans: they didn't imagine the Italians would be great rivals in Europe. On the other hand, and more importantly – this is something I've never spoken about in detail – I was in dire need of a little business because Cysterszpiler had had such bad luck with figures that I was down to zero. Yes, sir, broke ... stony broke. When I arrived at Napoli I had nothing except debts. That's another reason why I didn't go to Juventus, or Milan, or Inter. The Napoli deal came up and we had to hurry it through. Over the years Jorge had invested in any old thing, petrol, houses, bingo halls in Paraguay, all with my money. What's done is done. I fell, I got up. I was twenty-five years old and I didn't have a penny. I have never explained it to anyone, not even Claudia: all I'm saying is that I was left with nothing and it was my fault. I had to start again. The truth is I owed here, I owed there. Things were so bad that, of the 15 per cent of the transfer which was due to me, I didn't see a single penny. And I ended up having to give away the house in Barcelona to pay off debts. So Napoli it was.

Eighty thousand Neapolitans turned up at the San Paolo stadium just to see me on the day of my presentation. It was Thursday 5 July 1984. I said the only thing I'd been taught to say in Italian: 'Buona sera, napolitani. Sono molto felice di essere con voi ...' (Good evening, Neapolitans, I'm very pleased to be here with you), and I kicked the ball into the terraces. The crowd went mental and I didn't know what was going on. I was wearing a pale blue track suit, a Napoli scarf, a Puma white T-shirt and I was standing on top of a flag they'd laid out on the floor. The fans sang a hymn which they'd composed especially for me: Maradona, take charge/ if it doesn't happen now, it will never happen/ your Argentina is here/ we can wait no longer. And then they played another song on the loudspeakers to the

What a tiger! Evita Tournament, Rio Tercero. In those days the Cebollitas beat everyone we played. And I was already getting my picture taken.

There it is. That was my house in Villa Fiorito. It rained more inside than out, but I have wonderful memories of it because it was what my folks could give me and for me that was enough.

Ah, the christening. It must be the oldest picture of me there is.

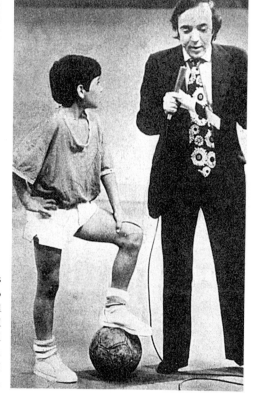

I was twelve years old and I was already famous. Or at least so they told me. Because I played keepy-uppy in the stadiums and people loved it, I got invited onto *Sabados Circulares*, a programme everyone watched. I enjoyed it, I enjoyed it a lot.

There we are, there's the whole crew. We played so well! There's Dalla Buona, Chammah, everyone. And look how I'm standing ... what a swagger!

A Cebollitas derby against Huracán. We went 136 matches without losing a single one.

The one who's got his arm round me is Tomate Pena, may he rest in peace, a phenomenal guy. He really looked after me! To think I later played against him, and much later against his son.

What a moment! 20 October 1976, ten days before my sixteenth birthday, and the manager, Montes, called me and said: 'Go and do what you know best.' My first touch, I nutmegged Cabrera.

My first two goals in the First Division: 14 November 1976 against San Lorenzo in Mar del Plata. I felt sure of myself, but celebrating those two goals was the best, the best.

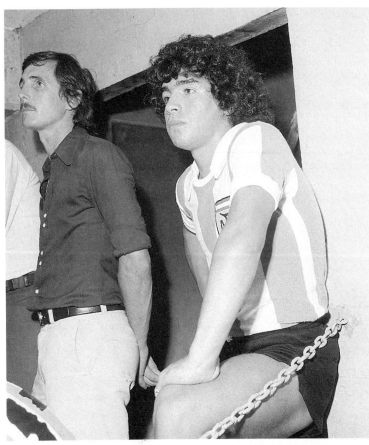

I look scared, don't I? But I wasn't. My one worry was that I knew Menotti would only give me my debut with the national side if the match against Hungary went well. And it did, so I went on. People shouted 'Maradoooo, Maradoooo', and on I went. 27 February 1977. We won 5–2.

What a lovely run. And behind me in the stands, madness … All those people coming to watch Argentinos. Wonderful.

I still think that was the best team I was ever part of. The Youth Team, World Champions in Japan '79, my first important title. Here I'm kissing the Cup with Tucu Meza.

El Loco Gatti, poor guy, had said I was a fatty. He didn't know *bronca* was my fuel. Cyterszpiler asked me to put two past him and I said: 'No, I'm going to score four!' I did, and this was one of them.

Menotti had left me out of the World Cup in 1978 and just a year later I started to show him what a big mistake he'd made. At the Monumental in a friendly against the Rest of The World, I scored this beauty against Leão. And I celebrated …

How could I celebrate any other way? I didn't know it at the time, but jumping like this would become my trademark.

My first goal in the first team. An enormous joy. It was 2 June 1979 in Glasgow. We won 3–1.

I love this picture, I love it!
I think you can see
written all over my face
what a big Boca fan I am.

If I had dreamt of a *super-clásico* it couldn't have been better than this one: April 1981, in the rain, 3–0 at the Bombonera. I love this goal. I'd already dummied Tarantini, Fillol had been left for dead, and I'm finishing.

My debut with Boca was in February 1981 and I scored twice against Talleres de Córdoba. My romance with the people, with the Boca fans, had started long before, so when I celebrated the goal I felt I was hugging each and every one of them.

When I transferred to Boca we played a friendly a week. And not just round the corner. We went everywhere. That's how we got to the Ivory Coast in Africa.

At Napoli I did any old thing, like this. No, really, my years in Italy were spectacular. We took Napoli from near relegation to the top of the *scudetto*.

Ever seen anyone dance a tango on top of a ball? You have now.

This was the San Paolo party when we won the *scudetto* '86/'87, two years after I signed for Napoli. Unforgettable.

Italy wasn't big enough for us, that's why we wanted to conquer Europe. In '89 we beat Stuttgart to pick up this beautiful Uefa Cup.

My last title with Napoli, the Italian Supercopa in 1990. We beat Juventus 5–1!

What a lovely celebration. Antonio Careca and I understood each other in our hearts and we had many opportunities to celebrate goals like this one.

The Hand of God, heh … Not even the photographers managed to capture what really happened. And Shilton, jumping with his eyes shut, was outraged! I like this goal. I almost like it as much as the other one. I felt I was pickpocketing the English.

I was in such fine form at USA '94. Thank God I scored this goal, thank God. At least I left one good memory behind: it was my last goal in a World Cup, after a spectacular one-two with Redondo.

What can I say about this goal? Simply this: I dreamt it. I dreamt it in Fiorito, I dreamt it in the potreros, when I didn't even have boots to play in … and I scored it in a World Cup, against the English. I started back there in midfield and then I beat one, beat two, on and on. And I scored.

The most sublime moment of my career, the most sublime. When I was there, with the World Cup in my hands, I felt I was touching the sky; all my dreams had come true.

tune of 'El Choclo', a famous Argentinian tango. It was perfect: I'm so in love with tango. I was there for fifteen minutes, fifteen minutes only, because we had to catch a flight to Buenos Aires for a holiday. When I went back down the stairs into the tunnel I saw Claudia and I hugged her, weeping. My legs were shaking again, like the time I played my first game in the first division, like the time I started at Boca. Everything had been very intense and Claudia and I knew we were gambling our lives, we knew we were starting over. And we were doing it in a place, in a city, that meant a lot to me. This is why when I talked to the journalists I said something which came from the bottom of my heart: 'I want to become the idol of the poor children of Naples, because they are like I was when I lived in Buenos Aires.'

I fall into Napoli, and without knowing it, I fall into a Serie B team. Of course, they were in Serie A, Italy's top flight, but it was as if they were a Serie B team. I was only told Napoli's history after I had already signed for them: that's when I found out that in the last three seasons they'd been fighting relegation and that the previous season – '83/'84 – they had managed to avoid it by just one point. I asked them then if they could at least guarantee me a quiet life. They said yes, so I went ahead with the deal. While the negotiations were going on the fans had even staged a hunger strike in order to get me. And one of them, I think his name was Gennaro Espósito, had chained himself to the railings of the San Paolo. So I started to get myself sorted physically – I knew that in order to win in Italian football I needed a different body. Italian defenders aren't like the Spanish: in Spain they would kick and elbow you to death. Even my tongue was at risk in Spain! Not so in Italy, because the TV could send them all to jail and because they were trained to mark. I still had memories of Gentile in the 1982 World Cup! I adapted slowly, slowly, and there, at that stage, my personal physio Fernando Signorini turned out to be crucial.

I called Fernando Signorini 'El Ciego' (the blind man) because he couldn't see a cow in a bathroom, but he knew a lot more than anyone else about physical training. He came to me when I was in a bad way after the injury in Spain. He helped with my rehab there, which was why I was able to make my comeback in just 106 days. In Naples, our work was different: our aim was to get my machine, my body, in perfect working order. And we made it. I went for pre-season training with Napoli at Castel del Piano and I was made to feel like any other Neapolitan: they applauded my heel flicks, nutmegs, scissor-kicks – I scored with a scissor-kick at the very first training session – my dummies, they celebrated my every move . . .

Rino Marchesi was the manager. My debut was an away game against Verona, in the north of Italy, on 16 September 1984. They hammered three in against us. They had the Dane Elkjaer-Larsen, and the German Briegel, who could get me off the pitch with the simplest of moves. They greeted us with a flag that made me understand, suddenly, that Napoli's struggle wasn't just a football matter: 'Welcome to Italy', it said. It was north against south, racism against poverty.

In the first half of the '84/'85 season – in Italy the season breaks up for Christmas – we barely managed to get nine points. Nine! I went off to Buenos Aires for Christmas and I was so embarrassed I could barely talk about it. When I returned in January it was so fucking cold that I froze my bollocks off. On 6 January we clashed against Udinese who had eight points and were fighting us for relegation. We were playing for a place in Serie B, for God's sake! We beat them 4–3: Ricardo Daniel Bertoni scored two goals, and I scored another two from penalty kicks. From then on, after Christmas, we scored more points than Verona, who came out champions. We got twenty-four points to their twenty-two. We missed qualifying for the UEFA Cup by just two points. I scored fourteen goals and came third in the table of top goalscorers, only four behind Platini. There were some great kids in the Italian league: Platini himself, Rummenigge at Inter, Laudrup at Lazio, Zico at Udinese, Sócrates and Passarella at Fiorentina, Falçao and Toninho Cerezo at Roma.

So – getting a little bit big for my boots – I confronted the club president, Corrado Ferlaino, and said: 'Buy three or four players and sell the ones the crowd whistle at. That should be your thermometer, if I pass the ball to a guy and he gets whistled, *chau* . . . and if not, start thinking about selling me, because I'm not staying like this. Buy me a couple of players. Get me Renica, of Sampdoria, who comes on as a 3, a defender, and in fact is a fucking first class *líbero*.' And that's how we started building the team up.

My second season in '85/'86 saw the arrival of Alessandro Renica, Claudio Garella – who had been goalie for Verona when they won the championship – and Bruno Giordano, from Lazio. Garella saved with his feet, it was incredible, he didn't use his hands. Which is why I begged him, pleaded with him: 'OK, so don't catch it but don't let it bounce.' He never ever left a ball hanging, to be pushed in. I started an era at Napoli, I branded the club with a stamp of respect. Before my arrival Paolo Rossi had refused to join because he said Naples wasn't a city for him, because of the Mafia. The truth is before my arrival nobody wanted to go to Napoli.

The first time I saw Giordano I realised he was a player for us. He'd been involved in the Totonero mess, a huge scandal about clandestine football bets. They said to me, that's Giordano, this and that . . . he plays for Lazio, he's got a good touch, he plays down the right, down the left. I said: 'This one's for Napoli.' And I confronted him: 'Giordano, please, come play for us.' And he said: 'Whenever you like.' Lazio asked Ferlaino for three million dollars for Giordano, and the guy was crying all over me, saying he didn't have the money. 'Make the effort, old man,' I said to him. And he did, luckily, because Giordano was a phenomenon. Bruno and I understood each other really well;

he'd go back a little and I'd go a bit more up front. I scored eleven goals to his ten, we qualified for the UEFA Cup and finished third in the *scudetto*, just six points behind the champions, Juve.

By then Ottavio Bianchi was our manager. Well, we were the managers really, because I didn't like him from the start. He was hard, he didn't seem Latin, more like a German, you couldn't get a smile out of him for anything. He didn't get on my case too much because he knew that when he started talking his nonsense, I would leave. He was an authoritarian guy, but he showed quite a lot of consideration towards me. One day he said, 'There's an exercise I want you to do.'

'Which?'

'I'll throw the ball and I want you to go down to the ground in a sliding tackle. Practise on both legs.'

'I'm not doing that, I'm not going to the ground . . . I only go down if the opposition push me down . . .'

'OK, well, we're going to have problems all year.'

'OK, well, you'll have to leave then.'

That's what our relationship was like, although we always managed to get results. Fortunately, by then, God had already put Guillermo Cóppola in my path. I'd signed him up as my agent in October 1985. The changes in my management team came about because of the money problems I'd had when I left Barcelona completely broke. I insist it wasn't just Jorge Cyterszpiler's fault; at the end of the day, the reality is that the decisions were and are always taken by me. Jorge didn't want to resign because he had faith that we would recover, but I'd been working too hard for too long to have nothing to show for it. *Things will change*, he kept saying to me. And I would answer: 'No, things don't change, this isn't working out . . .' In fact, I'd made a plan with La Claudia: we knew we had our whole lives ahead of us and we needed to make the most of it.

I'd known Guillermo since my transfer to Boca, although at

that time he'd been on the other side of the counter, working at a bank. He was also looking after the interests of most of the players who were due to transfer to Argentinos Juniors, particularly Carly Randazzo, who was the least keen to go, and I was impressed by the way he made sure Carly was a priority. We finally got together in 1985: we were at the *concentración* in Ezeiza, preparing to play an international qualifier with the national squad, and he heard through Ruggeri that I was looking for him. In fact I'd asked Ruggeri what he was like, how he worked. I was interested in him partly because I always remembered a gesture Guillermo had made to Barbas years earlier, which I'd been particularly struck by: after Barbas was transferred from Racing to Zaragoza, Guillermo appeared one day in Alicante, at the *concentración* for Spain '82, and he gave Barbitas back some money, having shown him a load of figures with detailed accounts of his expenses. He was incredibly meticulous. I reminded him of that when we first sat down to talk about the possibility of working together. Guillermo was chatting with Fillol, whom he also looked after, and I called him up to my room. I explained that my relationship with Jorge wasn't working any more and asked if I could count on him. Guillermo said he didn't want to step on anybody's toes and I stopped him short: 'You don't have to talk. I'm going to talk.' At that time he had almost two hundred players on his books and he also still worked at the bank. I was asking him for exclusivity. He asked me for some time. He closed one more transfer, Insúa to Las Palmas, I remember, and when he came to Naples he had already studied all my figures, all my fuck-ups. The first thing he did was put my old man and Claudia's dad to work in our Buenos Aires office: sorting out what was there, what was missing, doing a sort of inventory. If I couldn't trust them, who could I trust? It was a way of uniting the whole family, even though neither Claudia's dad nor my old man understood the first thing about numbers. They both acted as inspectors of a sort.

Many years later Guillermo confessed to me that for him, working with me was the ultimate dream.

Guillermo, over and above everything else, was order, management, presence, the intelligence to know what to do with my money, how to invest it. He never took a percentage of anything, because he had more money than I did! We always joked that we would start a race to see who made more. Guillermo transformed my situation, turned me into gold. When people say that Cóppola took me to this, that Cóppola led me astray, I answer: 'Cóppola took me from zero and got me to ten.'

And with regard to drugs: Cóppola could never have got me into drugs because when I started, in Barcelona, he wasn't even with me. Full stop.

So we finished third. That, for Napoli, was glory. Juve were champions, Roma in second place and we were third. I thought back to that Verona flag, at the first match of my Italian career – the 'Welcome to Italy' addressed to the Neapolitans. Well, the time for revenge, for the vendetta, had come . . .

It was 23 February 1986. The whole *curva*, the away stand, was shouting at us: *Lavatevi! Lavatevi!* (Wash yourselves! Wash yourselves!) Verona were winning 2–0; the Neapolitans were indignant . . . one touch, *pin*, *pan*, a defender makes a mistake, I score. And four minutes from the end of the game, bang, a penalty. I take it, two all. We celebrated as if we'd won the *scudetto*! And of course, instead of coming to celebrate with us, the whole bench ran towards the stands that had been shouting *Lavatevi, lavatevi!* That's what we were like, that's what the team was like, and that's what the city was like. They were in your face.

I'd asked Ferlaino to buy Carnevale, Andrea Carnevale, from Udinese and, since he knew by now that I never let him down when I got what I asked for, he brought him to me. He asked me what else was needed to crown ourselves champions and I said: 'A little bit of luck, President, a little bit of luck, that's all.' The others, the big clubs, were running scared. They had Platini, they had a load of talented players, but they were also afraid, really afraid! They kept displaying racist banners, but they were acting out of fear: they couldn't believe that a bunch of poor southerners were taking a slice of the cake that up to then only they ate: the biggest slice!

To have won Napoli's first *scudetto* in sixty years was, for me, an incomparable victory. Different from any other, even the 86 World Cup. We built Napoli from the bottom: it was proper workmanship. The *scudetto* belonged to the whole city, and the people began to realise that there was no reason to be afraid: that it's not the one with the most money who wins but the one who fights the most, who wants it the most. I was the captain of the ship, I was the flag. They could mess with anyone but not with me. It was that simple. When we started building that team, the results came: Inter came, we thrashed them; Milan came, we beat them. We beat everybody.

On 9 November 1986, an incredible thing happened: we travelled to Turin to play Juventus. We were 1–0 down and when we equalised the stadium exploded, everyone was celebrating, going mad . . . we couldn't understand what was going on. When Juve scored the crowd shouted: goal, just like that – no flares, no delirium. We scored a second, and again there were huge celebrations. Then the third, and it went even crazier. Then I realised: the stadium was full of workers, southerners the lot of them! *Napoli, Napoli!* they were screaming. Amazing. We had truly become the club of the working class, of the poor. Even in the north we could count on the support of the southern workers who lived there.

We were already champions when I heard about a statistic (because Italian journalists are fanatical about that kind of thing): at that point only two teams had ever won the *scudetto* and the Copa Italia in the same year – two northern teams, Torino and

Juventus. So, just before playing the final of the Copa, I faced the press and said: 'Yes, of course it would be nice to win the Copa Italia. It seems hard but the explanation may be the fact that the contenders have always been from the north. Us here, in the south, we don't tend to miss chances. Not in football, not in life . . .' I was right, and to top it all off, to achieve it we beat the team with some of the most racist fans in Italy, Atalanta of Bergamo. It was perfect.

But there were problems too. The Napoli directors were reluctant to spend money. And after that *scudetto*, in the European Cup, we almost knocked out Real Madrid. We had to play a match behind closed doors in September 1987 at the Bernabéu for the first leg, and at the second leg, people went mad. It seemed every Neapolitan in the world wanted to be at the San Paolo: we made four million dollars in box office takings – which, with resales and touts, in the best Neapolitan style, was probably more like seven or eight – but the club didn't use the millions and we missed out on the opportunity of turning Napoli into something big, big, big . . . they didn't even replace the turf on the training pitch at Soccavo.

The Centro Paradiso di Soccavo, Napoli's training ground, was more like that of an Argentinian second-division team than a European first-division one. It reminded me of my house in Villa Fiorito: the walls in the changing rooms were falling apart, there was a tin roof with room to park four cars underneath it, and the ground of the pitch was so hard it broke your tendons. Which is why I always say that Salvatore Carmando, who was the masseur, the physio, and everything else, deserves 50 per cent of the recognition for any title we won.

My contract ran until '89 but in '87 it occurred to Guillermo that we should hurry to renew it. And anyway, the Napoli I had arrived at two years previously was nothing like this one, after coming third and winning a *scudetto*. The negotiations started in Madrid, at that match behind closed doors we lost at the

Bernabéu in the first leg of the European Cup. Because we were knocked out, Ferlaino started backtracking. But there was a surprise in store for him: Silvio Berlusconi wanted to take me to Milan, and a tug of war started. In my heart of hearts I knew I couldn't play for any team in Italy that wasn't Napoli, because the fans would kill me and whoever bought me. That's what I said to Berlusconi, when I saw him, and he impressed me as a gentleman, as a winner. I said: 'Berlusconi, if it comes off we'll both have to leave Italy. You're going to lose business because the Neapolitans are going to bust your balls every day and I'm not going to be able to live.'

At the beginning of November 1987, we were in the *concentración* at the Hotel Brun, in Milan, to play against Como, and an amazing Mercedes arrived to pick up Cóppola. He was taken to Milano 5, where Berlusconi himself had a little ranch all of his own, a mansion like you see in the movies. He told Guillermo he wanted me, at any cost, when my contract expired, and that he had spent almost 50 million dollars and hadn't yet managed to get a fucking title. Without even asking how much I was getting paid at Napoli he was offering double for me! An apartment in Piazza San Babila, the poshest bit of town, any car I wanted – and I don't mean a Fiat 600, I mean a Lamborghini, a Ferrari, a Rolls-Royce – a five-year contract and a deal with Fininvest, his communications business.

My journalist friend Gianni Miná heard about the meeting and in December published it in his magazine *Special* . . . By Tuesday morning everyone knew Milan wanted me and was offering whatever I dreamt up. That same Tuesday night Ferlaino accepted all the conditions we imposed and we'd signed a new contract, with three times more benefits than we expected to start off with. We agreed $5 million a year until 1993, excluding other incomes from advertising and merchandising, which would be another $2 million every 365 days – a few pennies and a little gift on top. Ferlaino even turned up one day at my house with a black Ferrari F40 – the only one in the world at that time.

I don't know what would have happened with my career if I had finally agreed a deal with Milan. I don't know if it would have turned out different, better or worse. But I knew the Neapolitan and I knew he would give his life for me. Beware – if anyone touched Maradona in Italy, all Neapolitans would smoke them out, in Turin, in Milan, in Verona, wherever.

Actually, if there was one thing I didn't have in those days, it was money problems. It was around then that the International Management Group conducted a poll on who was the best-known person in the world. And my name topped the list so IMG offered one hundred million dollars for my image rights. But there was one stipulation: they expected me to have dual nationality – Argentinian and American. My nationality is priceless. No one can pay me enough to stop me being Argentinian, no one. So I rejected the offer. It was *my* decision, like every other in my life. Guillermo could guide me, but I had the final say. This was always the way. Other people, even Henry Kissinger, had got involved, and they'd raised the hundred-million-dollar figure. But to me it wasn't an issue of money: being Argentinian had no price tag.

I didn't lack money, I told them. In those days I had a programme on RAI, the Italian television channel, which paid me $250,000 a month, and I'd signed a contract for $5 million with the Japanese firm Hitochi, for a sports-clothing label which carried my name. And I had another advertising contract for some kind of cold coffee drink. They wanted to shoot the adverts in the Grand Canyon in Arizona. When I found out I said: 'Let's do it in Argentina, I want to do it in my country!' and I took the Japanese to La Rioja, to Talampaya. *We need models*, they said to me. 'I've got them. My brothers, El Turco and El Lalo,' I said to them. The then governor of La Rioja, Carlos Saul Menem, lent us his helicopter every day to fly from La Rioja to Talampaya. That's how we shot it and it was spectacular

– and they sold a lot of cold coffee in Japan. We also did some shots on the edge of Vesuvius for Asahi beer, another Japanese brand. With all that we made a fortune but in every contract I demanded the inclusion of a clause: that it should not affect the development of my professional life. We endorsed TV programmes, school stationery for children, confectionery, whatever I wanted.

I asked for cars that weren't available and soon afterwards I would get them delivered. It happened with a Mercedes Benz which wasn't being released on to the Italian market. I mentioned it to Guillermo and he phoned Mercedes. They took the bait; they always did. Some time went by and one day Guillermo told me to look out of my balcony. I looked down and there it was: the Mercedes, with all the guys who'd brought it over around it, all bigwigs from Mercedes. It was the first one they brought into Italy. So I went down, everything lovely, hugs here, hugs there, I asked for the keys and got inside. Touched everything, the steering wheel, the controls, fucking amazing, then I looked down and saw the gear stick: 'It's automatic,' I said to them. Guillermo's face paled. 'Yes, Die, yes, it's automatic. Latest model.' I got out, handed the keys back to the guys, said thank you very much, and went back up to my apartment: I didn't like automatic gears. With hindsight I can see it was madness.

Life in Naples was incredible. I couldn't go out on to the street because they loved me too much. And when the Neapolitans love you, they really love you! *'Ti amo piu che i miei figli'*, they would say to me, I love you more than my own children. I couldn't go to buy a pair of shoes because five minutes later the window would be smashed and a thousand people would be in the shoeshop. So La Claudia would buy all my clothes, everything. And she really commanded their respect: *Don't anyone touch Maradona's woman, or he won't play on Sunday*, they said. And the journey from my house to Soccavo and back was a real adventure. I had to get out, one way or another, so I would be ready behind the garage door with the engine roaring and accelerating ... when I gave the order the door would be opened and I rammed into the crowd which would then open up and I'd go through the middle. Madness! And the ones who already knew my tactic would follow me on their mopeds until I lost them. In Naples, those little *motorini* were everywhere! It was crazy, but in my Mercedes or my Ferrari I would lose them.

Things went so well for me in Naples because I brought them things they didn't have: in footballing terms I brought them heel flicks, dribbles and titles but more than that, I brought them pride. Pride, because before I arrived nobody wanted anything to do with Naples, they were afraid. I arrived believing it was a beautiful bay on the Mediterranean and nothing more, but I won them over because I faced up to everyone. That's why, today, any Neapolitan can tell you: *Those teams weren't built by the directors, they were built by Maradona.*

Those were the days, during my fourth season in Italy – '87/'88 – of the formula Ma-Gi-Ca. Giordano and myself had been joined by Antonio Careca from Brazil. Ma for Maradona, Gi for Giordano, Ca for Careca: Ma-Gi-Ca. People had got used to seeing us fight at the top and that season was no exception, which is why I got fully prepared, perhaps like never before, to face it.

In October '87 I became an in-patient for the first time at Doctor Henri Chenot's clinic in Merano. I hadn't stopped since my arrival in Italy: I had played almost two hundred matches on the trot, what with the championship, the cups, the friendlies and the internationals. My adductors (the muscles in my thighs) hurt so much that not even Doctor Oliva, who had always worked wonders with me, could find any solution other than rest. The pain made my eyes water, but I played on, played on, played on, always at the cost of injecting painkillers. That's why it pisses me off when people talk about footballers, saying we earn too much, that we're lazy. Do they have any idea what it means to have a ten-centimetre needle prodding in near your groin? Your ankle? Your knee? Your waist?

The explanation for my performance in that championship can be found in the treatment I received at that clinic. What I will never understand, granted, is why we fell the way we did at the end. That was a strange season: I look back on it with a weird mixture of feelings. To this day I remember it as one of the best, if not *the* best, in my whole career, because physically I was on tiptop form, like I had never been before, like a bullet. But it's also one of the most bitter, the one that gives me the most *bronca*, because it was said that Napoli sold out. That we'd given the title away under pressure from the bookies.

But first it's worth talking about all the good bits. I managed to score in six consecutive matches, something, I believe, that hadn't happened in Italy since the days of Gigi Riva, at Cagliari. I scored against every Serie A team, which had never been achieved before, and some I even scored with my dud leg, the right one, against Udinese, for example. We got 87 per cent of the points on offer in the first nineteen fixtures, an historical record. We were a machine! My performance even managed to convince Ottavio Bianchi, who had to put his authoritarianism in a file and shut the drawer. In training I just played with the ball and I did full sessions only three days a week; and on Fridays only massage and a little free-kick practice. And Bianchi had also forgotten, finally, about timidity: we all attacked, with me, Careca and Giordano in the lead. I ended up top goalscorer with fifteen and Careca came next with thirteen. We didn't have many fixtures left and we were five points ahead.

Then, on 17 April we lost 3–1 against Juventus in Turin. We didn't win a single match after that: week after week it was the same, each result worse than the last. We drew with Verona, 1–1; we lost against Milan, 3–2; against Fiorentina, 3–2, and against

Sampdoria, 2–1. We picked up just one point in five games. We lost a championship that we couldn't lose and that's when people started talking crap.

The decisive match, I think, was the one against Milan at the San Paolo: we went 1–0 down and then I equalised with a free kick like I think I've never taken in my life. Then they killed us with a couple of goals by Virdis and Van Basten. Then Careca scored one to make it 3–2, and finally the ref, Lo Bello, stopped Antonio when he set off on his own again against Galli, their goalkeeper. Maybe, if we'd drawn . . . but it was all a done deal. Bianchi, the wanker, had started experimenting and had left Giordano out. Everything went to shit. To top it all off I was fucked, injured, there was nowhere left around my lower back or my knee for a needle to go in and I couldn't even go on the pitch for the last two games.

It's not a question of looking where to point the finger of blame for what happened. I do think my team-mates made a mistake when they issued a statement to get Bianchi sacked, after the defeat by Fiorentina. They were right, really, because Bianchi had let the tortoise get away from him with some of the decisions he'd made. So it was a noble idea on Garella's, Ferrario's, Bagni's and Giordano's part, but it was mistimed. Their statement said we'd never had a good dialogue with him, and that's true, but Bianchi wasn't to blame for everything, in the same way that we weren't – the players I mean – which is what people were later led to believe. I could never stand being accused and I was willing to leave Napoli if people thought there were any players who had sold out. I don't accept it today and I didn't accept it then. I stayed in Napoli, once the championship was over, because I was willing to face the situation. I remember I sent Claudia and Dalmita, my one-and-a-half-year-old daughter, to Buenos Aires in case some motherfucker wanted to take it further. And I took the opportunity to attend Platini's testimonial. I didn't really want to go because I wasn't up to it physically, but Platini called me fifteen times a day at my house asking me to play. Above everything else I stayed to face the situation, to talk with Ferlaino, to say everything we had to say face to face. There was talk of the Camorra, of the Totonero, the Italian football betting system. And the unbelievable thing is there'd been talk of exactly the same thing the year before, the year we'd won the championship.

All continued to be well with the people, with the fans. But if people were saying that the *squadra* had sold out then they were saying that Maradona had sold out, and if they really thought that, I wanted to leave. In the match against Sampdoria, the last one of the season, the crowd were chanting: *Bianchi, Bianchi, resta con noi!* (Bianchi, Bianchi stay with us.) So I thought: OK, let Bianchi stay at the club. It made me really angry because the thinking among the squad – even though I hadn't signed that statement – was that the manager should go. The minute the *scudetto* was lost Ferlaino should have said 'Go' and the matter would have been resolved. But instead the statement turned Bianchi into a martyr. We made him bigger than Maradona. Napoli ended up renewing his contract immediately.

I had nothing to hide from the manager, we had a strong exchange of words when we argued, we even nearly came to blows. But what happened to us in those last few matches was about football: we didn't have much strength in the midfield. Romano had a torn muscle, Bagni was not in shape and de Napoli, who usually did all the running, was knackered. Up front we weren't giving the midfielders the support they needed and the manager refused to play four midfielders. By the time we realised this it was too late, we were finished. Bianchi wanted to change just before the crucial match, against Milan. That was his fault. It was our fault to have endured the whole championship with Bagni playing on injections of painkillers. I left saying to Bianchi: 'You work it out. Maradona scored fifteen goals, Careca thirteen, Giordano ten, so *hah*, you know? It's impossible to lose the championship. But if you score ten and let twelve in, well . . .'

Eventually I went back to Buenos Aires with all the anger in the world. When I left for the summer break the club had made their position clear: they backed Bianchi, were renewing his contract for another year and were leaving the door open to give the four players behind the statement a kick up the arse: Garella, Ferrario, Bagni and Giordano. It felt to me like a kick in the balls: they were giving the manager all the credit for everything we'd achieved. They'd forgotten so quickly. I'd arrived before he had, I'd fought against relegation, I'd fought with Ferlaino, told him to buy this player and that player . . .

When I returned to Italy in July, I went in with my studs sharpened. The little village chosen for the pre-season training was Lodrone, in the north of Italy. I wanted some explanations from the manager. I wanted to defend the four players who'd engineered the statement, and to advise everyone not to say anything else because if we went on like that they were going to renew Bianchi's contract for another five years. I spoke with Bianchi. I didn't apologise, but I did realise that the only way out for Napoli was to march on, onwards and upwards. That's what I did, and we set off on to the next stage.

In the early days of the '88/'89 season – my fifth in Italy – there were two matches, on two consecutive Sundays, that I shan't forget for as long as I live. First, on the sixth match day, 20 November 1988, we had a field day against Juventus, 5–3, in Turin, with a hat trick from Careca. And then, a week later, we scored four in a 4–1 victory against Milan at the San Paolo. The Napoli fans went crazy; nine goals in two games, against Juve and Milan! And so we marched on. In one game against Bologna, around that time, I invented a celebration dance, a tango . . . that same day my folks had arrived to watch me and I dedicated my dance to them. But our main rivals that season were Inter, Ramón Díaz's Inter.

And at the same time we began our race in the UEFA Cup.

I was dying to get an international title, that was what I was missing.

At Christmas time, I realised that 1988 had been a turbulent year. I was working with UNICEF. I would do anything for the children of the world, especially those who need it the most, I like seeing them joyful and happy. So I dressed up as a clown and became one more among them at the Medrano circus, in Naples. There were over 3,000 children there and among them was my daughter, Dalmita. I also brought my parents to Naples for Christmas, because we're never apart at this time of year, or at New Year. I had suffered a great sadness because of Napoli's defeat in the Italian championship, but also many joys: my best season on the one hand, and on the other seeing my daughter grow day by day and having my whole family with me. That's the most important thing Maradona can have.

I asked nothing more for myself as I looked forward to 1989. As I always say, I'm scared of asking for too much. I just hoped my second child, who was about to be born, came to a better world, with no wars and no hunger . . .

And it was then that the idea of leaving Napoli arose. Bernard Tapie appeared, the president of Olympique Marseille, and he offered me everything I could possibly want and more. At the Hotel Brun in Milan, where I was doing some ads, I sat down with him, Guillermo and a businessman called Santos.

Tapie said to me: 'Let's not talk figures. I'll give you twice what Napoli give you . . . I want you no matter what!' But it wasn't just the issue of money. Or at least, not for me it wasn't, because Napoli would walk away with $25 million. There were other small details which interested me more: a villa, and not Villa Fiorito exactly, a real house, with a 6,000m park for my daughter to run around in, for my family to enjoy, with a swimming pool. Naples had always promised us that but they never delivered. I was tired of hearing my daughter say: 'Daddy, shall we go and play on the balcony?' And also, I said it then and I recognise it today, I wanted the calmness of a championship such as the French one – more . . . mild. It would mean a month-long break in January, which would enable me to go back to Argentina. It felt like I could start over, do something totally different. It was ideal. The problem was who would take the flak for letting me go, and I think that was Ferlaino's greatest fear. The Neapolitan who signed over my freedom would be condemned for ever. Everyone would say: *that's the motherfucker who let Maradona go.*

In the meantime we continued to move forward in the championship, continued to progress in the UEFA Cup. We played the second leg of the semi-final against Bayern, in Munich on 19 April 1989. Ferlaino came up to me and we chatted for a little while before he dropped it in: *If we win the UEFA Cup I promise I'll let you go to Marseille.* I was dancing, I was so happy. I didn't want to hurt the Neapolitans, I knew they loved me, but I thought if I left for a club that wasn't Italian it wouldn't hurt them as much. We drew and qualified for the final because we'd won the first match in Naples 2–0. Now we had to play against Jurgen Klinsmann's Stuttgart and I was bursting at the seams. Our level was the fucking highest and we were convinced we could win the cup. On 3 May we beat them 2–1 in Naples. In the last match, the decisive one, on 17 May we drew 3–3 in Germany. I headed the ball to Ferrara, for him to finish, a very strange move because I headed it from outside the box and on the bounce. We had done it – we'd won the Uefa Cup. It was almost too much at once: I had won my first international title with a club. I had stamped Napoli's name on Europe and I would finally have my transfer!

But Ferlaino didn't want to let me go. Right there, on the pitch, he came up to me while I still had the cup in my hands . . . He held me by the shoulders and whispered into my ear. He said, 'We're going to respect our contract, right, Diego? We still have so much to do.' I wanted to smash the cup over his head but all I managed to say was: 'This isn't the time, President, this isn't the time ... I've kept my promise and now you must keep yours.' And he answered right there, on the pitch: 'No, no, no ... I'm not selling you. I just said it to motivate you.'

Right then and there another war started. Actually, bombs went off from previous battles, which for one reason or another hadn't exploded before, and everything that was left from there on was a minefield. When the championship was over I travelled to Argentina to join the national squad for the Copa América in Brazil, and I decided I wasn't going to keep my mouth shut. I would say everything I was thinking and feeling. Ferlaino had called Cóppola in Brazil to tell him that I should forget about my transfer, that he wouldn't let me go for anything in the world. I couldn't bear it any more, couldn't bear it any more. It was hard to forgive Ferlaino at the time, the fact that he doubted me, after knowing me for five years. I remember that May, there was a match against Bologna which I was unable to play because my damned lower back meant I couldn't walk. Ferlaino stated that he didn't think it was so serious, but I had been carrying that problem ever since I had played with Los Cebollitas. I even learnt the scientific name for it: professional arthritic lumbago. I'd been having injections with ten-centimetre needles in order to play! To this day it hurts, still. But of course in his eyes I was the unprofessional one, the one who lacked respect ... I would love to have a statistic of all the games I played injured, injected with painkillers, in a cast practically.

Before I left for the summer break, Albertino Bigon had been signed to replace Bianchi, thank God, although I had nothing to do with it. I was pissed off, still am, that he left a winner, that when we won it was thanks to the manager and when we lost it was Maradona's fault. There are still people who think managers win matches: they're wrong. There are no tactics without players, and I think that's not open to debate.

I wanted to leave Napoli, but I also knew if it didn't come off, I would stay and fight.

And that's when the never-ending holidays started. After the Copa América I went fishing in Esquina, in Corrientes; I went skiing in Las Leñas, in Mendoza, and I enjoyed it, I enjoyed my first holidays for years. Napoli had messed me around and now they were going to have to dance. What did they think? That it was the first time I was caught in a bit of strife? It had happened at Argentinos, when the crowd had insulted my old man; at Barcelona, when they threw themselves against me with everything they had. This time I'd reached my limit. In the penultimate match of the *scudetto*, the crowd had insulted Cóppola and Claudia. It seemed they'd forgotten, suddenly, everything I'd given them: the *scudetto*, after sixty years; the Copa Italia; the UEFA Cup, and their first ever European title. It seemed they'd also forgotten that they'd paid me just over ten million and they'd already made over a hundred. In truth I was willing to throw grenades at their heads.

It was then – what a coincidence – that my name started to be linked to drugs and the Camorra, the Neapolitan Mafia. Some pictures appeared in the newspaper *Il Matino* and some other magazines, pictures of me with Carmine Giuliano, who was accused of being the leader of a *Camorrista* group, Fortella. I don't deny the Camorra was in the city. But it's a big leap from that to the idea that I did deals with them. They never bothered me. They saw me as entertainment – they said: *Don't mess with the kid*. I admit it was a seductive world. It was something new for us Argentinians: the Mafia. It was fascinating to watch and of course they offered me things but I never wanted to accept them: because of the old dictum that first they give and then they ask. They offered me visits to fan clubs, gave me watches, that was the link we had. But if I saw it wasn't all above board I didn't accept. Even so it was an incredible time: whenever I went to one of those clubs they gave me gold Rolexes, cars. They gave me the first Volvo 900 to come into Italy, and I asked them: 'But what do I have to do?' They said: *Nothing, just have your picture taken*. 'Thank you,' I would say, and the next day I would see the picture in the paper. That's how I came to be pictured with Carmine Giuliano and his family.

Rumours that we were trafficking started to spread. I didn't want to go back to Italy, I felt I was in danger. I sent a statement from Buenos Aires detailing a load of things that nobody knew. We gave details of attempted assaults we'd been subjected to, which had never been properly investigated (such as when a steel ball had been thrown against the windscreen of one of my cars), and thefts which had never been solved, like the one in which my Golden Ball from the 1986 World Cup had been taken. I also asked for protection before returning to Italy, because unless I was guaranteed some security there was no way I could go back there.

So the Neapolitans didn't love me any more, eh? It was dangerous for me to go back? They spoke of the Camorra and of drugs? I decided to return and face them, to see who was the toughest, to see who was lying. Once again I was ready to play almost immediately thanks to Fernando Signorini, who had prepared an impressive work plan while I had been on holiday. I came back against Fiorentina, on 17 September 1989, and sat on the bench for the first time, with the number 16 on my back. I came on in the second half, unshaven as I was, and I missed a penalty. But no one whistled me, none of those whom the papers claimed hated me insulted me, no one. Quite the opposite. That's why the only ones I forgave were the people: the rest, the ones who spoke, the ones who wrote, they wanted to put right what they had put wrong. I missed a fortnight of training and was accused of being a *Mafiosi*, a drug addict, and a *Camorrista*. Upon my return, at the receiving end of the applause once again, I was a good kid – all because I did my job. I was a footballer, and had at that point been one for thirteen years. It really annoyed me that Ferlaino and the club didn't come out in my defence. But all the time I was preparing my revenge, a revenge they wouldn't imagine in a million years. It was different from anything I'd done previously in all my years of rebelliousness.

After that match against Fiorentina I played twenty games in a row, each one better than the last. On 1 October at San Paolo against Milan – whom we were supposed to have sold the previous championship to – we scored three, and one was mine. 3–0 – one of those games you dream of as a kid. And when it looked like Milan was walking away with the *scudetto* (because they paid us back for that 3–0 at the Giuseppe Meazza stadium), God – the Beard – once again gave me a helping hand. Or rather, threw me a penny.

It was 8 April 1990. In those days I was flying, really flying. We went to play in Bergamo and once again we made the Atalanta fans, the most racist in Italy, pay with their own currency. They threw a coin at Alemão as he was walking off to the dressing room. They cracked his head open and the match was suspended. Afterwards, the inquest gave us the points. Towards the end of the *scudetto*, when everyone was taking it as given that Milan was going to win the title again, we hit the pedal and began to overtake, the *sorpasso*, as the Italians say. On 22 April we beat Bologna. The fact is that, while everyone thought that first *scudetto* of ours had been a miracle, something that would never happen again, there we were, on the verge of the second. The season which had started in the worst possible way, with the drug addict and the *Camorrista* on the edge of the abyss, was ending up with the title. I had never – and nor have I ever – been physically better, never.

We had to play our last match against Lazio but it was all a done deal. I remember the Italian journalists confronted me in Soccavo, coming out of the last training session, and asked me if Napoli would have suffered less if I hadn't had all those troubles at the beginning of the season, if I regretted anything. I burst out in my best Italian: '*A me piacere vincere cosi*' (I like to win like this). On 29 April, with my national squad team-mates already in Italy to battle for the World Cup, we played Lazio. It was just paperwork. We won with a header from Baroni and we got payback, payback again.

I shut everyone up. Nobody could say a word. Only I did: I said that neither Maradona nor Ferlaino was to blame for everything that had happened; that the best thing that had happened to us was to have brought in a manager like Albertino Bigon, who knew how to talk with the players. In the changing room, after the victory lap, I sent a message to Argentina: 'This title, this new joy, is for my old man. As soon as the match was over I spoke on the phone with him and we both wept a lot . . . a lot . . . He told me he was happy for me and for those close to me. But for no one else. He doesn't forget that the last time I left Argentina it was as if I was a delinquent. They called me irresponsible when everyone knows that everything I achieved was the result of struggling up from the bottom, that when I started out I couldn't even afford the bus fare. Very nasty things have been said all over . . . and Don Diego is a wise old man, he doesn't forgive; he's not as soft as I am. I'll tell you something: I wish I had 5 per cent of his honesty and his principles. I cried, we cried together . . . This win is for him, because he suffered for me. And I thank God for the parents He gave me.'

Earlier, on the pitch itself, as soon as I heard the final whistle I shouted, from my soul and with all my heart: 'This is proof that I know myself better than anyone! And this is the down payment to be allowed to live my life! I want to live my life, please!'

They didn't let me. The last season at Napoli '90/'91 was a nightmare for me. By the time I left Naples the critics were attacking me from every angle. There was that nasty story about the European Cup game in Moscow, against Spartak. I hadn't trained well all week, I was at home and the whole team went to Russia without me. Everyone was hanging on to see whether I travelled or not. And I went. I may have got there on a private plane, but I was there, I played. We drew 1–1, went to penalties and lost, otherwise we would have stayed in the European Cup . . . But the thing was, I was already doomed.

On Sunday 17 March Napoli played Bari at home at the San Paolo: one more match in a championship that we were fighting from way down the table. We beat them 1–0, with a goal by Zolita, Gianfranco Zola. He was my substitute, usually, and on that Sunday we played together . . . We never imagined, neither one of us, nor anyone else, that it would be one of the last opportunities we would have to do so. I got picked for the drug test.

I call it Antonio Matarrese's dope test. There's no doubt in my mind that it was Italy's vendetta because Argentina knocked them out of the World Cup in the summer of 1990. I should never have gone back to Italy after the World Cup. That match against Italy, in Naples, with Canniggia's goal, that was my crime. After that match, Matarrese, who was the president of the Federcalcio, a man born in Bari, didn't look at me with anger or bitterness. He just stared at me the way the *Mafiosi* do . . . and I thought, at that moment: It's going to be very difficult to carry on living here.

I had a drug problem, yes, but for that very reason I tested myself. And anyway, cocaine is no good for playing football – it's no good because it pulls you back instead of pulling you forward. I took care, I did my own analyses . . . and in that fatal game against Bari, I was clean, clean. Today, there is an investigation still pending on the lab that carried out the tests, not just mine but so many others. Nothing, anyway, will ever give me back the years of football they made me lose . . . Nothing.

In the meantime, on Sunday 24 March, without even knowing it, I played my last match at Napoli. It was in Genoa and we lost 4–1 against Sampdoria, who would become the champions. I scored our only goal, from a penalty kick. The saddest goal of my life.

I said good-bye to Napoli with that goal. I was pushed out of Italy like a delinquent. And that's no way to end the story, certainly not.

6

The Glory

Mexico '86

I was watching him out of the corner of my eye because I knew it wouldn't be long, it wouldn't be long at all . . . I was watching Arppi Filho, the little Brazilian referee, and when he put his arms up and blew the final whistle, I went crazy. I started running this way and that. I wanted to hug everybody. In my body, in my heart and in my soul I knew I was living the most sublime moment of my career. 29 June, 1986, Azteca stadium, Mexico; that date and that place are now imprinted on my mind, on my skin. I remember the feel of the cup in my hands, I was shaking it, I was lifting it, I was shaking it, I was kissing it, I was shaking it, I didn't know what I was doing. I lent it to goalie Nery Pumpido for a bit but I immediately asked for it back. I wanted to be sure it was true – that the World Cup belonged to us, to Argentina.

We risked so much to achieve this. It cost us so much. Nobody believed in us, everyone was knocking us, even our own government. We felt insulted and criticised. Even the Mexicans turned against us, cheering the German goals. Solidarity among the South Americans? Solidarity my arse! Even right there in the Azteca, alongside our fellow Latin Americans, it felt like an away tie. What nobody has understood, ever, was that our strength and our togetherness were born from just that, from our *bronca* . . . the *bronca* we felt from having had to fight against everything. That's how it had to be. This was my team, a team built from scratch and in the face of fierce opposition.

For me, the Mexico '86 World Cup, the greatest joy of my whole career, had in fact started three years earlier. Well, actually, for me it had started the very minute the previous World Cup in Spain ended because revenge had been on my mind since those terrible days. But anyway in January 1983 something decisive, something fundamental, happened to me. I was in Lloret de Mar, on the Costa Brava in Spain. I was recovering from the hepatitis that had stopped me playing for Barcelona. I was with Fernando Signorini and a doctor. We lived in a beautiful house, that's true, but in reality we spent all day working. Then suddenly Carlos 'El Narigón' Bilardo appeared. He was the new manager of the national squad, having replaced El Flaco Menotti, who quit after Spain '82. He was walking with Jorge Cyterszpiler from the house towards the beach . . . right towards me.

I was getting ready to go running and El Narigón said hello, kissed me and asked:

'Have you got a tracksuit top for me?'

I gave him one and he said: 'Can I come running with you?'

The first thing I thought then was the same thing I later thought many times, over so many years of our relationship: This guy's crazy, this guy's sick in the head . . . It seemed so incongruous to me that the manager of the national squad should want to borrow a tracksuit top and come running with me. We ran for a while and, when we got back, he asked me: 'I want to know how you are and also to tell you about my plans for the national squad, in case you're interested in taking part.'

'What? Of course. Rest assured that my contract with Barcelona says very clearly that I must be released for the qualifying rounds and the occasional other match, as long as the club doesn't have some other important commitment.'

'I thought as much, that's lucky. The other thing I'd like to know is whether you have any financial demands.'

'Financial demands to play in the national team? Please don't worry about that, Carlos. For the honour of playing in the Argentinian strip I will never make things difficult.'

'Great, great, great. I also want you to know that, if you agree, you will be captain.'

I was petrified, really and truly petrified.

'You are a symbol, the most important player of your generation,' he said.

I burst into tears. And I was still weeping when I told Claudia, La Tota, everybody. Captain of the national squad. What I had always dreamt of being. Representing all Argentine players, all of them. I had said, in interviews, that I wanted to end my career as captain of Argentina. And immediately I would make it clear that that would only be the case once Daniel Passarella had retired. He was the captain of the national squad, had been ever since Argentina won the World Cup in 1978, and I was willing to respect his captaincy. But I had been captain at Argentinos Juniors, captain of the youth team, captain of Boca ... I had always loved being the captain, honestly. And now my dream: captain of Argentina's national squad! Every trip I went on, whether it was Austria or New York, I always bought captain's armbands, more and more of them. So when Bilardo confirmed I would be captain, Claudia ran off to get the two hundred armbands that had been kept in a drawer, waiting for the right time to be worn. In truth, I had expected it to happen at some point, but later on in my career. I was only twenty-four and Passarella was still around. He had been my role model as a captain; he had been the captain, the skipper, Menotti's number one. I wanted to be the captain, the skipper, Bilardo's number one. And finally I was, I was ... I don't know if Passarella's anger actually started then, over that. It could be. But for me the captaincy went beyond that, far beyond my relationship with him. For me, it was a dream becoming reality.

The first thing I said to myself at the time was that we had to try to build something, a certain frame of mind: playing for the national side would be the most important thing in the world. If we had to travel thousands and thousands of kilometres, we'd do it; if we had to play four games a week, we'd do it; if we had to live in little hotels which were falling to bits, we'd accept it ... we'd give everything, everything for the sake of the national side, for the blue and white. That was the message I wanted to send out.

I don't want to put myself up as some kind of role model but people have to recognise what we did for the squad. I was at Napoli during the qualifying rounds for Mexico '86. Although every game wearing the blue and white was important, in May 1985 we had two friendlies against Paraguay and Chile that were really crucial for many reasons. They would mark my debut in Bilardo's team, as well as my return to the national side, and to Argentinian pitches. I hadn't played for Argentina since the World Cup in Spain. The last match I had played was against Brazil, on 2 July 1982. Since El Narigón had taken over he had only been trying out boys who were still playing in Argentina. It sounds odd now, but for almost three years I hadn't put on a blue and white shirt, right from being knocked out in Spain up to these friendlies. But I felt calm because Bilardo had been very clear from the start. He hid nothing from me nor from anybody else. Throughout all of '84 he stated publicly that the only certainty in his squad was me, the only definite starter, and that was because I was the number one in the world, I was the symbol. Wherever he went in the world, Singapore, China, Germany, anywhere, they asked him about me, they wanted to talk about me. At a press conference in Germany, for example, he was asked if I would be included in the team and Beckenbauer stepped in, because he was sitting next to him, and answered: 'If he's not going to play him, I'll have him.'

But even though I hadn't played all that time, I was still with the team in a sense: I'd send them telegrams before each game, encouraging them, so they'd know I was part of the group. I still felt close to them.

As the two matches against Paraguay and Chile approached I said that they were very, very important, because after those two games we would actually be playing for a place in Mexico '86.

But even as long ago as that, Antonio Matarrese, the president of the Federcalcio, the Italian league, had already started putting stones in our path. He claimed that even if our clubs allowed us to travel, the Italian league reserved the right to suspend us. So I answered back: 'What?! Even Sandro Pertini, the President of Italy, couldn't stop me from travelling to Buenos Aires!'

Passarella was playing at Fiorentina at the time, and they didn't want either of us to travel to Argentina. They said it was madness. Madness to play for my country? Madness my arse! I prepared a thorough schedule. I wanted to be everywhere. My mind was made up.

The marathon began on Sunday 5 May. Napoli drew 0–0 at home to Juventus. From the stadium I zoomed in one of my cars, I can't remember which one, to Rome, 250 kilometres away, to Fiumicino airport. I'd been promised a police escort but they didn't deliver: I had to endure Sunday traffic but did it my way, and I made it in an hour and a half. I took the plane, landed in Buenos Aires and on the Thursday I stepped out on to the pitch, at the Monumental, to face Paraguay. We drew 1–1 and I scored the goal. I went back to the training camp with the lads and the following day at five in the afternoon I took a plane to Rome which stopped over in Rio. Saturday 11 May I was once again in Fiumicino and another plane: this time to Trieste. Then seventy kilometres from Trieste to Udine, which we did by car. I got there in time for dinner, had something to eat, and went to sleep. The following day, Sunday the twelfth, on to the pitch against Udinese: we drew 2–2; I scored both goals. Celebrate? No, no time! Travel! Seventy kilometres by car to

Trieste airport, airtaxi to Fiumicino and, just in time, the Aerolineas flight to Buenos Aires, again.

So on Tuesday the fourteenth I was back at the Monumental, as if I'd never left, this time to face Chile. We beat them 2–0; I scored a goal. I took a breath, and flew back to Italy. On Sunday the nineteenth, in Naples, we beat Passarella's Fiorentina 1–0. He was a little bit more rested than I was because when the whole dance started he got himself booked and saved himself one trip. So I didn't stop at all between Sunday the fifth and Sunday the nineteenth May because I wanted to do the right thing by both my club and my country, the one who paid my wages, yes, but also the one who loved me and needed me.

Of course even in those days they invented stuff about me: it was published somewhere that for playing those two games I was paid $80,000 – even Frank Sinatra wouldn't have got that for singing naked at the River stadium!

The minute I got to Argentina I joined the group of lads already at the *concentración*, at the national training ground in Ezeiza. The process of building the national side had already started and it wasn't turning out to be easy. The lads had been on one tour which had started like shit, with a draw with Colombia, although it had ended brilliantly, with a victory over Germany. I'd come willing to be just another player in the team and was happy to play wherever Bilardo wanted me. The mad guy seemed convinced and I was going to follow him, to the death.

The qualifying rounds began in Venezuela. Easy? Bollocks was it easy. For us nothing was easy. Our opposition might have been weak, but that time we didn't play against just eleven players. It's the only explanation I can find even today for what happened. The thing was, no sooner had we landed in San Cristóbal, the crowd got out of control. There were police around, but of course they were also Venezuelan. Some madman found his way through the crowd towards me and when he crossed my path he kicked me really hard on my right knee. Gentile, who had tackled me

so famously during Spain '82, couldn't have done it better! I
limped to the hotel with Doctor Raúl Madero running after me
and everyone scared. The son of a bitch had buggered the
meniscus in my knee.

I spent the whole night before the game lying in bed with a
pack of ice on my right knee. I didn't get to sleep until five in
the morning. At first I thought it was nothing but it got worse
and worse. And to top it all off, during that bloody match and
all the subsequent ones everyone aimed at my right knee,
everyone had a go at that knee. I say bloody match because it
took an arm and a leg to win it, as was our style. We finished
3–2, anxious for the final whistle.

Then came Colombia, in Bogota, on 2 June. It was such pressure, I'd never experienced anything like it. We beat them 3–1
and everything seemed like a bed of roses, but it wasn't like that.
Nothing like that at all. Most of the players had never before
taken part in the qualifying rounds, me included. To this day I
think if we'd lost then, in Bogota, we would have been out of
the World Cup, because it would have been too hard a blow to
bear.

A week later, at the Monumental, we beat Venezuela. The way
they badmouthed us gave me the creeps. I couldn't get my head
round it. Trassero touched the ball, they whistled him;
Burruchaga touched it, they whistled him; Clausen touched it,
they whistled him. It was terrible. We ended up winning 3–0 but
the last two goals were scored in the final four minutes.

The two matches against Peru, the ones that were going to
define everything, were awful. The first one in Lima, on 23 June,
was Reyna's match. I say Reyna's because he was the Peruvian
who followed me everywhere, to the loo practically, it was
madness! At one point I landed heavily on one leg and had to
leave the game for the doc to have a look at it, and the guy
followed me to the edge of the pitch. When I went back on he
stood right next to me, the moron. He talked to me, just kept

on talking to me. Everyone's got their tactics, I know, but these weren't mine. Everyone does what they can to get a result, sure, but this kid overstepped the mark. He punched me a couple of times as well. Reyna was amazing: after that experience, over the years, I started to realise that I preferred to be marked man to man, because I could get rid of them like that, *tac*, quickly, and stay alone. Zonal marking on the other hand was more complicated. But Reyna . . . to think that when I arrived in Cuba I got sent a get-well ball signed by all the Peruvian footballers wishing me a speedy recovery, and there was his signature! Aged forty and in Havana I still couldn't shake him off!

Then came the match in Buenos Aires on 30 June, the qualifier. How we suffered! The fear I felt that afternoon at the Monumental I had never experienced before and I doubt, at this stage, that I ever will again on a football pitch. I can't explain it. We were playing well, for the first time we were playing well, but they managed two counter-attacks and they got two goals, two goals in the first half. On the way to the dressing room we were all swearing at each other. We could see we were losing because of our own mistakes. At half-time El Narigon said nothing about the goals, nothing about the first half, he just shouted at us to forget everything, to start again, to go out there and qualify for the World Cup, to stop fucking about.

But I knew it wouldn't be easy. We were so nervous. The same thing had happened to us in the matches against Paraguay and Venezuela. We went back out after half-time with all guns blazing. Pasculli scored straight away but it wasn't enough. At one point, after a run, I looked at the electronic scoreboard and saw that there were only twenty-three minutes to go. I passed the ball, looked again: thirty-two minutes! It felt like these Peruvian sons of bitches were moving the clock back. And at the end, with ten minutes to go, Passarella's playmaking came into its own. And Gareca gave it a little push. I don't know who scored, but I had Pedrito Pasculli near me and I hugged him, I hugged anybody . . . But it was Gareca's goal, because if it wasn't for him the ball would have gone out.

Up until that moment, I'd think of the word play-off and my soul would break into pieces. I was ruined, physically ruined, and carrying around that damned right knee. I dreamt of kicking the ball and hammering it into the goal from an angle but I couldn't do it, I wasn't up to it . . . Luckily, eventually we made it, all of us. We qualified for the Mexico World Cup and right there, I swear on my mother's grave, I said to Gareca: 'This is how the World Cup is going to end for us . . . we'll suffer for it, but we will win it.'

We needed to get the people of Argentina on side. And it wasn't that we didn't understand what Bilardo asked of us, we understood perfectly well. But we couldn't let go, we couldn't find the freedom to express ourselves on the pitch. And on top of it all, the conflicts arose.

I think Daniel Passarella could never accept the fact that I was the only certain starter and the captain of Bilardo's team, never. So he started to put on pressure. And in an interview with *El Grafico* he said: 'Either I'm first-choice or I'm not playing for Argentina.' That was in October '85. I was fed up with the bickering, the jealousy, and all the bullshit, so I stepped out with my boots on. I called a press conference in Naples and I said everything that was on my mind. I spoke like the captain but not like the owner of any absolute truths, and I did it without having spoken either to Bilardo or to Passarella beforehand. It was a real mess, and I was in the middle. For Bilardo, apparently, the only first-choice player was Maradona. Well, as far as I was concerned, Bilardo had been very clear from the outset, and I didn't know what Daniel thought. The only thing I could say to him as a friend off the pitch, as a team-mate, as a man and as a player, was that we had to respect our different career paths. And I thought Daniel knew that Bilardo had respected us all from the moment he called us for the qualifiers. After that, if

he'd promised things or not, I didn't know, that was something they'd have to sort out themselves. I knew because of
everything I'd read in newspapers back home, and everything
my mum had told me on the phone from Buenos Aires, that
something strange was going on. Daniel wanted to be a certain
first-choice, but all of us who were close to him and had seen
him fight like a lion for the Argentina strip knew that he was
a born winner. So, I asked myself: why was he making us all
suffer by threatening a resignation nobody wanted, not even
Bilardo?

Every manager has his special players. In Menotti's day if
anyone touched Passarella it was a national scandal, because he
was the captain and he was everyone's favourite, like Houseman
had been before him, it was a given. I resigned from Menotti's
squad when he didn't include me in the 1978 first team, because
at that time I felt we should all be on the same level. But I came
back. That's why I didn't want to criticise Daniel for what he
was doing, because he was a grown-up and I wasn't going to tell
him what to do. The only thing I was going to ask of him as
captain and as a team-mate was to try and solve it in the best
possible way. At the training camp he knew he was a definite
starter because he was a leader and because of everything he
represented on and off the pitch. We needed him, all of Argentina
needed him.

What I asked Daniel at that press conference was to decide
for himself, not for others. I knew him well and that's why I
kept repeating that there was something very odd going on
behind all of this and I just didn't know what it was. If I'd
known, I would have said it, because I've always liked things to
be out in the open.

I didn't know and I didn't care if Bilardo's decision was a
whim or what, but we always respected what the manager said.
I asked myself, why should things change? Daniel, due to the
simple fact of being among the twenty-two, and knowing what

he did about that squad as an insider, didn't need Bilardo to say: *you are definitely in the starting line-up*. He had been in the starting line-up for ever.

I said, 'It's not good that when we need to unite we are disunited or that we go on and on about the pros and cons of Bilardo, or of Menotti. Can't you see that we're destroying ourselves for no reason? I was left out of the World Cup '78. There were twenty-five of us, three had to go, and I was one of them, but I am still grateful to Menotti for everything he has done for me.' I wanted to set the record straight.

In the middle of all this mess I had to face Passarella on the pitch: Napoli against Fiorentina, in Florence, on 13 October. The Italian newspapers had spent all week going on and on about the duel between us, the fight, it was a total circus. In the end we drew 0–0 and I said what I really thought at the time. 'I don't understand all this fuss, all this polemic ... Daniel is a friend, we've all loved him and still love him very much. For me he is unarguably in the first team. That's enough, don't you think?' He said something similar but the saga continued.

But over and above all these hassles, it was a magical time for me. In spite of the knee that I'd had bashed in Venezuela (which incidentally had sparked off a fight among the doctors because there were those who said I should have an operation and those who said I shouldn't), in spite of that, I was moving forward. Thanks to Doctor Oliva I had once again been spared from going under the knife. He decided that it wouldn't be necessary to have surgery on that damned knee that had brought such fame for that Venezuelan dickhead who kicked it in. But I had other worries. During that period we beat Juventus, every Neapolitan's dream, and I scored the goal. At the time I said: 'Right now, if it's between Naples and the national side I choose the national side.' I said it, yes, but that didn't mean I wouldn't kill myself for Naples as well when I had to play for them.

The big issue was which players would and would not get called up to go to the World Cup. I backed the ones who had already been playing in the squad because they had taken a lot of shit, too much: Pedro Pablo Pasculli, Ricardo Gareca, Jorge Valdano, Julian José Camino, Miguel Angel Russo, El Pato Fillol, Oscar Alberto Garré, Jorge Luis Burruchaga, Jose Daniel Ponce. And I also stated publicly that I would like Ramón Díaz to come on board. I was convinced that under Bilardo he would be a different player, even more complete. He was exactly the type of player who could do well with Bilardo as boss. Contrary to popular belief, I was never opposed to Ramón Díaz joining the squad, any squad. The one who never considered it was Bilardo.

Another player who I thought would thrive under Bilardo was Bocha, Bochini. He was one of the newer members of the squad, a weird guy, Bocha! He was my idol as a kid, I'd always dreamt of playing with him . . . but it hadn't happened. We had been together in exhibition games for the players' union and suchlike, and he'd been part of a tour prior to the qualifying rounds, and I thought we might finally play together then, but no, he got pissed off and left.

Then there was Bichi Borghi, also new to the squad, but an old team-mate of mine from the lower divisions of Argentinos. He had been quickly promoted to the first team and quickly demoted as well – he was audacious in the extreme on the pitch but had the mind of a brat. He needed to get hurt in order to realise that playing in the first team was different. The thing is, sadly, we Argentinians always need to invent idols, to fatten them up . . . I was always saying, even in those days, that you couldn't hurry Borghi. And in the matches in Mexico I was always shouting at him to pass the ball more, to be more of a team player, because otherwise dribbling is useless.

That's how we were building the team, always suffering, always under pressure. Truth is, nobody liked us . . .

I was trying to defend a group of players that was not *fuori-classi* – not out of this world – but who would never stop working hard. They were the ones who had come all that way fighting any way they could, and now the moment of truth had arrived. I wanted Bilardo to respect them as men, rather than just as players. He couldn't leave Barbas or Pato Fillol out of the World Cup – they were too well established in the national squad. In February I was already asking him to release the final team sheet, so we could stop worrying about who was going to be selected and get on with our work. I spoke to him about Ramón Díaz but he never even went to see him . . . So all that stuff about me controlling who was in or who was out of the squad . . . Please – it's just not true.

The truth is that by March '86 I wasn't in good shape. I felt vulnerable and exposed. Bilardo had come to see me in Naples and the only thing he was worrying about was my physical condition. As if I was going to let him down . . . But he had also gone to Florence looking for Passarella, which pissed me off. Passarella had been threatening to leave and I couldn't understand why Bilardo didn't just leave it at that. I was fucked-off with the whole thing and felt I'd had enough. I'd let my stubble grow long. Since then they say that when my stubble gets too long . . . bad sign!

There were some friendlies looming and I was even being teased in the Napoli dressing room: a team-mate, Penzo, kept asking if we weren't afraid of being humiliated against France. I wanted to kill him. But he had a point, no one could see if we had a clear game plan. We were a motley crew and Bilardo wasn't adding any of the players I liked, like Tolo Gallego or Guaso Domenech.

I felt alone, completely alone. I even thought – as I have on so many other occasions – of packing it all in and fucking off. Thankfully during those days my old mum arrived. Turco, Lalo, Claudia, my old man and my nieces and nephews had all left

Naples. Only she was with me. Many times I woke up in the morning and I would say to her: 'Tota, what if we go back? What if we just fuck off?' I don't know, maybe I was trying to think about too many things and not everything was being dealt with the way I would have liked.

Then Fernando Signorini came up with a physical exercise plan that I got really enthusiastic about. It would start with an evaluation of my current condition and, in theory, would get me into tiptop shape for Mexico. And I thought: What the hell, let's push forward. So I did.

We travelled to Rome, to the Italian Olympic Committee's medical centre where my friend Professor Antonio Dal Monte was the boss. Every Italian Olympic medal winner had been through there and I started to think about the cup, about holding the World Cup in my hands. In the end, Penzo wasn't right about us needing to fear France in that pre-world cup friendly, but they still beat us 2–0. Passarella ended up playing and he elbowed Tigana badly, really badly! We immediately travelled to Zurich, to play against the Swiss Grasshoppers. We beat them 1–0, but only just.

We wanted to know where we stood physically. There was a lot of talk about the differences between South Americans and the Europeans. For me, and I put all my faith in this, the month of May was going to be crucial, the time when we would all finally be together. Bilardo had said so, and I believed him. All us forwards had to get it into our heads – and this seems obvious now but at the time it seemed revolutionary – if we lost the ball we couldn't just stand there staring, we had to dig in and pull together.

I was aware we weren't particularly inspiring people back home . . . in truth, more than enthuse them we pissed them off. But what nobody understood was that we needed time, that this team had a lot of valuable players. On the other hand it didn't surprise me: the Argentine fan is like that; they also had made

Menotti's life impossible before '78. I always respected the opinions of others, but it bugged me, it bugged me that the same people who criticised so harshly would later be the first to jump on the bandwagon of victory.

But we were used to fighting alone. We were focused and we knew what we wanted. The feeling within the squad was that we were being persecuted, and some were on the verge of being unable to take it any more. People thought Borghi was no longer as promising, that Pasculli couldn't score against anyone, and that Maradona was just some small guy ... We were persecuted, yes, let there be no doubt about that. But at the same time we were more united than ever, we had an indestructible solidarity.

The April of '86 was terrible. On the thirtieth we lost against Norway, we really took some stick for that. The only good thing about that match was that it was Negro Hector Enrique's debut. Then we went to Tel Aviv to play against Israel with all the cannons pointing at us: the Argentinian government wanted to knock Bilardo down! Raul Alfonsin, the president at the time, had commented that he didn't like the national squad, while Rodolfo O'Reilly, who was the Secretary for Sport, was lobbying to stir things up. It was terrible, really. Football had never been a serious issue for politicians but it had suddenly become a matter of state. I had said: 'If Bilardo leaves, I leave.' I hope it was useful and had some effect because it would have been absurd for the Argentinian government to fire the national football manager, a disgrace of global proportions. Anyway, on 4 May we beat Israel 7–2 and I was already convinced that in the thirty days remaining we would prepare to win the World Cup. I was convinced, also, that the other teams would fall one by one.

I really loved that squad. It's easy to understand: I was the captain and they were an exceptional group of people. I felt luck had been with us, so far, and that we had more to come. But I felt, also, that there was a total lack of respect towards us.

When we at last settled in the training ground in Mexico's Federal District, I realised, just like that, in a flash, that everything that was happening wasn't just a dream. We were in this together, and we were going to be World Champions.

We played against a team from local club America, and we lost, and then we went to Barranquilla and drew 0–0 against Junior. But it wasn't about results, it was about much more. We had a heated meeting in Mexico where we really had a go at each other, getting everything out in the open, telling it like it was ... that's how we were and how we lived, from meeting to meeting. Before Passarella's controversial departure from the World Cup we had one such meeting. This is what happened and let's hope nobody makes up any more wank. I arrived at the meeting fifteen minutes late, together with the other 'rebels' (that's what we were, according to Passarella) Pasculli, Batista, Islas ... we were fifteen minutes late, hardly late at all by Argentinian standards. So we had to swallow a lecture by Passarella, with his dictator-like style: how could the captain arrive late, this that and the other. I let him go on, I let him go on. Finally I said, 'Have you finished? OK, so now let's talk about you.'

And I told them, the whole squad, everything he was, everything he'd done, everything I knew about him. And the ensuing mess was big, big, big! On the one hand there were those who supported Passarella. His gang. That was Valdano, Bochini, a few of them. Passarella had filled their heads and therefore they were saying we were late because we'd been doing drugs.

So I said, 'OK, Passarella, I'll admit I do drugs, OK.' All around us, a tremendous silence. I went on, 'But on this occasion, I haven't been taking drugs. Not on this occasion, would you believe. But you, you're landing others in the shit, the kids who were with me, and the kids didn't do anything! Have you got that, grass?'

The only truth is that Passarella wanted to win the group over like that, by sowing discord, making things up, putting spokes into the works. He wanted to win them back ever since he'd lost the captaincy and the leadership; it had really stuck in his throat. He'd been a good captain, yes, and I always said so. But I was the one who displaced him: the great captain, the true great captain, was, is and always will be me.

After that, any chance he got, Passarella played dirty against me, very dirty. He got hold of Valdano, who is a very intelligent guy, whom everyone listened to, including me, I could spend four hours with him unable to get a word in edgeways, and he filled his head with the idea that I was leading them all into drugs. So I got up and in the name of my team-mates and in my name of course I shouted at Passarella: 'No one's using here, *viejo*, no one.' And I swear on my daughters that we didn't, not in Mexico. But since we were airing our dirty linen I thought I'd have it all out: 'But let's see, while we're here. That 2,000 pesos phone bill we've all got to pay between us, why is no one owning up? Who made the calls?' No one got up, no one answered, maybe someone stared at the ground, you could have heard a pin drop. What Passarella didn't know is that in those days, 1986 – it seems a century ago now – Mexican phone bills were itemised: the bills came with the dialled numbers, one by one, and it was his number, the wanker! He was earning two million and he was playing the idiot over two thousand. Now that really is taking the cat's milk.

I'd rather be an addict, however painful that is, than take advantage of others or be a bad friend. I say bad friend because of another episode that ended up distancing us from each other and that also ended up tarnishing Passarella's image in the eyes of the others. When he was in Europe everyone talked about the fact that he used to run off to Monaco to see the wife of another well-known player. He used to do that and then he would boast about it in the dressing room in Fiorentina, like it was an

OK thing to do! So when Valdano came to ask for explanations in Mexico, at that meeting, about the drugs, and also to harangue me, telling me that I couldn't do this, that I couldn't do that, I stopped him short.

'Hang on, Jorge, for fuck's sake, whose side are you on? So now what Passarella tells you is true and what I tell you is a lie, right?'

So he said: 'Alright, tell me then.'

And I told him about Passarella's affair with another man's wife, but at a meeting with Passarella and the rest of the squad there. I told everything I knew about him and there was a deep silence. And then Valdano jumped up: 'You're a shit!' he shouted at Passarella. That's when all hell broke loose. That's when Passarella got diarrhoea, Montezuma's revenge, when the truth is that we were all pissing out of our arses. He left without playing a single match of the tournament.

We decided then that it was us against the world, so we'd better all be pulling in the same direction ... And we pulled, how we pulled! I've always felt suffocated and tied down at training camps, but now it was different: because we all opened up, and told each other everything face to face. From that moment on it all started to come together.

I would have loved it if my daughters had seen me play in Mexico. How they would've enjoyed it! During that World Cup, the only thing in my head was that I wanted to demonstrate to Argentinians that we had a team which might or might not become champions but which was without question up there with the rest of the world's great footballing nations.

I am convinced that for the first game, against South Korea on 2 June 1986 at the Olympic Stadium in Mexico most of the Argentinian people watched with their eyes half-closed. They didn't even know who was playing. Passarella had left, Brown, Cucciuffo and Negro Enrique had come into the squad. We trusted, we trusted, but we had not yet had a single positive result to build on. But the truth is we left the dressing room with conviction – that's the word, conviction. We believed we could take on anybody. All Bilardo's meticulous plans, all his tactics, his obsession with positions, suddenly it all fell into place, and we were putting it into practice against Korea. I think it made the Koreans angry . . . How they kicked me! They fouled me eleven times, practically once each. Eleven doesn't sound that much but some of the challenges left me bleeding, I'm not joking. Forty-four minutes of the game had gone before a defender got booked, number 17. I don't remember his name but I'd already christened him Kung Fu. Another one came in so hard with his studs they went right through my sock, and my bandage. And my bandages are more like casts.

It was exactly then that I started my battles with FIFA: over the fouling and the timing of matches. The referees, by allowing kicking and hacking, didn't defend talent. To make matters worse matches were being played in the morning, at noon, at any old time just to please European TV schedulers. Do you know how hot it is in Mexico, at that height, at twelve noon? That's ravioli time, not football time. I always went to bed late before a match, and woke up at eleven, but when we played at midday I had to get up at eight in the morning. It was a life-time habit, even if I went to bed early, I couldn't get to sleep. But it was a more serious matter than just a personal habit. That's why we kicked up such a fuss, Valdano and me.

Everyone kept asking if I hadn't gone too far against the powers-that-be, with no real protection for myself and at the wrong time . . . What did they think, that I was a politician? No. I never was and never will be. To top it all João Havelange, the president of FIFA himself – a waterpolo player, for Christ's sake – had come out saying that you had to respect the top guys. To my mind he got the wrong end of the stick. Either he was misinformed, or he misheard me, or maybe he was deaf and he hadn't heard me at all. My intention wasn't to fuck up their TV deal, that was their business. What I was asking was that we be consulted, the players, the true owners of the show, because without us they were and are nothing. Without Maradona, without Rummenigge, and even without the last reserve from Morocco, they are nothing. And I said, yes, that at twelve noon a guy could die, and I wanted them to see what would happen, what would happen then? I used to get terrible chest pains during the first games.

The fouling was unbelievable, too. I think in that first game the Koreans got scared and took it out on the biggest sucker – me. I was expected to praise the referees after all that? How could I if they allowed a guy to kick me twenty times? They did the same to Zico. Not so much to Platini because the Frenchman whacked the ball away, kicked hard and stayed put. How could I possibly speak well of the standard of refereeing?

The next two games of the first round were against Italy, 1–1, on 5 June in Puebla, and against Bulgaria, 2–0, five days later, once again at the Olympic. It was a stroll in the park for us, as if we were holding a footballing seminar. I scored a lovely goal against Italy, one of my best ever. They gave the goalkeeper, Galli, a really hard time, poor guy, nobody realised I just didn't give him time. Valdano's long pass landed right in front of me, in the area. I jumped up to meet the ball and volleyed it with the side of my left foot without waiting for it to touch the turf while all the time the defender Scirea, may he rest in peace, was running behind me. I struck it towards the far post before he could get to me. It wasn't Galli being slow: it was me being quick! I was so up for it. Bilardo had drilled it into the lads that they had to back me up. And I helped him with that, because I didn't stay standing still up front: if I had to press the defenders I did. My knees didn't wobble, tiger!

In the end we drew, because the Italians were awarded a penalty – Garré handled the ball. But we had played our best match so far under Bilardo. It was there, in that game, that Bilardo found the team he had been looking for. He finally found room for Batista, he left Checho playing alone as a central winger, he gave a more open role to Giusti and he freed up Burruchaga. I wasn't alone; we had a team.

After that, against Bulgaria, we made a few of our old mistakes – getting caught unprepared by the counter-attack, for example – but by then we were too strong for them. The Bulgarians' attitude confused us a bit, because we had thought they were going to attack us more. At any rate, we vaccinated them: first Valdano scored, he hung in the sky long enough to get his head to a cross from Cucciuffo; then Burru scored after I centred, one of those crosses I love . . . I go deep as a left wing and then, when I'm so close to the touchline it's like I'm standing on the edge of a cliff, I get the cross over with just a little flick of my ankle. And I'm looking up at the stands the whole time. We made them pay, 2–0. We were vaccinating them team after team all over, one after the other. We were through to the second round.

As a team we had everything: technique and tenacity. An Argentinian journalist, Juvenal, defined us perfectly: 'A European rhythm with a creole swagger.' That's what we were, very tidy tactically, with a novel defensive formation: a *líbero* – Brown; two stoppers – Ruggeri and Cucciuffo; two midfield wide men – Giusti and Olarticoechea; a central winger like Batista, who could stop everyone; Negro Enrique giving us the balance; Burruchaga – the link in the midfield; and up front, Valdano and me. With minor changes that was basically us: it was a great team.

My old lady, Tota, kept saying: 'Son, what are you on? You are running faster than ever! On the TV it's always you with the ball.' I was really fired up, in better shape than ever. Still, I couldn't bear to leave our bedroom! I was sharing with Pedrito Pasculli and every day we added something: a little picture, a photo, a decoration, a letter. We wanted it to be our home for a month, our home until the final. And it had our style, that room. It was humble, very humble – it wasn't Fiorito, but it had thin brick walls, small hard beds, just one phone – made famous by Passarella's phone-bill incident. But for us it was OK, because it was home. I lived that month intensely, it was all exactly as I had dreamt, no more, no less. At long last I truly felt that I was Bilardo's captain, just as Passarella had been Menotti's captain. Bilardo had really stuck his neck out for me, he had given me the captaincy, he'd stood by me ... Passarella had been big in '82 because he'd had everything I had in '86: captaincy, support, trust. I'd leave the training camp for the Azteca saying: 'Seeee youuu laaaateeeeeeeeeeeer!' It was like a ritual. I knew I was off to win.

We had our superstitions and little habits. Once a week we would eat at a restaurant called 'El Viejo', owned by Fat Cremasco, an ex team-mate of Bilardo's from his Estudiantes days. Also, the day before a match there was a compulsory outing to a shopping centre called Sanborns, or something like that. We'd done it before the first match, against Korea, and we couldn't stop. As we progressed through the tournament, more and more people heard of our ritual. To me it was like another training session: I'd run around the corridors of the shopping centre with three hundred people running after me, until I nipped into a shop – it could be an electronics shop or a hairdresser's – and I would stay there, feeling hundreds of eyes staring at me, focused on me, from the other side of the window. I was happy. Very happy. It was adulation but it didn't bother me, not at all. On those walks, a man called El Negro Galíndez was always by my side, ready to protect me. I remember Tito Benrrós, the kitman, would always let him in: he'd pretend to get cross with me, or shout at me, on purpose, and El Negro would jump in to stop him like a madman. When he calmed down again we made him sing boleros. His classic was 'Reloj me voy amor ...'

(Clock, my love, I'm leaving) or some nonsense like that, with a voice that, how should I put it ... well, my dog sounded better. Salvatore Carmando was also with me, of course: he was Napoli's masseur and he's always helped me a lot.

The truth is we had a good time at that training camp. We were a team, a good team. We understood each other instinctively. I had a perfect understanding with Valdano. If he went back, I'd stay forward and vice versa, and Burruchaga made his darting runs exactly when he needed to. Carlos had drilled that into our heads and things happened without us needing to say anything, like a carbon copy of the training sessions.

But at the same time it wasn't easy. The second-round match against Uruguay, in Puebla on 16 June, opened with a goal by Pedrito Pasculli, thanks to a pass from ... Acevedo, one of the Uruguayan defenders. That wasn't just another victory: the Uruguayans' paranoia really pissed me off in those days, and also we hadn't beat them in a World Cup for fifty-six years, not since the 1930 final. That bastard Luigi Agnolin, the Italian ref, wrongly overruled one of my goals. I never stamped on Bossio, no way. I beat him because I jumped over him. It was never an intentional stamp ... that Agnolin, he was a fucker. We tried to pressurise him from the start but the Italian wasn't a man to be intimidated. It was: *don't you try to fuck with me or I'll punch your lights out.* He pushed Francescoli, he pushed him! He even elbowed Giusti. I liked Agnolin, he was one of the few refs I liked. But he made mistakes, like most referees. We beat them 1–0, and we ploughed on, pushing all opponents aside, hitting harder than Tyson.

At that point in the competition I fancied Germany, I'm no fool, me. My brother Lalo liked neat little touches, which is why he favoured Morocco, who were having a good tournament. But the Germans pushed forward like crazy. They had Matthäus, who was already one of the best in the world; Völler, who was a tiger; and Allofs. El Turco preferred France and Denmark. What

Denmark did was amazing: they were like a bullet train with Laudrup, with Elkjaer-Larsen. But the manager went mad when they started losing 2–1 against Spain. He took off a defender and the team crumbled: they let five in, mainly because my mate Emilio 'Buitre' Butragueño was inspired for Spain. Bilardo always said: *One mistake can cost you the match.*

We had got to the last eight when nobody had believed in us. Someone asked me at the time if we were satisfied with that position. I reminded them – because I always had that phrase in mind – what the Uruguayan Obdulio Varela had said before the 1950 final: 'We will only have honoured our duty once we become the champions.'

The next game was against England, on 22 June 1986, a day I will not forget for as long as I live, ever. That game against England was so hard-fought, so tight, with Barnes making things difficult for us towards the end. And with my two goals. My two goals!

I remember many things about the second goal, so many . . . If one of my relatives tells it, there's always yet another English player involved; if Cóppola tells it he likes to make out that Bilardo had given me the previous night off and that I only got back in at lunchtime, just in time for the game. Seriously, though, I think it is a dream goal. When I was in Fiorito I used to dream of scoring a goal like that on the little makeshift pitch, for Estrella Roja, and I did it in a World Cup, for my country, and in a final.

I say a final because for us, because of everything it represented, we were playing a final against England. More than defeating a football team it was defeating a country. Of course, before the match, we said that football had nothing to do with the Malvinas War but we knew a lot of Argentinian kids had died there, shot down like little birds. This was revenge. It was like recovering a little bit of the Malvinas. In the pre-match interviews we had all said that football and politics shouldn't be confused, but that was a lie. We did nothing but think about that. Bollocks was it just another match!

It was more than winning a game, and it was more than knocking England out of the World Cup. In a way, we blamed the English players for everything that happened, for all the suffering of the Argentine people. I know it seems like madness and a nonsense now but truthfully at the time that was what we felt. It was stronger than us: we were defending our flag, the dead kids, the survivors. That's why I think my goal meant so much. Actually, they both did. They both had their own charm.

The second was, as I said, the goal you dream of as a kid. In the potrero, when we did something like that, we used to say we'd made the opponent dizzy, that we'd made them go crazy. It was ... whenever I see it again I can't believe I managed it, honestly. Not because I scored it but because it seems a goal like that just isn't possible, a goal that you could dream of but never actually score. Now it's become a legend, and as such there's been all sorts of shit said about it. Like the fact that I'd thought about my brother's advice to dummy it at the keeper. I didn't, but I did later realise that unconsciously it must have entered my head, because I finished like my brother Turco had told me to a little over six years earlier. As I've said, in 1981, during a tour with the national squad, against England at Wembley, I'd done a very similar move but finished by sidefooting the ball when the keeper came out. I'd missed by a fraction and was practically celebrating the goal. Turco phoned me and said: 'You moron! You shouldn't have sidefooted it ... you should have thrown a dummy, the keeper had already committed himself.' And I answered: 'You little shit! It's easy for you to say that, you're watching it on the telly!' But he really shut me up: 'No, Pelu, if you'd thrown a dummy, you could've dragged it towards the sideline and finished with your right, do you see?' The brat was seven years old! Well, this time I finished like my brother wanted.

One thing that was true, even though it has also become a

legend, was that I could see Valdano, running down my left, free on the far post. Here's how it went: I started off from the middle of the pitch, on the right; I stepped on the ball, turned, and sneaked between Beardsley and Reid. At that point I had the goal in my sights, although I still had a few metres to go. I passed Butcher on the inside and from this point Valdano was a real help, because Fenwick, who was the last one, didn't leave my side. I was waiting for him to stand off, I was waiting to pass the ball – the logical thing to do. If Fenwick had left me, I could have given it to Valdano, who would have been one-on-one against Shilton. But he didn't do that. So I faced him, then threw a dummy one way and went the other, towards the right ... Fenwick tried so hard to close in on me, but I carried on and I already had Shilton in front of me ... I was on exactly the spot that I'd been on at Wembley that time in 1981, the exact spot! I was going to finish the same way but ... but God, the Beard, helped me. The Beard reminded me, *tic* ... and Shilton bought the dummy, he bought it. So I got to the end and I went *tac*, inside ... at the same time Butcher, a big blond guy, caught up with me again and kicked me quite hard. But I didn't care, I'd scored the goal of my life.

In the dressing room, when I told Valdano I was watching him he wanted to kill me. 'I can't believe you were looking at me and you still scored that goal?! That's downright offensive, mate, that's humiliating, that's not possible.' Negro Enrique came up to us – he had been in the shower – and added: 'I'm hearing a lot of praise for him, a lot of praise, but with the pass I gave him, how could he not score?' Fucking Negro! He'd passed it to me in our area!

But that goal, that was an incredible goal. I wanted to put the whole sequence of that goal in stills, blown up really big, above the headboard of my bed. I'd add a picture of Dalmita (Gianinna hadn't been born yet) and below I'd add an inscription which read: *My life's best*. Nothing more.

I got a lot of pleasure from the other goal as well. Sometimes I think I almost enjoyed that one more, the first one. Now I feel I am able to say what I couldn't then. At the time I called it 'the hand of God'. Bollocks was it the hand of God, it was the hand of Diego! And it felt a little bit like pickpocketing the English . . .

No one noticed at the time: I went for it with everything I had. Even I don't know how I managed to jump so high. I struck out with my left fist behind my head. Even Shilton didn't see what was happening, and Fenwick, who was behind me, was the first one to appeal for a hand-ball. Not because he'd seen it but because he couldn't understand how I could have jumped higher than the keeper. When I saw the linesman running towards the middle of the pitch I did a beeline towards the stand where my dad was with my father-in-law to celebrate with them.

Don Diego was hanging over on to the pitch thinking I'd headed it in. I was a bit stupid, because I was celebrating with my left fist outstretched and watching what the linesmen were up to out of the corner of my eye. The ref could have cottoned on to that and suspected something was up. Luckily, he didn't even notice. By now, all the English were protesting and Valdano was giving me the *shhh!* with a finger over his lips.

Valdano had passed it to me, we'd played a one-two, they put pressure on him and he passed me a dud ball because he'd had no choice. I jumped. I jumped at the same time as the keeper with my fist outstretched but behind my head and . . . goal, gooooaaaaaaaaal, go weeping to church. As I told a BBC journalist a year later: 'It was one hundred per cent legitimate because the referee allowed it and I'm not one to question the honesty of the referee.'

The rest of the world wanted my head, of course. But when I returned to Italy after the World Cup an amazing thing happened. Silvio Piola came to see me. He'd been one of Italy's great goalscorers during the 1930s World Cup final, and he said to me: 'Tell all those who say you're dishonest because you've scored a hand-goal that if that's the case they have one less honest man in Italy. I also scored a hand-goal, playing for the Azzuri against England, and it didn't stop us celebrating then!' He was a great old boy. I later read he really had scored one like mine.

Poor Belgium were just another stepping stone for us. In the semi-final on 25 June we were so full of ourselves that we couldn't lose. That scared me a little bit, to be honest. We weren't used to being the favourites. During that match, what I'd been feeling all along was confirmed: all the others, my team-mates, helped me be the star. Maybe I am a star on account of the goals I score, but the team provided the space for me to play. In the first goal, for example, Burru played a crucial role. I lost my marker, he understood me, he paused, and then delivered it right in front of me. For the second, the credit was Cucciuffo's and Valdano's, who made it for me. This time, when I scored the goals, I thought of La Tota, of how happy she must be feeling about it all . . . because each game brought more joy.

During that game, I tell you, everyone was saying we were going to win and I was shitting myself precisely because it's so easy to relax and let your guard down, to rest on your laurels. That's why, after those two goals, I wanted to continue scoring, I wanted more. I would look up at the box where my dad sat; all we needed was the Beard to help us win the championship. We'd made the final, an achievement that only we – the players and the technical staff – had believed possible.

And in the final we were up against Germany, the team that yours truly had picked from the start. Germany. The Germans are always tough. They keep going even after they've been issued their death certificates!

I think that World Cup was the first where both teams stepped out on to the pitch together. We'd perform a load of stupid rituals in the tunnel: we'd shout and beat our chests. All the other teams had looked at us with fear. Except the Germans. I remember telling Tata Brown: 'This lot aren't afraid of anything'.

They put Matthäus on me in the final. He was a real pro; it wasn't normal man-to-man marking. Usually, the guys who do that job are clumsy, but Lothar knew how to play: he could be a number 10; he could mark; he ended up as a *líbero*. Phenomenal. I was desperately seeking the goal, I wanted my goal, but above all I wanted to win.

We scored two great goals to start. Tata Brown's header was a just reward. He deserved it more than anybody, because he had replaced Passarella and had played better than anyone. And so was Valdano's beautifully timed goal, because it was a brilliant summary of what Bilardo asked from us and a demonstration of what Jorge was, physically and in football terms.

When they drew level I got scared. Unwarranted fear as it turned out. Sure, they'd scored with two headers in our area – unforgivable for any serious team – but when I looked at Briegel's legs and saw they were like logs, I knew we could make it. Victory would come. When we got back to the centre spot for the kick-off, I squashed the ball against the turf, I looked at Burru and told him: 'Come on! Come on, they're knackered, they can't even run any more. Let's get the ball moving and we'll finish them off before extra time.' And that's how it was. I was still in our half when I turned, lifted my head and saw a huge wide avenue open up in front of Burruchaga for him to run straight on goal. He turned his back on Briegel and left him behind. Briegel lacked the speed to catch up. So I sidefooted the ball and off went Burru, off went Burru, off went Burru . . . Goaaal! Burru! I really shouted celebrating that goal, I really shouted! I remember we all piled up on top of each other, like a huge mountain. We felt like World Champions, six minutes left, and there it was . . . But Bilardo was shouting at us: 'Stop fucking about, stop fucking about! Go mark; you and Valdano, mark! Come on, come on!'

When at last Arppi Filho waved his hands – I caught it out of the corner of my eye – when the match was over and all you could hear in the Azteca stadium were Argentine voices singing because all the Mexicans had been left speechless, that's when I burst into tears. I had cried at every moment of my career, and this was the best, the most sublime. Once we had the cup in our hands we went back into the changing room and started singing the rudest chants from the terraces. We were directing them at everybody, absolutely everybody. We'd built up a lot of anger and in the middle of that resentment an amazing thing happened.

'Come on, Carlos, come on! Get it off your chest! Say everything you want to say, don't keep any of it inside,' I said to Bilardo, with bitterness, because we both knew how much we had suffered – too much. And he answered almost in a whisper, with his eyes full of tears, 'Leave it out, Diego. This is something I've wanted for a very long time and it's not *against* anybody. I just want to remember one person, and that's Zubeldía.'

He was remembering Osvaldo Zubeldía, his manager at Estudiantes de La Plata when they had won a truckload of titles, including a famous win over Manchester United in 1968. Zubeldía had taught him all he knew. He made me feel this small, all my anger vanished, I didn't know what to say. Bilardo had been rubbished, destroyed, and he didn't bear a grudge, he wasn't shouting for revenge. He was the World Champion, he'd won everything, and he felt no resentment, no anger. It's a great memory I have of Bilardo, that image. It's not the only one I have, but it's special. I carried on screaming, swinging my shirt, demented, in the middle of a changing room that was out of control. We always used to stand a little Virgin of Lujan on a corner shelf and Galíndez couldn't stop kissing her. We were all standing on the benches, screaming like madmen: 'And this one is for all you motherfuckers out there!'

I was really letting off steam. I'm never going to forget the atmosphere in that changing room: the bright green synthetic grass floor, the white benches and lockers, the sunlight coming in through the windows ... and us, happy old us.

And so we headed for the training camp to pack up our home. We accomplished what we'd hoped for: to be there at the end of the tournament. We were really hugging each other tight, and then we did one last thing we had promised ourselves we would do: we took a victory lap round the little pitch we'd been training on. Just us. It had been on that pitch that we set ourselves a goal when we first arrived in Mexico: 'We're the first here, let's also be the last.' There was hardly any time left for anything, except packing. But every so often, while we were folding our clothes, Pedrito Pasculli and I would look at each other and shout, grabbing our heads: *How're you doing, you World Champion motherfucker, you!*

World Champion, World Champion. I was a World Champion. A dream turned to reality. Now I always think that during those incredible days of Mexico '86 God was on my side.

When you're pissed off you can end up saying a load of crap but for me the greatest triumph was that the detractors had to line up in the end. There were many who stuck to their guns and said the World Cup had been mediocre and that's why we'd won it, or that Argentina had only won because of me. We didn't become champions just because of me. I did my bit, others helped me, we all won. That's why I wanted even those who had been on our backs to rejoice in victory.

I lived the World Cup to the full, like everything I've done in my life. But in some ways I think too much was made of it. It was an extraordinary success for Argentinian football – which sadly has not happened again since – but nothing more than that. By winning the World Cup we didn't change the world, we didn't bring down the price of bread. It's a lovely thought that football players can solve people's problems through playing, I wish we could. We'd all be better off.

I was thinking about that when I stood on the balcony of the

Pink House, Argentina's Presidential Residence. They had asked us there to greet the people assembled in the Plaza de Mayo, the square opposite where the crowds gather. I thought about that while I stood there feeling like I was the President. I was next to Raúl Alfonsín, the guy who had brought democracy back. The turncoats were there as well, of course, even O'Reilly, who had been trying to knock Bilardo down only a few months earlier. But now we were the kings. I already knew Alfonsín: he had granted me an audience before the elections. But truthfully, at that time I didn't care about Alfonsín or any politician. I was only thinking of the people. I felt very close to the people. If it had been up to me I would have grabbed the flag and run off with it into the crowd. Standing on that balcony everything went through my mind: Fiorito, Argentinos, Boca, everything. All the dreams which had come true.

When I finally got home there was another crowd gathered. They were treading all over Tota's garden, driving her bonkers, singing, honking, bearing gifts. My house had become part of the Buenos Aires tourist trail. And the mayor of the city, Julio Saguier, had named me an Honorary Citizen. People camped outside my house. Days went by and the people were still there. I couldn't believe it. I used to say: nobody deserves this, not Maradona, not anybody. Grown men and women, little children, I couldn't get my head round it. I kept trying to put myself in their shoes: maybe as a kid I would have gone to stand at the door of Bochini's house. I guess it's about identifying with your heroes: you like what a bloke does and you want him to know it. But it was also a bit spooky – my family hadn't done anything and they were forced to live under siege. One evening I invited two little boys in because they'd broken my heart. We kicked a ball about in my front room for a while while their mum stared at us in disbelief. I reckon they didn't even register the fact that they'd been with me, but I felt an enormous sadness. I felt it was too much . . . all I'd done was win a World Cup.

7

The Struggle

Copa América '87 and '89

When at last we went on holiday to Polynesia after Mexico '86, just like I'd promised Claudia, I imagined everything would be rosy. I was wrong. I was so wrong. The truth is that this time *I* let the tortoise get away. We had a phenomenal time, Claudia and me, the beaches were marvellous, I had a chance to indulge my passion with a few good kickabouts on the beach – we thrashed some Dutchmen – and I didn't have to sign as many autographs as I feared. The problem was elsewhere. After all the criticism and lack of support we had received as a squad before and during the '86 World Cup, a banner appeared on one of the terraces of the Azteca stadium, after the final. It read: SORRY, BILARDO. THANK YOU. But for me that wasn't enough. It was just a little banner. Sorry? Thank you? My arse! I don't know, maybe it was a trademark, or one of those stains that doesn't come off, but I felt the squad continued to be persecuted ... nobody could say we weren't World Champions, sure, but persecuted nevertheless.

I was doing OK at Napoli. We were on our way to our second *scudetto* and also aiming for the Copa Italia. The issue was with the national squad. Six months after our lap of honour we were still going round in circles, but this time over the prize money which we'd never received. Everyone was arguing. Was it too much? Was it too little? So I took a stand and sent very strong messages from Italy. Two friendlies were organised, supposedly to raise the money to pay us, but I was neither informed nor consulted by anyone. I wanted to play in all the national squad matches, as always, but I also wanted my captaincy to be respected and I wanted the other players who'd won the World Cup to be respected. All this was very important to me. Bilardo, for example, had asked me to play in the Copa América '87 six months before, and I said yes, I committed myself even though I knew it would come at the end of an exhausting season. Julio Grondona, the long-standing president of the AFA, on the other hand, owed me a chat. It seemed that he believed that winning the cup was enough. And I wanted to be absolutely honest: my team-mates had come to expect Maradona to stand up for them, and I'd never let them down, even if we were being accused of being *peseteros*, as they say in Spain of those who think only about money. All we wanted was to feel valued, our rights respected, nothing more. But the usual Argentinian moralisers would start mouthing off: *How can it be? With the state of the country? These guys want easy money!* But it was nothing like that, nothing like that at all. I played in Mexico without ever thinking about the money, but we had an agreement which, as far as I understand it, wasn't honoured.

I discussed all of that with Grondona at a meeting in Rome, in March 1987. We were both very hot-headed, Julio and I, but we always ended up understanding each other. And anyway, he gave me all the answers I needed and agreed to pay us a small amount. The only thing that pissed me off then was Bochini, who had said after the finals that he didn't feel like a World Champion. But that didn't stop him from being the first to turn up to collect the cheque. I don't mind him wanting his due, but he was the first . . . if at least he'd been fifth in line.

Just after that meeting, the national squad played a friendly against Roma and lost. The struggle was starting again, we needed to build from scratch. In the middle of the year, at the end of the European season, I was exhausted. But I had every title under my belt: World Champion, Italian champion, with a *scud-etto* and a Copa for Napoli, something which hadn't happened in *calcio* for fifteen years. I was exhausted and I felt like a winner, but I couldn't say I was happy, speaking purely in football terms. I can't deny it: I was thinking of all those who had attacked me saying I won nothing, and I wondered where they would be shoving their words right now. And it hurt me that, in front of everyone, in front of the press and the people, as a team we had to start all over again.

What had happened? Nothing, just that Argentina had played a match against Italy, in Zürich, a year after the World Cup, in June 1987, and we lost 3–1, that's all. But all the criticisms returned, all the doubts, everything exactly like it had been, a carbon copy. I remember the match as if it was yesterday: bumping into Pelé, with no controversy, each of us minding his own business. 'I never wanted to be bigger than him,' I declared, and we had our picture taken shaking hands, with Altobelli, Italy's captain. The only positive thing about that game was that I met Cani, Claudio Paul Caniggia. My brother El Turco had had some training sessions with him and had spoken very highly of him so the minute I saw him I said: 'I know you very well already, we're going to understand each other.' But Bilardo only brought him on for Siviski five minutes before the final whistle. I could see another fight coming over that one: to me Cani is like . . . a soulmate, that's what he is.

In spite of everything we'd achieved the press laid into us without mercy and it hurt a lot, I still feel that pain. The ghosts were returning, once again the national side was labelled as being incapable of beating anyone. No one could accept that we were starting afresh, with kids who were making their debuts. I was doing my best but I couldn't perform better. I remember distinctly looking for one of the squad, Juan Funes, on the pitch, wanting to communicate with him. But it wouldn't come out right, I'd only just met him. I'd read some interviews and articles about him but that was it. I wasn't able to say to him, 'Juan, do you understand me?' Same with Goycochea, I actually called him Goycochea, instead of Sergio or Goyco which is how the whole country knows him. And Siviski? I had never seen him play, I knew nothing about him or about that cunning Hernan Díaz. But of course I was introduced to all of them in Zürich. Afterwards, when we were all gathered together in Ezeiza preparing for the Copa América, I talked to the press about how I'd felt and said I thought things would be different as we got to know each other. But I wasn't making excuses for the defeat, OK? I've never been interested in excuses. I just thought in that first half against Italy we'd been a disaster. That was the state we were in, and that's how we arrived at the Copa América.

I was exhausted. Physically and mentally shattered. I hadn't stopped since my holiday in Polynesia. There had been a friendly against Paraguay, before the start of the Copa in June, to raise funds for the football players' union, Futbolistas Argentinos Agremiados. I didn't play because I was knackered. I was given a really hard time over that – they killed me! I'd even bought tons of tickets, I wanted to do my bit somehow. And what made matters worse for me was that I couldn't understand, I couldn't accept that the World Champion national squad could play a match, with or without Maradona, and that only ten thousand people would attend. I couldn't believe it. Dead as I was I wanted to play the Copa América, I wanted to win something for my country in my country. I just wanted the people of Argentina to accept us once and for all. Nothing turned out as I'd hoped.

Physically, I wasn't up to playing. I had tendonitis in my adductors and Doctor Madero had told me that in order to make even an averagely good recovery I needed absolute rest for two weeks. Two weeks! Our first Copa América match, against Peru, was sooner, so I played anyway. We were alright, but we drew 1–1. Reyna didn't follow me all over the pitch on that occasion but a bunch of them took turns to kick the shit out of me. I finished very beaten up and on top of that I caught the flu. It didn't help that it was so cold where we were staying in the Trade Workers' Union in Ezeiza. I was so ill I couldn't even join in the anniversary celebrations of the '86 World Cup title. I wasn't training, but I played anyway in the second match against Ecuador. We beat them 3–0 and Bilardo finally made his mind up to play Caniggia in the second half: he scored one, I scored two and we finished them off. Cani was amazing but Bilardo, I don't know why, was in some sort of denial about him. The people asked for him; they had a banner up on the stands that said: BILARDO, DON'T DO AS MENOTTI DID WITH MARADONA: PLAY CANIGGIA. The good news was that we had made it to the semi-finals and the bad news was that my flu had turned into a terrible bronchitis with fever and all. I had the lot.

That's the state I was in when I went out to play against Uruguay. At least having Cani by my side gave me some peace of mind. But Francescoli and his men beat us, they beat us well. We lost 1–0 and that was it, over. We were out of the Copa América. We had the third-place play-off but I've never enjoyed playing for that. What's the point? We played out of respect for the fans, but our soul had been destroyed. Colombia beat us 2–1 in a very strange Monumental, I don't think anybody there will be able to forget it. The fog was so dense that I never even saw Cani's goal, the one in injury time. I think that the image of the team in that Copa América remains wrapped up in that fog: a sense of frustration, of failure, even though we hadn't really played that badly.

It didn't take me long to get back into top shape again, have my desire to be back in the national strip re-ignited. I went on holiday, returned to Italy, and accepted a different invitation: the English paid me a fortune, $160,000, to play at Wembley for the centenary of the English League. They sent a private jet to Verona and put me in a hotel that was closer to Scotland than London, but it was very beautiful. Every time I touched the ball the fans heckled me like they did to black players: 'Uuuuhhhh!'. But if I took a nice touch they would immediately applaud me, like the English gentlemen that they were. Of course, in those days I still had to talk about the hand of God. Osvaldo Ardiles was my host, and in England he was the best thing since sliced bread. Also, he is one of the guys who, together with Valdano, I've always listened to.

After that match I had a little stay at Doctor Henri Chenot's clinic in Italy. I went straight back on to the pitch, and gave it everything I had. Argentina were due to play Germany for the home leg of a game we'd played in Germany and I'd asked Bilardo to save me a place among the sixteen selected for the match in Buenos Aires. It was another one of those trips of mine: a match in Italy with Napoli on Sunday 13 December (against Juventus, 2–1), a flight to Buenos Aires, a match on Wednesday in the Argentinian strip against Germany, and an immediate return to sport the Napoli strip again on Sunday the 20th (against Verona, 4–1). And again it was worth it. I felt indebted to the Argentinian fans, and that 1–0 victory over Germany, at the Vélez stadium, filled a very big void. Our country was once again in a terrible state: the economy and the politics seem to be forever up and down, and this was a down time. All we did was give the people a little bit of joy, as was always my main objective on the pitch. Not to make people forget the reality of what's going on, but to give them something, a smile, a little fun. And I'd also beaten Grondona in an arm wrestle: I'd asked him that the match be played at the Vélez stadium, so we could feel the people's warmth. In River's stadium, the Monumental, you never know if the crowd is insulting you or cheering you on, because they're two thousand kilometres away. At Vélez, it's the complete opposite, and we attracted a crowd of fifty thousand. I always say we would have come out better in the Copa América if that had been our home stadium. Burruchaga scored the winning goal against Germany and once again we felt we were the champions, the best. One thing is for sure though, Bilardo busted my balls so much he scared me. I don't know, he was on overdrive, obsessive, putting the pressure on me like crazy, burdening me too much. I wanted to say to him: 'Carlos, ease off a little', but I kept it in, I kept it in. I did say it in an interview and all hell broke loose but my love for the national squad could overcome everything.

I loved the national team so much that in April 1988 I took the risk of playing in an impossible tournament, a four nations or something like that, in Berlin. First the USSR humiliated us, 4–2, and then Germany beat us 1–0. Those results always made me so bitter, even if they were only friendlies . . . they hurt me as an Argentina fan. What's more, they obviously wanted to kill me in Naples, because I was playing all those other matches for Argentina – they were particularly pissed off about the time I'd stayed in Germany just to be there when we played for the fourth place, for nothing. And to top it all, our stars started to get injured: Valdano, Batista, Burruchaga, Enrique . . . and Bilardo was trying out the new kids. Building the team was a permanent struggle: the clubs wouldn't release players, they were selling the kids to Europe as soon as they'd played a couple of minutes in the first division. I felt the national squad was being betrayed all the time. That's why I always wanted to be there, even if I couldn't cope physically with the marathon of matches. Injured and all I played again against Spain, in Seville, a good draw, 1–1. I was dead, even my tongue muscle was torn, but I couldn't let the national side down, no way, it was too important. A lot of nonsense was being talked, as always, and I knew that if we got together we would shut them all up. And we did it: we played one half of the match as champions. But it was as if we were sitting an exam every day, and were expected to play 31 good games out of 30. So the struggle continued. I wanted the kids to understand what it was like to be part of a squad that was really battling. I wanted them to be prepared for Italia '90.

But before Italia '90 there was the Copa América '89, in Brazil. I was anxious for revenge. I had promised Bilardo I would be there for the national side. Almost six months earlier, just after a spectacular 4–1 victory against Milan, in November 1988, I had dedicated the win to him. I assured him that my next objective was to be there, with the best of the best, in the blue and white strip.

But it was as if destiny had fouled me – once again it was not to be. Napoli played already relegated Pisa in the penultimate match of the Italian *scudetto* '88/'89 and only a quarter of an hour into the game I felt something pull in my right thigh. I had to go off. Some imbeciles in the crowd whistled at me. Desperate, I called Doctor Oliva: I had the Copa Italia with Napoli coming up, and the trip to Brazil to join the national squad. My thigh hurt tremendously and Oliva was convinced it was a consequence of my chronic lower-back problem. I may have been whistled at but Oliva said if I'd carried on playing it would have been the fuck-up of the century – then it really would have been goodbye Copa América.

In those days I would joke that the reason I was getting injured so much was that I was old. But the truth is I had had an awful run of matches: by June, I'd played fifty-seven games. What's more, I knew that Bilardo had drawn the short straw: he was gathering us in Goiania, in the south of Brazil, but he would only be able to have us all there together just three days before the first game against Chile. There were players I had never even met before, like José Horacio 'El Pepe' Basualdo. One thing is certain: I was hugely satisfied that Bilardo had called up my brother El Turco to join the team. He was playing at Rayo Vallecano, a second division club, and had been chosen by the press as the best player of the second division. I also felt relieved to see that Brazil were going through similar problems to our own: I'd seen Antonio Careca, my friend and team-mate at Napoli, close up and the poor guy was as beaten-up as I was.

At any rate, I couldn't wait to be with all the lads, to meet the new ones like Abel Balbo and Alfaro Moreno and dive head first into the Copa. It was one of my dreams, like returning to Boca and winning the Libertadores Cup. It was also important because I was convinced that it would be the springboard for Italia '90. Bilardo had spoken to me of 'El Pepe' Basualdo and the other kids that were coming through. And I trusted Caniggia, too. He was just back from an injury, a fracture he had suffered at Verona. He was just a kid but he was treated badly, on and off the pitch. Like me, he was the sacrificial lamb, people accused him of selling drugs when the only thing he sold – and very well too – was football. As I said at the time, and stand by today, 'Why is it considered chic for rugby players to get pissed, to be seen in the trendiest nightclubs? If a footballer so much as touches a drink, even a Coca-Cola, he's considered a drunk. There's some kind of double standard going on. Let's stop this bullshit, everyone's got it in for Claudio and it's making me mad.' I said that over ten years ago and it still stands today. It would seem I'm not so stupid after all.

Perhaps, though, it was stupid to dream about the Copa América when deep down I knew I wasn't even up to putting a foot on the pitch. I felt I was going the wrong way down a one-way street – I even felt ridiculous being there at all. I had my reasons though, I wanted to build the team for the World Cup, I wanted to meet up with team-mates old and new, I didn't want to let down 'El Narigón' Bilardo, who was a real motherfucker when it came to pressurising, but a motherfucker in a good way, I use it as a compliment. I was finding a way round my injury, mainly thanks to the magic of Doctor Oliva, who had seen me off from Europe practically on crutches, but between the never-ending back problems and the pulled muscles, I wasn't up to much. I was far from full fitness and, as I said to the press mid-tournament: 'I'm not a superman, I don't eat glass. I'm not up to it ... and I'm not going to be.' In a sense that gave me a certain peace of mind: if we did end up winning the Copa everyone would finally have to praise the team the way they deserved. It wouldn't be possible to say it was just thanks to me. It's always pissed me off the way people say the World Cup was won thanks to me after the whole group had worked like mad, on and off the pitch.

We didn't win, of course, but it wasn't my fault or the other lads'. We started off well, beating Chile 1–0, on 2 July, with a goal from Caniggia. Then we played woefully against Ecuador. Bilardo wanted to kill us and he was right: he lectured us for two hours, you could hear a pin drop. We were pitiful.

Hope returned when we beat Uruguay, on 8 July. But it was just an illusion. Reality hit us hard. First Brazil made us dance, although if my shot from the midfield which hit the crossbar had gone in, history could have been different. Then Uruguay made us dance, they got their revenge when we met them again and *chau* Copa América. In my case, unfortunately, for ever.

In the end I said what I felt: third place for World Champions is nothing. We lacked preparation time, fitness and luck. Mostly luck, because if that ball that hit the crossbar had gone in, the story could have changed.

Surprisingly, when it was all over, deep inside I felt something similar to what I had felt at the previous Copa América in Argentina. We hadn't won it and we'd left a bad impression behind, nobody liked our Argentina. But once again we had built a team. Once again there we were, the hated ones, the misfits, Carlos Bilardo's chosen ones, united against everything. That's how we intended to go into Italia '90.

8

The Vendetta

Italia '90

I should perhaps have foreseen it, but I could never have imagined what actually happened in my football life in Italy during 1990.

After the Copa América in Brazil I took some long holidays. I was being rebellious, as I'd warned Napoli I would be. When I finally returned to Naples it wasn't easy. I had asked the club to sell me because I wanted a change but they had refused. When I say change I mean I needed a breath of fresh air, less demanding football, a less oppressive city. I always liked to think of a house with a park, with a swimming pool, something I couldn't find in Naples and which other clubs in other cities could provide. It wasn't so difficult to understand, I don't think, and those who couldn't understand it, well . . . they should give the dog its face back. I had no choice but to try to find strength where I had none. *Bronca*, which I had plenty of, would help. I wanted to start all over again, in my own way. Fernando Signorini was by my side and we constructed a training schedule that enabled me to reach Italia '90 in a better physical shape than I had been in Mexico '86, when I was four years younger. I was twenty-nine in 1990, neither young nor old: an expert.

Maybe because I wasn't just another player I dared question something that happened in the World Cup draw. I didn't want to dig for dirt but I wanted an explanation for what had happened. Before the draw it had been established that, in order to avoid

Colombia and Uruguay ending up in the same groups as Brazil and Argentina (who were both top seeds), the first European team to be drawn would play against Argentina and the second against Italy. Czechoslovakia came out first and instead of playing against us they were given to the Italians. We were landed with the Soviet Union. I asked FIFA to explain, nothing more, and the shit hit the fan. So I knew from the word go that Italia '90 was going to be difficult for us.

At the start of that unforgettable 1990 – unforgettable for many reasons – I was invited, as on so many other occasions, to take part in a TV programme. The presenter said to me: 'Diego, only 106 days to go to the World Cup.' And I replied: '106 days? When there's only 90 to go we'll get started . . .'

In fact, exactly three months and three days before kick off I was writhing on the floor because of the problem in my lower back. The pain was so bad that, though the painkilling injections in my hip helped, I could only run like my dad. In that state I would do more harm than good to the team (I mean to Napoli). I didn't play for two fixtures and after that, yes, I was off to a roaring start. On Sunday 11 March I played in a game against Lecce and from then onwards I didn't stop, I never stopped. Because of the injuries preventing me from training properly I was between six to eight kilos over my ideal weight. So I started a diet which Doctor Henri Chenot sent me. In just a few days I lost between four and five kilos. I travelled to Rome to see Professor Antonio Dal Monte, director of the Institute of Sports Science at the CONI (the Italian Olympic Committee), a guy who had already treated me before Mexico '86 and who had also worked with the record-breaking cyclist Francesco Moser. For one whole day he carried out every imaginable test on me. I tried out all his machines, which were spectacular, and it was already night-time when I got into my silver Mercedes-Benz to return to Naples, exhausted but happy. From then on I repeated the trip every Monday.

In the midst of those preparations I played in three friendlies. Against Austria, Switzerland and Israel – this last one a classic clash for us before each World Cup. We drew the first two (1–1) and beat Israel (2–1). The clash against the Israelis had become a ritual: it had been the last friendly we played before the World Cup we won, so it had to be the last before this coming one if we wanted to win.

I have an indelible memory of that trip, beyond the football and the anger. I visited the Weeping Wall, knelt down, one among the many, but I was terribly shocked by the armed soldiers surrounding us . . . really shocked. I couldn't understand that in a place such as that you could breathe in so much hatred. And, yes, I was asked for autographs as well. I signed every single one wearing a *kipá* on my head – it didn't look at all bad.

I did, however, feel uneasy. I still didn't feel 100 per cent, although I was sticking at following Dal Monte and Chenot's plans. Worse, I didn't feel the team was right either, something was missing. To my mind we lacked a finisher and I was convinced it should be Ramón Díaz. But it wasn't up to me to decide, it was Bilardo's call, though to this day people think I had something to do with it. Quite the opposite: in Switzerland, during a tour before Italia '90, I mentioned – and I have a journalist as a witness – that the only one who could save us at that time, when we badly needed a goal and a little something more, when we couldn't vaccinate anybody, was Ramón Díaz. I said: 'You know who should be in this squad and then the problems would be over? Díaz . . .' In '89, when Inter won the championship with Díaz as their big star I came across the pitch and I shouted at him: 'I hope Bilardo calls you, so you stop making up bullshit!' because he was going around spreading rumours about me. But a year later, when Bilardo picked the final squad for Italia '90, Díaz couldn't score in a twenty-metre goal.

Bilardo didn't even want to include Caniggia, who was my

baby! Although in his case I did give Bilardo an ultimatum: if he didn't bring Caniggia, I wouldn't play in Italia 90.

And Bilardo had finally decided to leave Valdano out of the squad. I was devastated. I knew Jorge's physical state and of course he was a risk. But who wasn't? We're always running risks. I saw that the motivation behind his exclusion was tactical, but with his decision Bilardo didn't just kill a football player, he killed a person that was very good for the group. He also killed another person, and that was me. Because of my friendship with Valdano; because together with El Tata Brown and Giusti we were the ones who held the group together. Now I had really been left alone.

That's why I decided to bring over Claudia and the girls, and my mother-in-law. I needed their support.

Despite my disappointment we finally settled in Trigoria, AS Roma's training ground. That would be our home for the following month and, as in Mexico, I expected it to be so until the end, all the way to the final. In my room, which had a balcony full of flowers overlooking the training pitches, I always had music playing: those were the days of *lambada* and my friend Antonio Careca had given me a spectacular tape. Trigoria was a beautiful place, really. It was on the outskirts of Rome, and the drive there was lovely, with curves this way and that, uphill then down, surrounded by trees . . . it was ideal for both my Ferraris. I'd taken them both to the *concentración* because I needed to feel at home. I kept them in the car park and when Bilardo gave me permission I'd go for a little drive: I'd go up to the Grande Raccordo Annullare, a sort of ring road that loops the city, and then I'd drive back. It was a pleasure, the pleasure of the speed and of enjoying something I felt I'd earned. Some people were bothered by that: they said I had privileges and I was undisciplined. So what? Wasn't the aim to reach the finals in good shape? Well, that small pleasure helped me be better; it bothered no one. More serious than whether or not I had my Ferraris was the fact that a bout of flu had forced me to take antibiotics. All the detox work I'd done went slightly to pot, but no one was talking about that.

Everyone said: 'The national squad depends on Maradona' or 'Argentina will only win if Diego is well'. To me this felt like a beautiful responsibility but I also felt the pressure that came with it. That's why I wanted to be well, in order to win. I've always had to prove myself. At fifteen years old I was the kid who had to prove he was going to make it; at twenty, if I was really as good as they said; at twenty-five, if I could remain the best in the world; and at twenty-nine – there, in Italy – was I going to fail or not . . . For the whole world, for a lot of journalists, for a lot of others who should do nothing but give the dog its face back, I was permanently sitting an exam. For me and for my loved ones that wasn't the case. It was simple: I knew very well what I was worth and in those days I would repeat, as if it was the slogan for a TV advert, 'They're going to have to rip the World Cup from my hands.'

To ensure victory I'd spent 60,000 dollars on an incredible training machine. Fernando had helped me set up my 'isokinetic ergometer' at the back of one of the Trigoria gyms. It was very useful to evaluate and control my physical condition, very detailed. In the early days of June we would use it a lot for exercises to develop flexibility. And there was a running machine which I had already fallen in love with. Doctor Dal Monte had also sent me a masseuse, Monica, who would leave me as good as new on a daily basis. I was hoping to arrive for the first match at my ideal weight, 75.5 kilos. But I made sure my diet included an *asado* organised by my old man in Trigoria. Meat barbecued by Don Diego couldn't be bad for anybody, quite the contrary. On the day of the barbecue he was interviewed – I think it was by Cadena Caracol from Colombia – and when they asked him about me he answered: 'I just want him to continue being like he is. And happy . . .' Great guy, Don Diego!

The only thing that was preventing me from being completely happy was actually something quite silly: the big toe on my right foot. A lot has happened to me in football, but a big toe! I think what happened was that in the matches against Israel and Valencia I'd received quite a few stamps on it and my nail was in a right state. During training I was suffering so much: we tried injecting painkillers, we tried cotton wool, I tried bigger boots, but nothing worked.

Our first match was to be against Cameroon on 8 June, but during training on Thursday 31 May I could no longer bear the pain and I came off. The following day I returned to practice and after a couple of set moves with Burru and putting a few past Goyco I took my shoes off because the pain was so bad. Immediately the journalists were on top of me and I stopped them short: 'Please, don't get too close, don't touch me! If any of you so much as brushes against my foot, I'll make a scene!' I was pissed-off . . . I was scared of missing the World Cup, that was the truth. Bilardo couldn't sleep a wink for worrying about my toenail.

On Sunday 3 June I went to Dal Monte's institute in Rome with Doctor Raúl Madero where they fitted me with an amazing splint to protect the toenail. It was like a shell, made out of carbon fibre, a hard but light material used in aeronautical manufacturing; that's why I said I was like a plane, fit to fly. I was able to return to training on the afternoon of Monday 4 June. Valdano, who should have been playing in that World Cup rather than working as a journalist, wrote in Spain's *El Pais* newspaper: 'There's nothing to worry about, the biggest footballing talent in the world is kept in a perfect site: the body of Diego Armando Maradona. The depositary of that treasure – a trove of bones, muscles and tendons which holds together uncountable footballing menaces – is in and of itself a marvel.'

On Tuesday the 5th I was running on my machine again for some tests Signorini was carrying out. On Wednesday the 6th, in the afternoon, we had a kickaround which we played to the death, just the way I liked them. Afterwards Bilardo gathered us at the centre of the pitch to tell us the final starting line-up: Cani would be on the bench. Everyone knew I wanted him to start, but I didn't say a word. I knew if he came on in the second half he would wreak havoc. I had incredible faith in him.

At any rate, playing with Abel Balbo, who would start, also gave me pleasure: for me, anyone wearing the national strip had to give their all.

I knew I was going to get whistled in Milan, where we were playing the inaugural match. Milan were my arch-rivals. But I'd also got a call from Naples asking me not to worry, and saying that the claps and cheers we would receive at the San Paolo, when we played there, would make up for it. I was very moved because looking at the draw I could see one thing very clearly: Italy's best chance of winning would be if Argentina were knocked out.

Our only problem was that Trigoria seemed more like a hospital ward than a *concentración*. We were all in a pitiful state: Valdano had already been left out, at the last moment we lost Tata Brown, Giusti could hardly stand, Ruggeri could hardly keep going on account of a lower abdomenal strain, Burruchaga was all wrapped up in cotton wool, as was Julio 'El Vasco' Olarticoechea. The spine of the team was broken. But at that point, I don't know why, I still had faith: maybe because I believed we were stronger than we had been at the previous World Cup. Once again, nobody trusted us: the Dutch and the Italians were mouthing off too much, they were sure they would win. Even Cameroon was claiming not to be worried by Argentina.

On Thursday the 7th we finally travelled to Milan, to recce the Giuseppe Meazza stadium. I walked right up to the centre of the pitch and crossed myself. Then I walked up to one of the goals and a Neapolitan who played with me at club level,

Tommasso Starace, gave me the boots I would wear the next day. I was already wearing the Argentina strip and I wouldn't take it off again. I wore it with light blue jogging pants, which I rolled up to my knees, like a fisherman. I knew that I would get sworn at there, although the place was more full of top totty than football fans – the models who would take part in the opening ceremony the following day. It was like a catwalk! Right there on the pitch I bumped into Gianna Nannini, who was the Formula One driver's sister – a friend of mine. She was also going to be a part of the opening ceremony, singing the World Cup anthem, 'Un estate italiana'. But the thing that I noticed the most, seriously, was how soft the pitch was. An image of Mar del Plata, in the '78 World Cup, immediately sprung to mind, when the players kicked the ball and chunks of grass flew up with it.

In the evening I went down to the hotel conference room. All the journalists were waiting for me, together with Carlos Menem, the President of Argentina, who awarded me an honourary title: Roving Sports Ambassador. He was wearing a suit and tie and I was still in my Argentina strip. I thought that was great. It highlighted the fact that I was still just a football player, and if my country was becoming well known it was because of the way I played, nothing more, nothing to do with politics or power. I clutched my new diplomatic passport and my diploma in my hand and said: 'I want to thank Mr President for this passport. Not so much for me as for my mum and dad, who must be very proud of this. Thank you. I will represent and defend Argentina ... on the pitch.' Some journalist mate of mine asked, half-jokingly, 'Diego, from now on will we have to call you Your Excellency?' I replied, 'No way! I'll always be the same guy.'

The time of truth was looming, the time to go out on the pitch. The following day, Friday 8 June, we were facing Cameroon in the opening match of the tournament. In the changing room, in the heart of the Meazza, while everyone outside was going crazy and the models were parading, I felt a strange atmosphere – in my skin, in my soul. I felt a silence too deep, too cold. I looked at some faces and saw them pale, as if they were tired already. I stood in the middle of the changing room, took a deep breath and shouted, loud, from my guts: 'C'mon, up! Fucking c'mon! This is a World Cup and we're the World Champions . . .' I felt I hadn't reached everyone, and as captain, I felt frustrated. I myself had said to everyone that whoever wanted the cup would have to rip it from our grasp, but now I felt we didn't have such a strong grasp on it after all.

I led the way out on to the pitch and I heard the whistling like few times before in my career. They were bursting our eardrums, but they didn't move a hair on my head. It gave me strength: to play against everything and against everyone was my speciality. I took a few steps and looked around to find the seats where my family sat. I blew them a kiss.

During our anthem, which I could hardly hear because of the Italians booing us, I tried to keep my head up high and run my gaze over the crowd. When it was over I stood in front of the rest of the players, and shouted once again: 'C'mon, fucking c'mon, eh?!' But more than one had his eyes fixed on the ground.

From the kick-off a huge black guy stayed right next to me, number 4, Massing. First he said hello, patted me, and then . . . he kicked the shit out of me. Two minutes in I passed to Balbo, but he couldn't finish; then Ruggeri got into the area, Burruchaga, Balbo again . . . but we couldn't vaccinate, we couldn't vaccinate. We had less definition than the old TV sets back in Fiorito. And Massing was continuing to say hello in a peculiar way, with a kick to the shoulder.

With a little less than half an hour to go, the game finished for me. When I saw Cameroon score I left the pitch. I was there but I wasn't there. I couldn't believe such a foolish defeat, so unjust, with only ourselves to blame. And I didn't mean goalkeeper Nery

Pumpido, who couldn't stop Omar Biyik's header, I meant all of us who'd played. Cameroon didn't win, Argentina lost.

I was used to the weirdest things happening in football but that defeat surprised and hurt me, truly. Cameroon had really given us a kicking but to talk about that was to make excuses. At any rate, it was a refereeing problem: they persisted in not protecting skill over brute force. It was meant to be the Fair Play World Cup but it started off with them kicking the living daylights out of us. To this day I continue to believe that if we had got the finishing right in that match, we would have had a goalfest. And if Caniggia had started, the story would have been very different.

I got picked for the drugs test, of course. How could I not? Afterwards I marched to the press conference, to show my face. It was ironic but true when I said, 'The only pleasure I got this afternoon was to discover that thanks to me the people of Milan have stopped being racist. Today, for the first time, they supported the Africans.' I was the last on the bus, half an hour after all the others, and we went off to the airport to catch the plane back to Rome. It wasn't far, but during the drive I didn't hear a sound, not a single voice, not a fly. We were all dead, dead of shame.

Nothing was working out for us, even at the airport we were told we would have to wait: there were so many presidents, directors and bosses who had come to watch the opening match that the private jets were clogging up the runways and our flight was delayed for over two hours. I took the opportunity to chat to Claudia and recharge my batteries. In those two hours my mood changed, I recovered my motivation. When I got on the plane I was a new man.

So much so that I managed to cut Bilardo short when he came up with something unbelievable: 'Lads, there are two possible outcomes after what happened here. Either we reach the final, or may the plane carrying us back to Argentina fall out of the sky.'

Bilardo, you fucking motherfucker! May the plane not fall out of the fucking sky! Let's make it to the final.

Everyone already thought we were out of the World Cup, but not me. We were up against the Soviet Union next, on 14 June. It would be our first match in Naples; it would be our first match at home. They didn't boo our anthem there, they cheered us all. I remember travelling down from Trigoria on the eve of the match, Wenesday the 13th, on our official bus. I knew the drive by heart, I'd done it a thousand times.

At the San Paolo there was a welcome sign. 'OK, boys, we're home now,' I told the lads. I heard the *¡Die-có!Die-có!* as always but now immediately followed by an *Ar-gen-ti-na! Ar-gen-ti-na!* which made me feel really proud. I sent the fans a message: 'If tomorrow all the Neapolitans come to cheer me, to support Argentina, you will see me truly happy. But I want you to know that you've already given me everything, I have no right to demand anything of you.'

But we did have to make demands on ourselves. There were no excuses, we had to get more points. We couldn't lose: with two defeats we would be out, there was no saving us. That match on Thursday the 14th against the Soviet Union was life or death. But fate was killing us on the counter-attack: twelve minutes into the game, when we felt slightly better positioned on the pitch, calmer, tragedy struck: Olarticoechea and Nery Pumpido clashed and Nery's leg broke as if it was a piece of wood. The noise, the pain! I couldn't believe it: first my toe – which next to Nery's leg was nothing – then the Cameroon thing, and now this. El Vasco Goycochea came on and we tried to go on, shocked as we all were. Luckily, Pedrito Troglio scored from a spectacular header and we won.

It was after that that I had to play goalie: I handled the ball again. The Russians were squeezing us, we were all inside our area, the way Bilardo liked us to be when the opposition had the ball. I saw a huge Russian waiting for a cross and shouted: 'Get the 6, get the 6!' Bam! The guy made an amazing header. 'I can't get there, it's a goal!' I thought, and the post was just there, and the ref was looking at me, and . . . *tac!* I put my hand out and stopped it. I immediately ran off looking for the rebound, and I kicked it into touch.

The Russians piled on top of the ref all at once, but I'd hypnotised the guy. I'd hypnotised him! 'Play on, play on,' he said. I shouldn't have been at that post in the first place, but we were all over the place. Later, Burruchaga sealed our victory with another goal and we finished the game as best we could, all of us still thinking about Pumpido lying there weeping. El Tata Brown, who had stayed in Italy with the squad, went with him to the hospital and called us from there. He wanted to cheer us up, so the wanker kept cracking jokes. I guess it was the right thing to do, we couldn't do anything for Nery anyway. 'It's OK, guys, I've saved him,' said El Tata. 'It wasn't easy but I managed. They're not going to sacrifice him. The Italians were ready to shoot him but I argued to the death and I won. Of course, when they heard they had a camel [that was Pumpido's nickname] with a broken leg, they wanted to shoot him like a horse.' I guess someone had to get a laugh out of it, because there seemed to be no end to our bad luck.

In the last training session before the match against Romania on the 18 June I got a nasty bang on my left knee. Afterwards I remember sitting on one of the sofas at the Paradiso Hotel, where we stayed when we went to Naples, hugging Claudia with one arm and holding a bag of ice to my knee with the other. I was laughing but only in order not to cry: it felt like we were in an obstacle race more than a World Cup. To ask us to play well, in those circumstances, was asking too much. We had to win any way we could. We couldn't do much during the first forty-five minutes of that game. We went to the dressing room as if we had already lost. We couldn't crack Romania's defence. Right there, in that place I knew so well, in the heart of the San Paolo,

I overheard Doc Madero telling Bilardo he should take me off: on top of my knee, I'd got a hard kick on my left ankle, and it was starting to swell. I jumped up as if absolutely nothing was hurting at all: 'What! Take me off? If I drop dead you won't be able to drag me off that pitch. I'm staying on, I'm st-ay-ing on!' In the second half I crossed to Monzón, Pedro Damián Monzón, nice kid, and he put it in. We were 1–0 up and we had to hang on in there, hang on in there. But then they scored twice from headers in our area, something that should never happen, and Balint equalised. We were through to the second round, sure, but in through the back door. Third place, only just.

I showered really quickly after the match and left the changing room wearing the same strip as always. I didn't want to talk to anybody. The same people always waited for us outside, it was like a ritual, our relatives and some journalists. I walked out of the exit tunnel of the San Paolo, where the bus would set off, and I sat on the side of the road. I didn't want to talk to anybody, not even to Claudia. I was fuming. Professor Echeverría, the physical trainer, saw me, came up and patted my head, warm as he was. I said: 'I'm really pissed off. I'd better not say anything or I'll make things worse.' And he understood everything. He understood that we couldn't be such *pichis*, such babies, that we could give our prestige away like it was nothing. If I'd said anything at that point I would have had to badmouth half the team, and that wasn't my style. It also wasn't my style to say 'I'm satisfied' because that would have been hypocrisy. Bollocks was I satisfied! It was better to keep my anger inside and to start thinking about our next match. Coming third in the group meant we had to face Brazil in the second round. We were also starting a dance of flights which I knew very well, because if there's something I've done for the national squad in my time it's fly. The time had come to leave our home in Naples. Now we were starting a tour of Italy that wasn't exactly a tourist trip. We were to play Brazil in Turin.

The day after the match against Romania, I called Guillermo
Cóppola in Buenos Aires where he'd stayed for good luck. I
said: 'Never mind about the luck. Get over here, I can't go on!'
It was true, I couldn't cope. The air in Trigoria could be cut
with a pair of scissors. I locked myself in my room, lay down
on the bed and stared at the ceiling as I went over everything:
the flu, which had meant I had to pollute my body with antibiotics; Valdano's exit, the only man capable of lifting my spirits
with a single word; the dammed toenail, an absurd injury that
robbed me of hours of training; the incredible defeat against
Cameroon; the kicks from my rivals, exposing the Fair Play lie;
Bilardo's stubborness in not starting Canniggia. But worst of all
and the thing I found really hard to accept, there were people
who enjoyed my defeats, who wished them upon me.

I couldn't take it any more. After Guillermo arrived I left the
concentración. I took one of my Ferraris and disappeared for a
few hours. I went to the centre of Rome, went for dinner. I
needed air. I needed to live my way. I'd done everything like I'd
been told and I'd lost. Why not do it my way? Win or lose, but
in my style, without betraying myself.

I went to the restaurant with Guillermo, and had three
bruschettas as a starter followed by a plate of spaghetti. As soon
as I walked in, the owner of the restaurant locked the door to
stop anyone else from getting in. After a while I saw a little kid,
blond and blue-eyed, staring through the window. The doorman
kept shooing him off and the kid kept coming back, so I sent
Guillermo to ask him what he wanted; I felt sorry for him.
Guillermo came back with a banknote in his hand: 'He wants
you to sign your autograph here, and because it's his birthday
next Sunday he asked if you would give him a goal. His name
is Ariel, like the washing powder, he said it like that so you
won't get it wrong.' I signed the autograph and gave Guillermo
a 100,000 lire note to give back with a message: 'As well as the
goal I'm going to give you the match.' When we finished I said

goodbye to the owner. 'You're a great player, but you would be even greater if you played for Roma,' he told me. And as I left the restaurant I bumped into Ariel: '*Auguri per il tuo compleanno y buena suerte*', happy birthday and good luck, I told him.

On Thursday the 21st I returned to Trigoria a few hours before the press were allowed in. El Tata Brown had flown back to Buenos Aires with Pumpido, so Prof Echeverría and Ruggeri had become the jokers, the ones who tried to lift the spirits, but even the dimmest among us could tell it was all forced. We were beaten, I was beaten. My left ankle was a ball, that's what it was, a football.

Signorini came up to me and said: 'Go out without shoes, so everyone can see you're not lying.' I went out dressed in a blue Adidas tracksuit top, white shorts, and Puma slip-ons. I stood on the side of the pitch to watch the others train and I could feel everyone's eyes fixed on my ankle like knives: they all appeared to be examining it. It was almost eight in the evening when the training session ended and I limped on to the pitch. I lay on the ground and started playing keepy-uppy without using my left foot at all. In no time I was surrounded by journalists. I knew they would come over, I was waiting for them. I wanted to send out a couple of messages. The first thing they asked me was whether that was how I was going to play against Brazil and I said: 'Like this or in a cast, but I'm playing.' And then I launched into my speech: 'I believe in miracles, and our victory will be exactly that. This should surprise nobody. But watch it: a lot of the favourites are dying on the pitch. The Soviets should be in the second round. Brazil should have scored ten against Costa Rica, Italy twenty against the US. None of that has happened . . .

'The Brazilians are in a much better shape than we are and they know it, but if they think we're going to give the game away they're mistaken. And it's not true that they no longer play as they used to, it's just that they're covering their backs a bit more.

'It will be strange playing against Careca and Alemão, my close friends and team-mates at Napoli. I'll go on the pitch and I'll give Antonio Careca a great big hug when I see him but the minute the whistle goes I'll try to beat him with all my might.

'I can't find an answer to what is happening to us, although I have been thinking about that question for a while. My experience tells me that this can't be the real us, that we'll have to wake up from this deep sleep, from this nightmare we are all in. All of us, OK? I'm not excluding myself and I don't want to be excluded. We still haven't justified why we are in Italy. I know it's easy to talk but now we have to act. The only solution I see now is to run, run and run. And not forget to play. Because this whole trend towards physical football has made us forget that the ball is the most important thing.

'I'm prepared for the whistling and booing in Turin. I'm prepared for anything. We have reached the limits of bad manners, even my injury has been questioned. Well, here it is, you can all see it now. But of course, you'd rather talk about my hand-ball against the Soviet Union and not about Murray's elbow. Or say my injury is a figment of my imagination and not the fact that at the Fair Play World Cup Cameroon didn't stop kicking us. Sometimes I think I'm going to be blamed for everything no matter what.'

On Saturday we flew to Turin. We settled in the Hotel Jet, close to the airport, and went from there to the Delle Alpi stadium. I was still sticking to the same clothes: my Argentina shirt and a pink and black bandana. I played keepy-uppy and started knocking it around, with my right, with my right, with my right . . . until I smashed it with my left and it hurt my soul.

I sat in the penalty area, chatting with Signorini. I was worried, in pain, but I was going to play anyway. The medical diagnosis also hurt, mainly because I didn't really understand it: 'Strong direct trauma to the bone, extending to the fibula, affecting a tendon.' I don't know, to me it was a kick in the arse with which they tried to leave me out, but they couldn't, they wouldn't.

That same night I telephoned Careca. He was my friend, I had nothing to hide from him. I told him my ankle was a disaster and that I was going to play thanks to painkilling injections. He was a coward about that kind of thing! Then I said to him: 'Antonio, tomorrow I'll say hello when we come on but after that . . . to the death, OK?' He was a phenomenon, he just said: '*Tudo bem, Diego*' (everything's cool). '*Now rest, rest.*' He was right: my ankle hurt even when I walked from the bed to the loo. El Negro Galíndez, who'd been with me in 86, tried to give me a massage and the minute he touched me I nearly knocked the walls down with my screaming. The only thing they could hear me say was: 'It hurts! It hurts!' But I felt happier. Guillermo had come. The atmosphere was a little more relaxed: I don't know whether it was because most were already resigned to losing. The night before the game, there was a wedding at the hotel and the bride gave me her bouquet. I don't know why but the smiles had returned to our faces. Even a piece of bad news didn't wipe them off: I found out that there were twenty-six tickets booked on a flight back home to Argentina the following day. I was promised that it wasn't an issue of lack of faith, that it was routine to book flights at that stage of the competition, when losing meant getting knocked out. I believed them but it wasn't a pleasant sensation anyway: it felt like we were condemned in advance.

In reality more than half of that match against Brazil on Saturday 23 June wasn't a match. For fifty-five terrible minutes they dominated the game with wave after wave of attacks: shots that hit the posts; incredible chances that Muller missed; Goyco saves. It took us fifty-five minutes to get stronger at the back. This was something I'd learnt from the Italians, to hang on, hang on, and never to waste a chance to counter-attack. And then we had a piece of play that was a beautiful example of counter-attack. I ran diagonally towards the right, dragging my markers Ricardo Rocha and Alemão with me, while Caniggia signalled that he was keeping up on the left. I passed it to him with my right and, just as Mauro Galvão and Branco closed in on me, Cani faced Taffarel and gave the world a lesson on how to finish. He dribbled round Taffarel's outside and caressed it in with his left ... a *golazo*! Huge joy!

It pissed me off that the Brazilian press accused Alemão of not having brought me down because we played together in Napoli ... nonsense! I surprised him with my short sprint, that's why he didn't catch me; otherwise, he would have brought me down. He wouldn't have tried to kill me because he's too good a guy to do something like that. That marvellous goal destroyed Brazil's spirit. It would have been impossible for them to turn the match around. Argentina was through to the quarter-final.

We were so happy back in the changing room I even forgot about the pain in my ankle. I forgot every pain. And we also proved that the Argentina squad wasn't just me: we'd had a great defence, a midfield that pressed with everything it had, and Caniggia's extraordinary finish. We couldn't have beaten a great team like Brazil with me alone.

After that, the only thing I asked of God was the speedy recovery of our injured players. Now we wanted everything: the only thing that would satisfy us would be to win the title. But we didn't want to become favourites: we'd always won as struggling underdogs. We dedicated our victory to Nery Pumpido and we enjoyed it. After such a long time, we were finally enjoying ourselves.

I really took pleasure in the elimination of Brazil in Italia '90. I thought of the fans back home in Argentina for whom beating Brazil means more than any other football victory. And the same goes for them: Brazilians enjoy beating us more than beating Holland, Germany, Italy, anybody. Same as us, same as me. Beating Brazil is lovely.

Brazil have sold the world this idea that they're the only ones capable of the *jogo bonito*, of playing beautifully . . . bollocks! We can also do the *jogo bonito*, we just don't know how to sell it. Brazilians always think everything is *tudo bem*, *tudo legal* and they're all mellow, whereas for us when it's not *tudo bem* it's not cool and fuck the lot of them. We stop people short and knock them out one by one. That's how we are and I don't have a problem with that. Don't get me wrong, I like the Brazilian way of life, I like them, but in football, I want to beat them to the death. They're My Rivals, with capital letters.

They're difficult on the pitch because they never betray themselves. In spite of the fact that they went twenty years without winning anything, they never gave up on their style of play, never. But one thing is true: Brazil became World Champions again in '94 with the ugliest team – ugliest to watch – in its entire history. The '82 squad would have scored at least five goals against that '94 one, but the '82 squad were too arrogant against Italy, whereas the Italians were playing by the book, as always. They were the masters of the counter-attack, thanks to them I learnt that when I played there: let them come, let them come, let them come, until the defence stands firm. And we all knew that when Napoli's defence stood firm, then it was time for the counter-attack, whether we were in Germany, in Holland, in Russia or wherever the fuck we were: when we came out, it was a goal. We'd come out, two touches, Careca, me, *pum*! goal . . . and Brazil didn't realise that in '90, just like they hadn't realised it in '82. In Spain, Brazil got fucked by Italy, and in Italy they got fucked by us with that spectacular bit of play that Caniggia and I produced, that's still among my finest memories, even today.

Our tour of Italy continued, but now in higher spirits. From Turin we went to Rome, and from Rome we flew to Florence. The next step was Yugoslavia, and they could play: they had Prosinecki, Stojkovic. It was one of our best games but we couldn't find the net. Luckily, neither could they. So we went to a penalty shoot-out and Goyco's story began, Sergio Goycochea. We started with the advantage because Stojkovic missed. Then came my turn. We had the chance of getting to a 3–1 lead. If I scored we were almost there.

Ivkovic was in goal for Yugoslavia and I knew him well. I'd played against him for Napoli when he was at Sporting Lisbon in the UEFA Cup. He had bet me 100 dollars that he could save my penalty. 'Deal,' I'd said like a wanker, and he saved it. But that shoot-out went on and in the end we won. Now I had him in front of me once again. I struck, a little beauty – and he saved it! At some stage afterwards I said I missed on purpose, to repeat the good luck of the UEFA incident, but that was bollocks. When I turned round to walk back to the centre of the pitch Goyco was already walking towards the goal. We did high fives and he said to me: *Stay cool, Diego, I'm going to save two.* He was serious but Savicevic scored and then Troglio missed. We were level when Goyco saved kicks first by Brnovic and then by Hadzibegic, just as he'd promised. I hugged him so much I nearly picked him up! We ran to the side of the pitch, looking up to where our wives were, we couldn't believe it. We were in the semi-finals!

We had to face Italy in Naples. I arrived at the press conference happy, and made a statement for which I would never be forgiven but which was true: 'I don't like the fact that now everyone is asking the Neapolitans to be Italian and to support their national team. Naples has always been marginalised by the rest of Italy. It is a city that suffers the most unfair racism.' I hadn't intended a revolt by the Neapolitans against the rest of Italy when we played there because I knew that the Neapolitans were Italians too . . . but I knew all too well what happened to Napoli when we played in the north, those banners that read WELCOME TO ITALY, LAVATEVI, TERRONI (wash yourselves, peasants). Why should I forget that racism? Why shouldn't I remember it just at the moment when the Italians, out of self-interest, suddenly wanted to include Naples on their map?

Then Gennaro Montuori Palumbella, who was the chief of the *Curva B*, where the Napoli *tifosi* sat at the San Paolo, publicly defined the fans' position: 'We will support Italy, but respect and applaud the Argentinians.' For me everything was cool. I asked for nothing. After everything we'd been through, just not getting booed and whistled at made us feel at home.

But the Italian newspapers took advantage of the situation: 'Now, it's Italy against Maradona', they were saying. Or: 'Dear Diego, see you at your home'. The 'dear' was bullshit, but the stuff about my home was, in part, very true . . .

When I stepped out on to the pitch, on the day of the match, 3 July, the first thing I heard was applause. I read all the banners: 'DIEGO IN OUR HEARTS, ITALY IN OUR SONGS'; 'MARADONA, NAPLES LOVES YOU BUT ITALY IS OUR HOMELAND'. The Argentinian national anthem, for the first time in the whole World Cup, was applauded from beginning to end. For me that was already a victory. I smiled, I was moved: these were my people, the ones who called me Diecó, El Diego. My people.

We were calm, calmer than for any other game in the tournament. Perhaps it was because nobody gave us a chance on this occasion or maybe because Italy's tactics were very clear so we knew how we were going to go about it. I wasn't worried when Toto Schillaci scored the first for Italy. I didn't worry at all, honestly. I went up to Caniggia and said: 'Stay cool, Cani, we'll keep playing our own game.'

We equalised when they were playing at their best. That's the way we were. A centre from Olarticoechea, a spectacular glancing header by Caniggia, and they paid the price. I think at that stage nothing scared our rivals more than the idea of going to a penalty shoot-out against us. We had nothing to lose by keeping the pressure on – Gringo Giusti had been sent off for Argentina so we played out the match and extra time with the aim of reaching that defining moment, that shoot-out for which we had our ace of spades, Sergio 'El Vasco' Goycochea.

This time I didn't miss my penalty kick. I hit it softly, as always, and it was a goal. The celebrations! And they weren't just from my old man, or Claudia's. I clearly heard celebrations with a distinct Neapolitan accent. But let's leave it there. Let's leave everything in Goycochea's hands, who first saved Donadoni's kick, then Serena's and the miracle was a reality. We were running around like madmen, hugging each other. On the way to the changing room, walking into the tunnel I knew so well, I raised my arm and waved at the terraces. They clapped me off the pitch. On the steps, I leant against a wall and kissed my strip. 'I love you! I love you,' I shouted at the shirt, clutching it in a clenched fist.

We were in the final. The happiness in the dressing room was such that we didn't notice our problems. Because of the red and yellow cards we had no Olarticoechea, no Batista, no Giusti and no Caniggia for the final. Cani had got an absurd yellow card, for a hand-ball in the middle of the pitch. To this day I think nobody could have beaten us if we had him among the eleven. El Gringo Giusti was a broken man, he knew he would never again wear the national strip.

But there we were, happier than anyone in the history of the world, in spite of everything. We, the motley crew, the injured, the persecuted, had made it to the final. For the second time in a row we were fighting for a World Cup title. That disastrous team had managed what few can, fighting from the bottom, as always. That was the way we were. And we'd knocked out Italy.

From that moment on, Trigoria stopped being a paradise and became a hell. The first sign that we were at war came just two days after the semi-final against Italy. My brother Lalo went for a drive in one of my Ferraris round Trigoria, with my daughters Dalma and Gianinna. He was stopped by the police for speeding. He told them he didn't have his papers on him, that the car was mine and that if they all just came back to the *concentración*, everything would be cleared up. They came to the *concentración*, but with the wrong attitude . . . and all hell broke loose. A scrap ensued with Mario, the security chief, and the rest of the guards joined in. They let the tortoise get away, actually, because they never imagined my brother-in-law, Gabriel 'El Morsa' Espósito, would turn up. He swung a couple of punches and left a few on the ground, and they needed four men to stop him.

The day after that, Friday the 6th, I got up, looked out of my balcony, and I wanted to die. What I saw got me going, it really made me angry. I ran downstairs and asked the guards to open the gates and let in all the journalists who were doorstepping us. 'Come along, come and see,' I told them, and they all followed me not knowing what was going on. We went round the back, behind the building and then I pointed at the three flagpoles. As they looked up they could all see what I had seen from my balcony: the Roma flag flying on one, the Italian on another, and on the third a tiny scrap of the Argentinian flag, ripped up. I got a little impromptu press conference going, my way:

'Where is it? You say we are treated well here! From the first day we've been fighting against this absurd campaign. My brother's problem yesterday afternoon and now this with the torn flag. This goes beyond football, I think the embassies should intervene . . .'

The Italian journalists immediately asked me: 'Who do you think tore the flag?' They put the ball in my court.

'There's a lot of security here. It's impossible for someone from the outside to get in. So it has to have been someone from inside, from Roma. Ever since we got here everyone's been against us. I told Bilardo: "We made a mistake choosing Trigoria as our *concentración*." Roma's president, Dino Viola, doesn't like us and he promised to make our lives impossible. He has. He's given every sign that there is indeed a campaign against us, against me, by periodically coming to check up on us. He comes to see if the chairs are all still there, if we've broken any glasses, if the grass on the pitch has been stamped on too hard. He has treated us like gypsies. We are just like everyone else. We live in homes and in those homes we have plates and glasses. If they think we're barbarians they're mistaken ... very mistaken.'

We were cannon fodder. We were cannon fodder because we'd knocked Italy out of the World Cup. They weren't going to forgive us for that. We'd buggered up the final the business interests wanted: Italy v. Germany. And as if that wasn't enough, we'd knocked Brazil out! We were cannon fodder.

We still had to face Germany, who'd had a nice, consistent little campaign, in their typical style. They'd knocked England out in the semi-final in Naples. And now we were facing them once again, just as we had four years earlier. Only Burruchaga, Ruggeri and me were left from the '86 campaign – not many of us. We'd lost a lot of soldiers in the war.

They robbed us, they stole that match from us. It felt like the winners had been picked out in advance. I'd spoken about my suspicions about the draw; I'd fought with Havelange; I'd demanded that the award money for the federations be distributed among the players. It was all too much for those in power.

That match against Germany was a farce from the start. The disrespectful insults during our national anthem got even louder when my image appeared on the giant screen. I knew everyone could see me, I knew ... that's why I mouthed, very clearly, so I could be understood in any language: '*Hijos de puta, hijos de puta*', sons of bitches, sons of bitches. I didn't shout it out loud, I said it under my breath, really quietly, as if I was whispering in each and every ear, willing to fight anyone, anyone who came up to me ... *Hijos de puta* ... that's what they were.

Germany were the better team, sure, but we were dignified.

Very dignified. Right at the start, Buchwald kicked me hard, to let me know what the match was going to be like. And the ref didn't book him, didn't give a single foul in our favour for twenty minutes. When the first half was over I went up to the Mexican and said, 'Book someone, please.' Yeah, he booked someone alright: he sent off El Negro Monzón after he fouled Klinsmann. And that's how the game got away from us, it got away from us. Of the World Champions I was the only one left on the pitch. We were a fragment of what had once been a team. Germany beat us 1–0.

I'd promised my daughter Dalma that I would come home with the World Cup, but instead I had to explain to her something hard, ugly and painful: that in football shit happens. It was never a penalty. Edgardo Codesal, the Mexican referee, thought he saw Sensini knocking Völler over but he never saw how Matthäus brought Calderón down earlier in the move.

And at the end of the match I wept, yes, without shame. Why should I hide my tears if that's how I felt? Bilardo sent Goycochea to cover my face so no one would see me crying. Why? They continued to whistle as my tears appeared on the giant screen. What did they want? To step on me while I was on the ground, to kick me when I was down? They'd defeated me already, that was it. It didn't surprise me: that's how they've always treated me in Rome and Milan. Afterwards I refused to shake Havelange's hand because I felt robbed and I felt he had something to do with that. And I refused to celebrate the second place because for me that was useless.

I knew, I was convinced, that my life would change after all that. I had to return to Italy, I needed to do it to seek revenge and to show who I was, but I never imagined I would live through everything I did after the World Cup 1990.

They were terrible months. And, as if the World Cup experience hadn't been enough, I came to a deadlock in my relationship with Cóppola. It was October 1990, five years after we'd started out together. We had our own reasons for splitting up. But it was decided that one of the guys who'd been working with us should remain with me, and that was Juan Marcos Franchi. I felt I needed a break from Guillermo and the feeling was mutual. Time proved us right. I returned to Buenos Aires in October and signed all the papers. I announced my new business set-up and decided to give out another bit of news. On 11 October 1990 I said: 'I will no longer play as an international. I've thought about it a lot and I have made my decision. It hurts my soul, I'm leaving the captaincy of a team I love, but I've been forced into it. They lied to me, they've cut the ground from under my feet. João Havelange came to Argentina and he was greeted like the finest man in the world, as if nothing had happened. But has everyone forgotten what happened in the World Cup? Have you forgotten the people who greeted us when we came back to Argentina, shouting "Heroes" and saying we'd been robbed? I think they've let the tortoise get away . . . and on top of everything Julio Grondona wrote a letter to Viola, the Roma president, thanking him for the way he treated us and I don't know what else. So Ruggeri, Giusti, Brown, myself, we're idiots then – they didn't even register how badly we were treated when we were there. Grondona is the vice-president of FIFA, and when we had the final stolen from us he wasn't capable of lifting a finger. Despite the pain in my heart, because I love being the captain of the national squad, I'm leaving.'

It was like ripping out my own heart.

9

The Comebacks

Sevilla, Newell's Old Boys

'Please, what do you mean number one? Today, I'm more like footballer number 10,000. That's how you should think of me.' That's what I said to journalists after they got excited by my latest comeback, this time in Sevilla, following negotiations that resembled a soap opera more than a business transaction – a *culebron*, as they're called in Spain.

I felt like number 10,000 – seriously, tiger, how could I not feel like that? By 1 July 1992 I'd only just completed the unfair ban imposed by the Italians. I'd finally come through those terrible fifteen months, among the most terrible of my whole life.

I returned from Italy to Buenos Aires on 1 April 1991. I didn't run away: I went back because I wanted to, because I couldn't take any more. I have the date imprinted on my mind because I didn't deserve to leave like that, like a delinquent, and because it marked a very clear before and after in my career. Barely a week later the Italians announced that they were suspending me for fifteen months. I wouldn't be allowed to do what I know best, to play football, for fifteen months. It was a terrible sentence, unjust.

I returned to Buenos Aires where I thought I would finally find peace, and instead I found war.

I was out of the scene, I wasn't news, but there were too many other problems going on in the country, it was all too serious. It seems they needed me to distract attention from the situation. On 26 April the biggest farce I can remember around me was staged. I was arrested, arrested!* In a flat in the Buenos Aires neighborhood of Caballito, on Franklin Street, where I was with two friends who are as pure as mineral water: Gérman Pérez and El Soldadito Ayala. I thought it was strange that the police didn't come alone to the operation: it was more like a press conference after winning the World Cup!

When they came in, knocking everything over, I was asleep. And I woke up asking for Claudia, which is natural I think. They got me out of bed, I got dressed, and when we were in the corridor on our way to the street I saw the lights, the cameras and heard the press shouting, everything. I asked the cop in charge:

'All the journalists are outside, aren't they?'

'Yes, Diego, yes, there's a lot of them.'

'Well, straighten your tie in that case because you're going to be on all the channels, they'll see you at home.'

Unbelievably, the thermos-head actually did straighten his tie.

They kept me locked in a cell and afterwards I kept myself locked in on the seventh floor of the building where I lived, in Correa and Libertador in Núñez. And all the time I promised myself I would return. In the room where I was detained there was a little stool, like the ones boxers get between rounds, and the only light was a shitty bulb hanging from the ceiling. Suddenly, I heard footsteps, someone coming. It was Marcos Franchi:

'Diego, you're going to play in the World Cup '94.'

That's what he said to me. I told him he was crazy but somewhere inside me I felt that it wasn't such a mad idea. It was possible, just possible. It would be more than a year before I would even be allowed to step on a pitch. But I would get opportunities to fight my vice, and I would make the most of any chance I got to play football.

On 9 July I played *papi,* indoor football, once again. I played

---

* In 1994, Maradona was arrested for possession of cocaine.

on the little pitch of the Club Social y Deportivo Parque, where the Argentinos Juniors story had started and where I had danced with Claudia for the first time. This time we made our rivals dance: we beat them 11–2 and our team, Parque, won the Metropolitano Indoor Football tournament. That title needs to be included among my others, eh? Even though I only played one match.

Then things happened to me which make me think that in a country like Argentina and in a world like the one we live in even trying to show a little solidarity can become a torture.

On Saturday 3 August 1991, La Tota's birthday, I played a charity match in aid of the Fernandez Hospital, to enable them to buy a scanning machine which they badly needed, something which became even more apparent after the actor Adrian Ghío had his accident, poor guy. Boca, at the time managed by the maestro Tabarez, allowed me to train with their first team for that match. But the press wouldn't forgive the club. They drove them mad. They said that I would break their concentration, that I would steal the limelight, that I couldn't . . . Fuck's sake, I'd given Boca so much, why couldn't Boca lend me a hand now? Then there was the issue of the sponsors: the organisers had broken their backs to find some support, to get someone to throw them a few pennies in exchange for publicity, and they hadn't got anywhere. When I said I would play, *bam*, there was suddenly loads of interest. So I said to the organisers: 'Accept their sponsorship, that's fine, but I'm not wearing any adverts on my strip. I'm not playing their game. Let them donate the money, that's fine, but if you get it with me on the pitch you should have got it without me on the pitch too.'

Luckily the terraces were full and I was able to play. It was my return to an eleven-a-side pitch – in Ferro, on a Sunday morning. What a sensation! Spectacular! The press may have kicked up a fuss but the people gave me everything, everything. I told them to forget about me, to think that this was just for the hospital, but they gave me everything. For them, El Diego had returned and everything was cool.

In April '92 I got involved in organising another match. This time the proceeds would go to Juan Gilberto Funes, who had been an extraordinary player at River and had just recently lost his long battle with illness. Today I could add El Búfalo to the list of my greatest friends, the closest ones, although we only felt deeply and truly together during the last fifteen minutes of his life. He'd been in hospital for some time, in the Güemes Sanatorium, with a broken heart, poor man, with his heart torn. To see that good bear, that enormous man, prostrate in his bed, it was a terrible image, very very painful. Claudia and I kept tabs on everything, asking his wife Ivanna if she needed anything, letting her know that she could count on us. And on his last day, 11 January '92, through one of those twists of fate that the Beard always keeps in store for me, I was there, right there, next to the bed. Juan had called me, he wanted to see me. He told me that he'd dreamt of a red Mercedes Benz, that he was going to buy it. I got close to him and said: 'Don't worry, Juan, I've spoken to some mates and they've reserved it for you. Don't worry, Juan.' And he died, just like that. Practically in my arms, just like that. I truly felt that at that moment I was very, very close to him. More than ever. We were with Ivanna for all the paperwork, all those terrible things that have to be done on top of everything else when someone close dies. Then we went to San Luis, the province he was from and where he was buried.

From that moment I started to think about a tribute match, about doing something to remember Juan and also to help his family: Ivanna and his son Juampi, who had the saddest little eyes I've ever seen. Maybe I could have just given them money and left it at that. But I wanted to give him something more, something Juan would have enjoyed. What better than to organise a football match? I was in the Moreno country house with La Claudia, still very beaten by what we'd been through, and I suddenly said to her: 'You know what I want to do for Juan? A match, a football match, and I'll play.'

Of course, I was still suspended but that never even crossed my mind. It wasn't a FIFA game, it was a game the players had organised for another player. And I knew if I was there, on the pitch, with my shorts on, more people would attend. We'd make more money, and it was all for Juan.

From the country house I rang El Flaco Gareca, El Cabezón Ruggeri and El Mono Navarro Montoya. The three of them, along with Raúl Roque Alfaro and myself, had been the only ones to travel to San Luis for the funeral. It seemed logical to start with them. This time round I knew the advertisers wouldn't be a problem because the people from X-28, an alarms factory, were with us from the word go.

When everything was ready, less than a day before the set date, Wednesday 15 April, the fax arrived, the damned fax from FIFA. I swear to start with I couldn't believe it, I thought it was a joke, in bad taste but a joke nevertheless. It was addressed to Julio Grondona and it said they'd heard about the match in which I was to participate. And it ended with a threat – nasty, ugly: 'For the good of the family of the deceased player [for the good of the family of the deceased player, for God's sake!] the presence of Maradona on the pitch together with other players registered in the AFA could cause FIFA-imposed sanctions to be brought against the latter according to the statutes and regulations.' It was always the same: I was the rotten apple, the one who ruined everything. I decided to step aside, I was full of rage but also of sadness. Once again they were making me feel like a delinquent. I said to Franchi: 'OK, Marcos, tell Grondona to stay cool, not to shit himself, I won't play. But let him know I'm doing it for the lads, to avoid complicating their lives. I'm not doing it because of the AFA or FIFA. Go on, go tell him.' He went and told him.

In the meantime the lads had heard about the whole mess.

El Cabezón Ruggeri got in touch with Grondona to see what was going on and to plead with him to allow me to play. He said that I'd organised the whole thing and that with me on board they would generate a lot more money. At first Grondona told him I wouldn't be allowed to play under any circumstances, and then he offered fifty thousand dollars to pay for Funes's hospital bill and suggested we played the match in June, once my ban had been lifted. And to finish off, he said: 'Diego can't play. If he does, you lot will have to pay for the consequences.'

El Cabezón rushed to the hotel where we were all gathered. There were forty-one of us in total and when he told us about the conversation he'd had with Grondona, El Mono Navarro Montoya said to me: 'Diego, now you have to play, more than ever.' I hadn't said a word throughout the whole meeting, I'd been listening to Ruggeri really attentively, but when El Mono spoke it was as if he'd pushed my play button and I heard my voice, slightly crackly in fact: 'Yes, I'm going to play, let's fuck them over . . .'

Some players, like Diego Latorre, went pale: 'What's going to happen to us?' the wanker asked, scared.

Nothing was what they could do to us, nothing. Ricardo Calabria, the ref, wasn't a member of the AFA because he was already retired, and it was the same with his linesmen. It was us, the players, organising the event, not AFA. We had paid for the insurance needed to stage the event, and we'd even had the tickets printed ourselves. So we marched out of the hotel and headed towards the Vélez stadium. I was going to be there, on the pitch, with my shirt on, with the ball. With the people.

The Grondona thing had hit me like a kick in the balls. In a sense he'd offered 50,000 dollars for me not to play! At the time I said some very strong things, perhaps with hindsight, seen at a distance, too strong. But I said them, that's what I'm like. 'No one in Argentina is going to cry for Blatter, Havelange, and some other execs, after they die.' I also said: 'While Grondona remains President of the AFA I shall never return to the national squad.' Very strong words, yes, but they came from my heart.

Everyone came to the dressing room, even the officials who were shitting themselves because they were afraid of losing all their players. If AFA carried out the threat of suspending them all, they would be out of the official league games. Now that I think about it, it would have been a good thing, because once and for all it would have been clear who really runs the show.

When I came out on the pitch I shivered. It was a dark night, heavy with fog, but the stands were crowded. We'd gathered over 100,000 dollars from box-office takings alone; with the advertising it went over 200,000. All of it for Funes's family, to pay the hospital bill and to continue what Juan had started: his little football school.

As soon as I stepped on the turf I waved at the Boca fans on my right. They wouldn't let me down. But there were more fans, clearly, not just Boca fans: all football fans were there – with me till the end. I was very moved, very moved, because I had Juan's image in my head ... Juan, happy because of that match which was forcing those in power to clench their arses, the ones who think they own something when in fact they own nothing.

I played quite well, actually. I scored two goals, gave Beto Acosta an assist and my team, which was playing in blue, won 5–2. I left a few minutes before the end of the game, to take some air and to say to the journalists gathered, 'Today, us footballers have started to grow.' I really believed it. We'd put our foot down on the dark forces. We'd beaten the powerful.

That night I took home with me the support of my kind: of my teammates, of the players. It was as good as taking home the World Cup. They put their balls on the line to stand up to what had been an act of pure malice. In the end, those in power had had to back down.

*   *   *

I'd started training, taking it slowly, assisted by Professor Javier Valdecantos and Doctor Luis Pintos. And I was also playing a little – on TV, five-a-side on synthetic turf: they were those matches on *Ritmo de la Noche*, Marcelo Tinelli's programme. As always, I played them seriously and had loads of fun. In January '92 I went to the Marisol resort for the first time, in Oriente, 550 kilometres from Buenos Aires. There, on 27 February 1992, I played my first real match since the ban. It was a very special match, Amigos de Marisol against Mercado Los Tigres, two local amateur teams, in aid of disabled children. It was there, in front of 5,000 people, all from the surrounding villages, that I scored my first goal as a banned player. The prize was a million kisses from disabled but happy children. Happier than anyone.

After that, and also after the famous match in aid of Funes, I once again put on my shorts for charity, this time in the city of Posadas, in the northern province of Misiones, for the benefit of a local hospital. That was my life, that was the only way to stay close, very close, to football – helping others, which was also a way of helping myself.

I was – and felt – far from Naples and Napoli. They sent me messages saying they expected me back on 1 July, when my Calvary was over. But I was starting to think about other possibilities for when that moment came. So much suffering couldn't last forever.

On Saturday 4 July 1992, three days after my liberation from the FIFA chains, I took my own personal team and went off to the Estancia El Sosiego, in 25 de Mayo, a city in the south of the province of Buenos Aires. I started my comeback and an incredible soap opera ensued: the negotiations to change club, to leave Napoli, even though I didn't know where I was going to go. One possibility was Marseille, again. Bernard Tapie, who had once offered me his life, whatever I wanted, wasn't doing so well now: he'd lost Adidas and he was also out of the government.

Out, and unpleasantly so. But Marseille was still tempting because what I was looking for was peace, and French football continued to offer me that.

Another possibility, but more remote, was the same as always: Boca. The issue was the money. A year and a half of not playing had left me a dead weight in financial terms and Boca was in no condition to lift such a weight. The only way was if an investor appeared on the scene.

The final possibility was that a door might open in the shape of another European club: Real Madrid for example. Or Sevilla, because Bilardo had arrived there as manager – he'd got shafted with a business deal in Argentina and he got pissed off and fucked off – and he'd sent me a message through Marcos Franchi: 'See what you can do because this could be a good place for Diego. They don't put on too much pressure here, they don't ask for championships. Although with him on board I think we can win everything. I don't know, you think about it, you know I want what's best for him.'

My main goal was to detach myself from Napoli. And that was also the most complicated thing. The bastards called me up for the team presentation at the beginning of the season. It was to be on 15 July, with drums and cymbals for all the new sign-ings, the Uruguayan Fonseca, the Swede Thern, like nothing had happened, like I was any other player. They were really pissed off because I'd said some very strong stuff to the Italian media, but I had good reasons not to return.

During an interview with Telemontecarlo I fired off some heavy ammunition. I said, very clearly, that my time with Napoli was definitely over, that I wouldn't be doing the Neapolitans any favours by returning, that the only one who would be richer would be Ferlaino, and that he had made enough money out of me already. For me, Napoli had learnt to play without Maradona and they could go on like that: if Maradona left, Napoli wouldn't die. True, they were relegated after that, but don't blame me for that: the blame, as always, was Ferlaino's, who can't even steer a bus, let alone a team. They said Ferlaino wanted to come and visit me in Buenos Aires. *HIJO DE PUTA!* For a whole year he didn't give a shit about what was happening to me and now he wanted to jump on the bandwagon. If I had been at a club where they cared as much for the man as they did the player, I would have gone back to Napoli. But there were too many precedents of players who had been badly treated: Bagni, Giordano, Garella. Why should I be the exception?

And to boot, Claudio Rainieri, Napoli's new manager, spoke out before he met me and said that as long as he was manager Maradona wouldn't even go to Naples for a holiday. As we say in Argentina, he spoke for free. And Matarrese, Antonio Matarrese, had been the one to put his hand, his black hand, on my case. I was sure of one thing and I let them know it: I hadn't deserved my punishment. They'd made me pay because I was a foreigner and because I prevented Italy from playing in the World Cup final. There are very strong interests in football and in 1990 many millions of dollars had been lost. But they could have banned me for ten years and the result of the Argentina–Italy match wouldn't change. And my suspension was, in actual fact, an advantage for Ferlaino, because during that period I wasn't the Maradona he wanted.

'*Non c'e la faccio più*,' that's what I said: 'I'm not doing it any more.' I can't go on, enough, *basta*! I had my reasons not to return.

Those reasons were spelt out in a fax we sent to Napoli, to the Italian Football Federation, to the AFA and even to FIFA on the eve of the ban being lifted at the end of June 1992. We were trying to explain why it wouldn't be any fucking good for me to go back. The risk was too high, seriously.

But Napoli weren't convinced: a war of letters, faxes and more letters started. At one point I thought we would drown in all those papers. Just in case, I did the only thing I could: I presented myself before Judge Amelia Berraz de Vidal, in the courts, as she was the one who had been following my case ever since the whole Franklin Street incident. I secured, at last, an authorisation to leave Argentina: I wanted to be packed and ready to move when the time came.

The team was already formed: I was the *líbero*; Juan Marcos Franchi was my agent; Javier Valdecantos the physical trainer; Luis Pintos the doctor. Plus Rubén Navedo, a psychoanalyst; Carlos Handlartz, a psychiatrist; and Luis Moreno Ocampo, Antonio Gil Lavedra, Hugo Wortman Joffré and Daniel Bolotnicoff, my lawyers.

Franchi flew to Seville, to follow up on the contact that Bilardo had made with the club president, Luis Cuervas. And at the same time Bolotnicoff went to Marseille where he had already made moves to meet up with Bernard Tapie, through one of his assistants called Jean Pierre Bernés. All this flurry of activity around me was intended to pinpoint the ideal club, the club to return to.

While Marcos and Daniel negotiated, I weighed it all up. I liked the fact that the madman Bilardo was at Sevilla and that there seemed to be no pressure to finish the season with a victory lap. The city had a good vibe to it, a good vibe. But on the other hand, the club was demonstrating an inability to decide, which made me feel that maybe I was too big for them. What attracted me the most about Olympique was Marseille itself; the long-dreamt-of villa, snatched from my hands by Ferlaino; the possibility of playing the European Champions Cup with a competitive team; and at the same time the peace and quiet of a league such as the French. But I was concerned about the atmosphere in the city, which was a lot like Naples, and the obligation of learning another language. It would be a big adaptation.

Finally Napoli agreed to negotiate the annulment of my contract in a neutral place and with an arbiter, both to be provided by FIFA. At a distance, I understood very well what Ferlaino's policy was: the Italian was smart. He wouldn't be the one who allowed me to leave Napoli; he was pushing things to the limit so that he would be able to tell his journalists and his people: 'They ripped him away from my hands.' That's what he was doing, clearly. That was why he had answered my first message so aggressively, so he could then look like he had been under pressure from FIFA to agree to the meeting. To top it all off, in the middle of the negotiation, Napoli threw a bomb at me: they fined me 168,000 dollars and reduced my contract by 40 per cent. It was clear they wanted war. And they were going to get it. They were going to get it and they were going to be surprised.

And all the time in the background Old Havelange was saying that he loved me as a son, as a grandson. That he loved me, *bah* . . .

The Marseille deal was crumbling slowly, mainly because Bolotnicoff and Franchi – who had flown from Seville a couple of days later to meet with Tapie – had a terrible experience. There had been a very heavy atmosphere, and when Franchi finally flew back to Seville, he felt like he was coming home again. We came up with a new strategy: we offered the Napoli directors a meeting, a dialogue, in Barcelona, where the Olympics were being held at the time. A neutral place with the FIFA people nearby. We were showing the FIFA execs my willingness to conduct a dialogue and we gave the Neapolitans a deadline. They responded but it seemed they were taking the piss: they said they were willing to give us an audience, to have a meeting, and they gave us Napoli's headquarters as the address! And the bastards wrote down the opening hours, outside weekends and bank holidays, like it was an office. They also reminded me that they were still waiting for me at the camp where the team was doing their pre-season training. They were taking the piss, the bastards!

But the tone of their fax worked in our favour because FIFA

was then forced to hold the meeting in Zürich, at their head-quarters. My phone was ringing non-stop: Bilardo was calling me, despairing because nothing was happening. Marcos was calling me to ask me to stay calm. Bernard Tapie was calling me begging me to take up his offer. Grondona was calling me to tell me to trust him, that everything was going to work out.

Grondona himself travelled to Barcelona and met up with Franchi. They saw the Olympic final in which Spain beat Poland and they both made their separate ways, I think, towards Zürich, where the meeting was to be held on 11 August. This had all been going on since 1 July, when my ban was lifted: a month and a half had gone by, already. It was time it ended.

No sooner had he arrived in Switzerland, a day before the meeting, than Franchi rang me and nearly gave me a heart attack. 'Diego, I'm going to tell them you're going back to Napoli.' I went mad, I couldn't believe it and then Marcos was saying to me: 'Hang on, hang on, hang on, let me explain . . .'

I didn't understand what the fuck was going on. We'd got this far with the sole aim of detaching me from Napoli and now we were offering ourselves to them on a plate.

When he managed to calm me down Franchi explained: 'We're going to tell them you're coming back, but under certain conditions.' Aaaah, I began to understand, but, what if Napoli accepted? 'Well, that's the risk we're running, but don't worry, they're going to refuse,' Franchi replied. My legs were shaking.

The meeting took place and the headlines shook the world. I remember the Italians were celebrating. *La Gazzetta dello Sport* ran a front page saying: 'Diego: yes to Napoli. Ferlaino wins'. I couldn't see how all that euphoria would be turned round. La Claudia was weeping, my folks also; I decided to talk, to carry on with Marcos's tactics. I said: 'The idea was to try to resolve this with FIFA's help. But in view of how badly Napoli are predisposed towards me, and how many obstacles they're putting our way, and seeing that FIFA can't resolve anything, we've decided to return, subject to a whole load of conditions. Time is running out and the only thing I want is to get out on to a pitch again. I've been training for thirty-six days and I need a team, I need a manager. It would be great if Napoli accepted the clauses we've asked for, it would be great. But I don't know how good it would be for Ferlaino, politically or face to face with the people, to accept the conditions we've demanded.' Bollocks would it be great! I awaited Napoli's answer with terror: if they said yes . . .

Their answer came on Friday 14 August: Napoli accepted all our conditions about my personal treatment but not our financial terms, the ones related to money. And since it had been established in Zürich that Napoli's answer had to be yes or no, it was considered that their response to our proposal had been negative. It was my first step towards freedom.

We now needed Sevilla to formally request my transfer. Before they hadn't been able to because of fear, yes, fear: if UEFA took against the fact that yet another club was involved in my conflict with Napoli, least of all a small Spanish one, they might give Sevilla a kick up the arse. But now there were no more reasons to be afraid: they just had to buy me.

But Sevilla took their time. Franchi and Bolotnicoff were despairing, but the Andalusian execs were calm, for them it wasn't a drama. I started to realise my initial impression – that I was too big for them – was indeed the case. And to top it all off, Napoli was doing everything in its power to seduce me: there was talk of a villa on the island of Capri for me, with a view over the Tyrrhenian, and a private helicopter to fly me to Napoli every day, as well as a yacht of course. And they were also officially protesting to FIFA because they denied that they had said no to my conditions. And the fans were another story: the fans, the ones who were always with me, the ones who chained themselves to the railings or went on hunger strikes to get me there in the first place, were returning to their efforts, this time to get me to go back. They'd say: 'We have no homes, no schools, no buses, no sanitation, no ideas ... but we have Maradona.' Poor people, it wasn't their fault, it wasn't.

I was still waiting for the Andalusians to do something. On Tuesday 18 August Sevilla finally sent a fax to Napoli, asking how much they wanted for me. I was chewing my fingers to the bone, I couldn't stand it any more. Napoli was never going to reply to those bits of paper! For God's sake, they had to go after what they wanted like true Spaniards, like *matadores*.

Another unbearable tug of war started, and even Blatter's comments didn't ease the deadlock: on Wednesday 9 September Blatter said that the best solution to this problem was for Napoli to let me go, for Sevilla to buy me, and that they should all stop pissing about. I slipped in my ultimatum immediately: 'If by Saturday the 12th this saga isn't resolved I'm going to retire ... I swear on my daughters.' Franchi must have got scared because on Friday the 11th he prepared the trip for the following day: everybody to Spain! *We* were going to go get *them*! Franchi hadn't actually hidden anything: 'If this goes on till after the weekend we're going to have problems with Diego,' he'd said. And he was right. He was getting to know me, the son of a bitch.

On Saturday I got up at lunchtime and I hardly ate. I said a really long goodbye to my daughters and left for the airport. Wearing a cerise suit, I looked a treat.

I landed in Europe once again at 7 a.m. on Sunday 13 September. Claudia, Marcos and me flew in a private plane from Barajas to Seville, to San Pablo airport. That's where I shook the club president Luis Cuervas's hand for the first time. I felt like saying: 'Why don't you speed things up a little, slowcoach?' but it seemed a bit much for a first encounter.

Later, at the Sánchez Pizjuán stadium, where Sevilla were playing at home, I watched a defeat against Deportivo La Coruña, and I suffered as if it were my own. Although the deal still had to be finalised, I had already started to feel at home. There was

El Narigón, going crazy on the bench; there was El Cholito Simeone, older now, pressing and pressing in the midfield. I remembered my debut with Napoli against Verona: how they really made us dance but we ended up winning two *scudetti*. Suddenly I felt all was well: Havelange and Blatter were sticking up for me because they knew I had served my time. I also felt I should be grateful to Sevilla, as I had been at the time to Napoli. It wasn't as if there were loads of clubs who wanted me after all.

I settled into a suite at the Andalusi Hotel, a spectacular place with an Arab vibe on the outskirts of the city on the road to Huelva, and I decided to train and wait. But although everything was OK, it could all turn sour in less than a week. Napoli wasn't giving an inch, Sevilla wasn't rushing things through, there was always a decisive meeting promised for tomorrow. The only reason why I didn't return to Buenos Aires was because one morning I found a piece of paper under my door: the hotel had left a fax sent by my daughters from Buenos Aires. It said: 'Daddy, don't come back. Wait for us, we're coming over there.' That piece of paper ended up being more important than the contract itself.

On Tuesday September 22 I was sitting at the table after lunch with my whole family in the hotel restaurant. It was nearly 3 p.m. I was playing with some crumbs or something on the table-cloth. Suddenly I looked up and saw Franchi coming. His face seemed full of laughter, bright. He stood next to me and said, looking down at me because I was still sitting:

'Kid, you're free.'

'I don't believe you, you're taking the piss . . .'

'I'm serious, you're free. You're truly free.'

He broke down, slumped into a chair and started weeping. I had tears streaming out of my eyes, looking at everyone around me: La Claudia, my folks, my parents-in-law. I held Gianinna tightly to my chest, and started whispering into her ear: 'I'm free, I'm free, I'm happy. At last you'll be able to see me on a pitch, with a ball. At last.'

Six days later, on Monday 28 September, I was a football player once again. The presentation party was organised against Bayern Munich, where my friend Lothar Matthäus played. I finally stepped on to the turf at the Sánchez Pizjuán with the 10 on my back.

We won 3–1 but the scoreline didn't matter. At least not to me. I enjoyed passing and playing with the Croatian Davor Suker, waiting for Simeone, listening to Bilardo, smashing a free kick practically from the corner which hit the bar, giving Monchu a pass for a goal . . . I enjoyed playing football again. And I celebrated in style, with Matthäus himself who came over to the hotel and joined us. Just by being there he made me feel football was happy because I had returned.

The next thing was to establish when I would have my proper debut in La Liga. I looked at the fixtures calendar and there I saw it: Sunday 4 October, Athletic de Bilbao, San Mamés stadium. That had to be my debut, history demanded it. No rival meant more to me, none. As soon as I signed with Sevilla the Athletic Bilbao manager, Jupp Heynckes, decided to invent some stuff and even went as far as stating in public that he knew that in my contract with Sevilla I had demanded not to play at the Camp Nou, Barcelona's stadium, or at the San Mamés, Athletic's stadium. I wanted to play there more than anywhere else! So I wanted revenge against that German, too.

There were so many things that separated me from and tied me to that Basque club it couldn't be any other rival. In the first place, Athletic had been the club which took from me the opportunity of winning both leagues when I played in Spain. We lost the Copa del Rey against them, the last one, the one that ended up being my last match with Barcelona, with the *blaugrana* shirt, where we all ended up fighting because somebody from Athletic gave me the two fingers. And of course, there was the player be given the full kit, the full blue and yellow kit, and to listen to Maestro Tabárez's technical chat. He was a phenomenon, the Uruguayan, he asked them to do everything possible to provide me with a goal. And I harangued the lads: 'Keep pushing, keep pressing! That's how we bust River's arse.' Of course a few days earlier, on Sunday, I had watched from the stands as they beat River the way it should be done, with authority. I went crazy watching, just like any other fan. Boca saved a penalty. So with that ringing in their ears we stepped on to the pitch. When it was all over, a lot of people told me I ran more during the second half and I gave them all the same answer: 'It was for the jersey, tiger.'

On my return to Spain I had to roll up my sleeves for real. So I asked Fernando Signorini to work with me again, the man who knows my physique better than anyone. I celebrated my thirty-second birthday in my new house, in Seville's best neighbourhood, Simon Verde. I'd rented it from the Spanish bullfighter Espartaco. Villa Espartina was amazing. The gift I was most grateful for was the peace the Andalusians gave me during those days. I had some tests done, those I like, where you check everything with the best machines, running strips and all that jazz, at a clinic which belonged to Xavier Azkargorta. The results were great: I was barely two kilos over my ideal weight.

Those were good times, until the end of the year. One day a Barcelona newspaper published a report saying that I did only what I wanted, that I never trained, that I lived at night. I answered back with a victory against Celta, in Vigo, and a *golazo* from a free kick. I was the centre of attention once again.

I remember a huge fuss was made before the match against Tenerife. I'd had some outspoken confrontations with Fernando Redondo, the Argentinian international now playing for Tenerife. I just shook Redondo's hand before the match started and that was it, there was no fight, we left everyone wanting. One thing's for sure: we let the tortoise get away from us that afternoon of

3 January 1993, on the island – Tenerife beat us 3–0. Another mad circus was made of my re-encounter with Barcelona, but on the other side: the hassle served to pack the Sánchez Pizjuán like never before and to get us a 0–0 draw – dignified, no more than dignified. And I ended the first half of the season at full gallop with a great match against Real Madrid. A great match, one of the ones I like. Then, I remember I dared say: 'I felt whole once again, able to fight hand to hand. I was able to go to ground to recover possession, I was able to sprint. And win. I felt sure.' Everyone latched on immediately and some Spanish newspaper carried the headline: *The Maradona of Mexico has returned*. They went too far, that's what I thought, and everyone who knew me well thought so too.

But that's the mood we were in until the time came to respond to what I loved more than anything: the summons from the national squad. Coco Basile had taken over from Bilardo as manager and he had promised me privately that he would call me up as soon as he saw me fit. He kept his word: he asked me to join the squad to play two international friendlies: one against Brazil to commemorate the AFA's centenary; another against Denmark in the Artemio Franchi Cup, a clash between the winners of the European championship and the Copa América.

I travelled to play for Argentina against Brazil. I was better used than anyone to crossing the ocean in order to play for the national squad, then flying back and playing for my club. Nobody could tell me what to do. But the Sevilla directors intended to do just that: they didn't want to allow me to play the second match against Denmark. They stood firm, threatened me with a fine and I don't know what else. Of course, I played against Denmark and returned to Sevilla but by then nothing was the same. Bilardo and I had been told that Sevilla always fell behind after Christmas: it was as if the players, after going for the champagne and all the toasts, weren't the same again. That's what happened to me but for another reason: something broke all that: if you pay up, they cheer for you; if you don't, they tell you to motherfucking fuck off. That's how it works. For protection, for getting cheered, for not getting beaten up, I've never, ever needed to, although it is definitely something that happens in Argentina and all over the world. If they wanted to clap me, they could see what I did on the pitch.

So I said to Franchi: 'They insulted Claudia? They asked me for money that I don't know who promised them? Fuck them; I'm going to Newell's.' And I did. For less money. But it was useful, because it was a sensational thing, the Newell's thing. My ex-Argentina team-mate Gringo Giusti had had the idea and he'd proposed it to the club president, Walter Cattáneo. At first the guy thought he was joking, he didn't believe a word of it. But Giusti insisted and the guy went for it. In the meantime everyone was saying I was already at Argentinos; nobody had any idea about the incident at my front door.

Giusti spoke to Marcos, Marcos spoke to me, I said let's do it. I don't know why, I'd made up my mind that I was going to make my dream come true: I was going to play in the Libertadores Cup with Newell's. I felt like a machine: I'd started a diet in Uruguay with the Chinese Liu Guo Cheng, and I had Daniel Cerrini by my side, who looked like a body builder but knew a ton about nutrition and training.

That's why I was the way I was: I weighed 72 kilos. I was like a kid again.

Grondona called Marcos and told him that we were running out of time, that we had to finalise everything because an international transfer had to be requested. Less than a week before, on 5 September 1993, the national squad had suffered the worst defeat in its history against Colombia, a 5–0 that hurt my soul. That was when I said: 'Newell's, Newell's ... and let it be as the Beard wishes.'

It turned out that the Beard wanted an incredible party which reminded me of when I arrived at Napoli, when 80,000 people packed out the San Paolo stadium just to hear me say two words in Italian and kick a ball about for ten minutes. Something similar happened here on Thursday 13 September, and if there were no more than 40,000 people there it was because the Parque Independencia stadium couldn't fit any more. How beautiful! They'd come just to see me train!

Indio Solari – Jorge Raul Solari – a great man, who as manager was very involved with my arrival, made sure it was a spectacular party. I remember the lads lifted me up into the air, in the middle of the pitch, to welcome me, and the people were delirious. The truth? I think of those times and it moves me.

Officially, my debut in the Newell's jersey was against Independiente, in Avellaneda, on Sunday 10 October 1993. After almost nine years I was playing in the Argentinian league once again; me, I'm the one who always says that if there's one thing I owed and am owed, it's more minutes played here, in my land, before my people. We lost 3–1 but, even though I don't like saying these things, I felt I'd won: I scored two goals with back-heels, although one of them was saved by El Loco Islas just as it was going in, when it was already a goal. I said it at the time and I can say it again now: I felt I was on a cloud, I couldn't believe I could feel so good, barely four months after my departure from Sevilla. It felt like a resurrection, another one. In Rosario, a beautiful city, I settled into the Hotel Riviera. That was my central base; from there I moved about. It was a very emotional time – it didn't feel like a day job, it was more like every match was a testimonial.

A match against Boca at the Bombonera was another emotional event – my re-encounter with Flaco Menotti. The truth? I felt so much respect at that stadium – from my team-mates, from our rivals – that I thought I was playing an exhibition game. But no, it wasn't, and against Boca we lost too, 2–0.

I also returned to the national squad. I'd played two international matches against Australia. When I came back to the club,

I wanted to play as many matches as possible for Newell's because thanks to them I had been able to go back to the national squad. Having a team round me had turned me into a player once again and that had been decisive in showing what I could do, what I could offer.

But the machine couldn't take it. My machine, my body. Then came the fatal night: Thursday 2 December 1993, Huracán stadium against Globo. I was worn out. We were 1–0 up, I sprinted after a lost ball and I heard the unmistakable sound of a muscle tearing, like a zip opening inside my leg. Ripped! Ripped! After almost thirteen years – unlucky thirteen – I'd torn a muscle again.

Because of that I missed an international against Germany in Miami. It wasn't Germany that I craved playing against, it was the anti-Castro Cuban *gusanos* [worms] in Miami, some of whom had said that if I set foot there they were going to kill me on account of my friendship with the Comandante Fidel Castro. I would have liked to meet them close up, face to face, but I missed out.

My last match for Newell's was a friendly in January against the Brazilian club Vasco da Gama in Rosario. I played for seventy-two minutes, two more than I was contractually obliged to by the club's TV deal, and I came off. I never went back on for them again, ever.

Indio Solari had brought me to Newell's and we'd agreed that I would have certain freedoms, logical ones I think at that stage in my career. After Solari left Jorge Castelli came in, with this, that and the other. The whole thing began to rot. He didn't want big players: after I left they got rid of Tata Marino, Chocho Llop, Gringo Scoponi, the ones who had truly carried that team and turned Newell's into something big. He wanted young kids instead.

On 1 February I ended my relationship with Newell's.

That same day I had one of the saddest experiences of my whole life: a group of journalists violated my privacy by shoving their cameras into my country house in Moreno. They weren't satisfied with my explanations of why no one had seen me in public over the past month and I reacted ... I reacted in the same way that anyone might. It was the episode with the air rifle, yeah, that's right.* It's not relevant to my football story – none of my private life should be.

A shame, a shame that chapter ended like it did. I left. I had the World Cup round the corner, less than five months away. The hawks and turncoats had dared to say that I wasn't going to play. That it was impossible that I, Maradona, would play in the World Cup in the USA.

* The incident referred to here is the much publicised affair when Maradona responded to persistent doorstepping by firing an air rifle at congregated journalists.

10

The Pain

USA '94

The truth, the only truth about the World Cup '94 is that my personal trainer, Daniel Cerrini, made a mistake and I took the brunt of the fallout. That's the only truth. No one had promised me anything. Some people went around saying that FIFA had left the road clear for me to do whatever I wanted and then they betrayed me with the drug test. That's a lie.

The only thing I asked of Grondona afterwards, when it had all happened, was that they take into account the fact that I hadn't intended to gain an advantage, that they allow me to finish my last World Cup. They could have treated me the same way they had Calderé, the Spanish player, in Mexico '86. I begged Grondona but there was no way: they slapped a year-and-a-half ban on me. A year and a half for taking – without knowing – ephedrine; exactly the same thing baseball players, basketball players, American football players take there, in the US, all the time. I didn't even know I'd taken ephedrine: I played with my soul, with my heart. The whole football world knew ephedrine wasn't a performance-enhancing drug.

I arrived at the World Cup cleaner than I'd ever been. I knew it was the last chance I would get of saying to my daughters: 'I'm a football player, and if you've never seen me play, you will see me here.' That's the one and only reason why I celebrated the goal against Greece the way I did, although some other idiocies have been suggested. I didn't need drugs to take my revenge and shout my happiness to the world! That's why I wept and I will continue to weep. We had been World Champions and they'd taken the dream away from us.

But for me the story of USA '94 had started a long time before.

In February '93 I had finally met with Coco Basile. He'd called me up to the national squad a month earlier, on 13 January, and of course I'd had to fight with a club president as usual to get permission to travel: in this case it had been Luis Cuervas, at Sevilla, but I told him to give the dog his face back and hopped on a plane. I'd already missed an international in Chile in 1991 because of the ban. I tell you, few things are as painful as that: you feel like you're in prison. It's different if you don't get picked for the squad, but not to be allowed to enter the race at all, nothing compares to that.

The thing is, I arrived in Buenos Aires in January 1993 to prepare for two friendlies: the one against Brazil to commemorate the AFA's centenary, and the Artemio Franchi Cup against Denmark. I went to the new sports complex in Ezeiza for the first time in my life, and the circus started. I was very firm, so there would be no room for doubts: 'First and foremost I want to thank Basile for bringing me into the team. It's like coming home. Although I have spent two and a half years without wearing the blue and white jersey, I've always felt like an Argentinian international. I know I don't have many years of football left and I will not waste this opportunity.'

But there were a lot of thorny issues as well. For example, the captaincy. I had already had a couple of clashes with El Cabezón Ruggeri and so I passed the ball to him and said that when we met he could decide what to do. The pull for me was to wear the number 10 once again. I hadn't done so since that damned match against Germany in Rome, two and a half years earlier, and I was looking forward to playing with all the little monsters who were emerging: Caniggia and Batistuta up front, Simeone at the back. That team hadn't lost once in twenty-two consecutive games since El Coco had taken over, and the nation loved them, followed them, and supported them. After so much suffering under Bilardo, it was a totally new experience for me. I wanted to go out and win, win everything, even in the training sessions.

What I did win, and this is one of the greatest sources of pride of my footballing career, was the AFA's recognition as the best Argentinian player of all time. I was ecstatic, who wouldn't be? But I was embarrassed to upstage names such as Moreno, Di Stéfano, Pedernera, Kempes, Bochini. I don't know, I'd wished for that recognition for a long time and at the same time it embarrassed me so much ... The following day the moment finally came: I was going out on to the pitch again.

On 18 February 1993, wearing the captain's armband that Ruggeri had finally returned to me, I stepped on to the turf at the Monumental, full to the brim, with the national strip on my back. We drew 1–1 against Brazil. Simeone and Mancuso played exceptionally well. Mancuso scored the goal. But I felt angry, I noticed that the team – including me – was lacking something, we hadn't given our all.

The next day another of the many stupidities that seem to follow me around hit the streets. There was talk of Diegodependency. What the fuck was Diegodependency? It turned out it meant that the team had altered its style of play on my account, that they needed me too much, that they looked for me too much. But what the fuck did they want? That I'd been born in Rio de Janeiro, or Berlin, so they wouldn't have this problem? Please! That kind of thing made me lose it.

I returned to Sevilla to play against Logroñés and found a tense, heavy atmosphere. It was all too reminiscent of the days when I would travel from Naples to Buenos Aires, to play here and then there, sometimes with the club, sometimes with the

national team. At thirty-two I didn't need to spell out that my
priority was the national squad. So I went out on the pitch, we
lost to Logroñés and I got ready to fly back to Argentina . . .
This time the directors really didn't want to know. They told
Simeone that if we travelled again there would be sanctions.
And Bilardo didn't know where to put himself. The only thing
he dared say to me was: 'You're only fit to play ninety minutes,
no more.' On 27 February in Mar del Plata, when the match
against Denmark was over after ninety minutes, extra time and
penalties, I was celebrating with the Artemio Franchi Cup in
my hands and nobody understood what I meant when I sang:
'El Narigón was wrong, El Narigón was wrong!' We'd won on
penalties. Once again I'd heard El Vasco Goycochea say to me:
Stay calm, I'm going to save two, just like in Italia '90. I scored
from my penalty kick and we celebrated, how we celebrated!

It wasn't just another cup for me. It proved to me that at
thirty-two I could still play three matches in ten days. Coco
Basile gave me the freedom to roam the whole pitch and attack
everywhere. I felt comfortable providing for Caniggia and
Batistuta, it was just fun to watch them running, criss-crossing
past each other. I loved passing the ball just so, for them to
finish. I've always had faith in myself: the thing about football
is you have to prove something every day. With this cup I'd sat
an exam and passed and I was going to move forward. I never
imagined that those would be the last games I'd play for a very
long time.

I should have guessed it, when I returned to Sevilla the shit
hit the fan. Simeone and I were sanctioned, we were made to
sign a piece of paper saying we apologised to the club and . . .
everything changed. I got injured, I fought, the lot. El Coco
included me in his line-ups anyway, out of good faith, but he
knew as well as I did that if I made it it would be a miracle . . .
The Andalusians were driving me crazy. The thing started degen-
erating until it exploded in my fight with Bilardo.

In mid-June the national squad played against Bolivia, in Guayaquil, in the Copa América. Without me, of course. They won it and, as was logical, for continuity's sake the same squad was kept for the qualifying rounds for the World Cup USA '94. I left Sevilla in June '93 and returned to Argentina. I was looking for another club, and in the meantime I was just another fan of the national squad, nothing more. I expressed my opinions anyway, as a lover of the national squad. I didn't have any problems with El Coco Basile. He believed in his men, they had given him a run of undefeated matches after all, and he bet on them. But I was pissed off because I felt I had been used in those two matches against Brazil and Denmark. The return of Maradona, all that jazz, and then they never came out on the balcony again.

On 5 September 1993 I went to the Monumental stadium – wearing the number 10 shirt, yes, but only to watch the World Cup qualifier between Argentina and Colombia from the stands with all the other fans. I walked there from my house in Correa and Libertador, with my old man, with my brother-in-law El Morsa, with La Claudia, with Marcos Franchi. It was an outing like any other. Argentina had a one-point advantage over Colombia. With just a 1–0 win that was it, the tortoise wouldn't be able to get away. But Colombia's goals started coming, one after the other, until they scored five. I couldn't believe it! I couldn't believe it! And when people started shouting *Colombia, Colombia!*, even the Argentinians, I wanted to kill myself. It really upset me, it disturbed me a lot! And I went back to my house, weeping the whole ten blocks. I was weeping and people were saying *Come back, Diego, come back!* But I hadn't gone to the game to be asked back, *viejo!*

The stadium was chanting *Maradoóó, Maradoóó!* But to me it felt like they were insulting me. I was crying because Argentinian football – the football of Argentina! – had lost 5–0 and that was a very big step backwards. It nearly knocked us out of the World Cup. What mattered at this stage were the

statistics, the results. It wasn't an irresistible Colombian team
– and in fact that result turned out to be their death certificate:
they thought they'd entered the history books and in fact
they've never done anything remotely like it since; quite the
contrary.

I was dead when I left the stadium because that squad of
Coco Basile's had been a credible and lovable squad. That's why
the stadium was jam-packed. The people had gone, like myself,
to party, to celebrate that we were in the World Cup. Instead
we were all left dangling on a thin thread.

We still had a chance to qualify, we had to play Australia over
two legs and get a draw. I wasn't sure I wanted to be involved
in that chance. I did want the lads to have it, to get their revenge.
In the end it was them and Basile who asked me to come back.
I accepted because of the people, who would have picked me
blindfolded. I saw it as a challenge for the football of Argentina,
a chance to jump forward after the huge step back of the
Colombia game. I got it into my head that I had to return, and
I did return. What's more, on 9 September, four days after
Colombia's goalfest, I officially became a Newell's player. It was
like returning to life.

I had already embarked upon one of my classic recovery plans.
This time using a Chinese method which enabled me to lose
eleven kilos in one week. Daniel Cerrini and I had set ourselves
the aim of bettering the physical level I'd been at in Mexico '86.
He was in charge of my diet as well, to complement all the stuff
the Chinese guy, Liu Guo Cheng, had given me. Every now
and then I would ask Daniel to slow down a bit. There were
times when we did three training sessions in one day! It made
sense, he was pure energy, a beast; and he got more confident
because he saw how focused I was. I had it very clear in my
mind: these were the last years of my career and I wanted to
play the best I possibly could.

I knew Coco wanted me but he didn't dare make the first

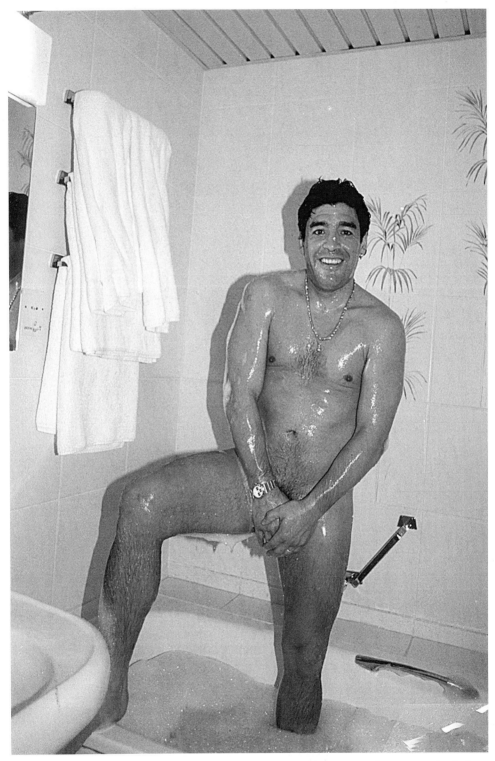

I have nothing to hide, nothing. I've always shown myself as I am and now I can look the world in the eye. That's why I'm willing to show myself like this. This was in Amsterdam on the way to China, and I thought it was fun.

Many say I was at my best at Barcelona. Unbelievable, no? I mean because of the way everything ended. But one thing is true: if everything that happened to me hadn't happened to me, I would have soared. Well ... I did fly a little.

The German Schuster and I understood each other totally. It must have been because we were both completely crazy.

Núñez was to blame for everything that happened to me at Barcelona. This picture was taken when I joined the club, we were already looking at each other funny.

At least I didn't leave Barcelona empty-handed. There it is, in front of all my people: the Copa del Rey.

Look at the medicine balls Lattek made us train with. Unbelievable. The more important the match, the heavier the balls: mine were already full.

The most painful moment of my career. I'm lying on the stretcher with a fracture. I heard the noise after Goikoetxea's tackle, and I knew, I knew. It sounded like a piece of wood cracking. They took me straight to the hospital from the stadium; nobody imagined that three months later I'd be back on the pitch.

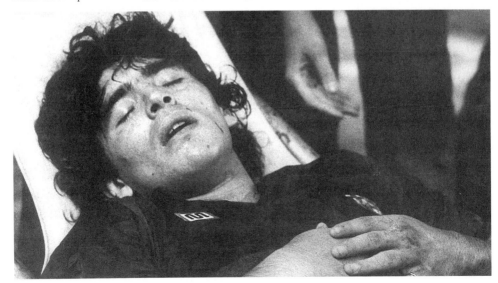

This is a good picture, because that's how it always was with Gentile, he was my shadow. Many years later he admitted that, with serious refereeing, he wouldn't have lasted more than twenty minutes on the pitch. He beat the shit out of me.

Little tongue sticking out, ball at my feet … but it wasn't enough. The Belgians beat us in my first World Cup. Spain '82 started badly, very badly, and that's how it ended too.

What a face, eh? A match against Brazil. We played the football and they scored. They wound me up and I got sent off. That was my exit from Spain '82. It was supposed to have been *my* World Cup.

Can you tell what I'm saying? '*Hijos de puta.*' I did it on purpose, so everyone would know.

I hated it when people talk nonsense, because at Italia '90 I was in perfect physical condition, better than ever. Look at that body!

How could I not weep? I'd had the World Cup snatched away from me. Robbed. And I was getting whistled, whistled. What more did they want? Afterwards, in Argentina, people wanted to celebrate: you don't celebrate second place, tiger.

Me applauding the Neapolitans, applauding them as always. At last Argentina was getting respect – on Napoli's home turf.

I shouted at the camera, yes, but not because I was off my head, like some idiots said. I shouted so everyone would know that I was back, that I was there. It was the goal against Greece in '94, my last one in a World Cup.

There she is, the nurse who led me to my execution. Have you ever seen a player going straight from the pitch to a dope test? I went along, laughing like an idiot. How they knocked me down.

When we turned the match round against the Nigerians, everyone realised we were serious, that Argentina was the best team at the World Cup. Afterwards … afterwards they kicked me out and ruined my dream.

What *bronca*! Bilardo took me off against Burgos and I left the pitch swearing at him. Later we beat the shit out of each other . . . but at any rate, there's a lot about him that has at times made me look to him as a father.

It was a shame that Sevilla didn't work out, because I had some good, some really good games.

The Newell's thing was lovely, really lovely. I'd like to do more with them, because I have the best memories. Those people in the background – they loved me very much.

It should have been a goal, but Loco Islas saved it. What a great backheeled flick that is. It was my debut for Newell's, at Independiente's stadium, 10 October '93.

I really enjoyed coming back to Boca. I stepped on the pitch and felt I owned it. Also, I was treated with enormous respect both by my team-mates and my rivals. And to be able to celebrate a goal for Boca again, well, this is how you celebrate …

Sometimes I have to do my shoelaces up, sure. If it was up to me, I'd play without laces. I think you can feel the ball better, you're freer. I love it.

One of the greatest satisfactions of my career, playing with Caniggia. A monster, a true monster of football. I also consider him my friend. This is in '95, when we played for Boca together.

I think it was the greatest recognition I could ever have received. I spoke at Oxford University and they gave me the title of 'Master Inspirer of Dreams'. I dedicated it to my folks and my daughters.

Being manager for Madiyú and for Racing was a great experience, and that was more important than the results. I learnt a lot and I know that one day I'll manage again, but kids this time. I want to teach, I want to pass on what I know.

A peck with Cóppola. Maybe people have made a big deal out of this – but what they don't realise is that we're brothers, that's what we are: brothers.

With Jorge Cyterszpiler, in our early days together.

I'll always be grateful to Bilardo, because he stuck his neck out for me when nobody else would have, nobody. He made me captain and the only certainty for his squad. That day I knew I would repay him with the World Cup.

My first tour with the national squad, with Menotti and Passarella. I'd admire Menotti deeply, but I would never forgive him for leaving me out of the national side in 1978.

I love Coco Basile (*above*) very much. It really annoys me that he was unfairly blamed for the national side's problems. And on top of that, they appointed Passarella to replace him. Please!

At one time, I considered Passarella my friend, and then he let the tortoise get away from him. I think he could never accept that I'd come to take his place. I was to Bilardo what he had been to Menotti, but he also took the cat's milk.

I haven't fallen out with Ramón Díaz, not at all. He got carried away with a load of nonsense, he thought I'd stopped him playing for Argentina. But I never did, and I told him so. To his face, in a match against Inter. 'Score some goals and stop fucking about, then you'll get the call.'

Aahhh, what a lovely picture. The dressing-room at Hampden Park, the day I scored my first goal for Argentina, with Tolo Gallego.

Two great honours, two, in this picture. One: the friendship of a truly great player, Alfredo Di Stéfano. And the other: that beautiful ball the French gave me in recognition of my career. I am grateful for both.

I'll always say that God and the Comandante, Fidel Castro, saved my life in 2000. The Comandante showed me what it really means to be there when someone needs you. Him and the Cuban people. Before I settled in Havana, I'd met him three times, and I would spend my life with him. He's a wise man.

I was with him, yes, and this is proof. And if I've said what I've said in this book, it's because I believe it. I know a lot of people would like to say the same and don't dare, but I mean no disrespect.

I became close to President Menem (*below*) when his son's tragedy happened. I didn't do it out of self-interest or anything like that, I didn't distance myself from him when he lost the election.

I know we could have done a lot of things together, but we're too different. I think the problem was that Pelé got scared when I appeared on the scene and he thought I was coming to rob him of something I've never wanted. The number one, the greatest, is up to the people.

Dona Tota and Don Diego, the best parents in the world, the best. I am grateful to have them and I'll say it again: if they asked me for the sky I would give it to them.

La Claudia (*right*), Dalma Nerea (*left*) and Gianinna Dinorah (*centre*). My family. They are the ones that matter to me, truly. If ever I've made a mistake and hurt them – which I have done – I beg their forgiveness.

Dal and Gian, the Princess and the Tank, my babies. They keep me alive. Although, on this occasion, they nearly killed me – popping out of a box on the middle of the pitch as I made my comeback for Boca in '95. I nearly had a heart attack.

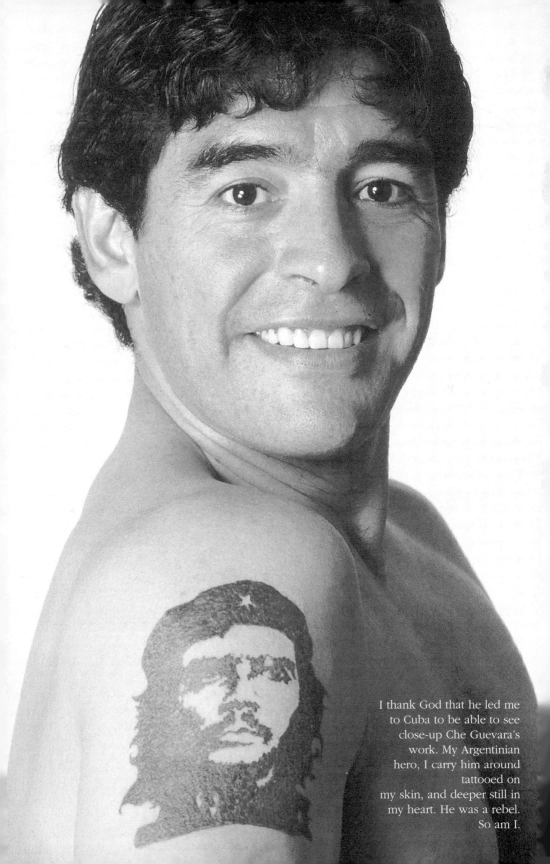

I thank God that he led me
to Cuba to be able to see
close-up Che Guevara's
work. My Argentinian
hero, I carry him around
tattooed on
my skin, and deeper still in
my heart. He was a rebel.
So am I.

move. Some people were filling his head with ideas: that I would break up the group, that this, that and the other . . . so I sent him a message through the media: 'Coco and I have never grown apart. We're both fiery tempered and we've sorted out everything we don't like about each other. Now I must improve my game before I can return to the national squad.' We met two days later, in September 1993.

Coco officially asked me to return to the national squad at a meeting which lasted two hours. Prof Echeverría was also there. He had spoken to me several times already and knew better than anyone that I was willing to do anything, sacrifice anything. Coco made it official: he asked me as the manager and I said yes.

I was enthusiastic because it might mean my country wouldn't get knocked out of the World Cup. But I was more enthusiastic about giving the squad a chance to make it to the USA than for my own sake. Then things began to fall into place because the lads started to understand me, the way I was . . . we were all new to each other. They had won two Copas América but they weren't THE great squad they later became.

The group I found on my arrival was broken, cracked. Their main worry was whether or not to talk to Victor Hugo Morales, the great football commentator, or whether or not to grant interviews to *El Gráfico*. I said to them: 'Stop fucking about, we're going to talk to everyone and we're also going to play, because we have to qualify for the World Cup USA!' And we qualified – only just, but we qualified.

It was in Australia where, for reasons known only to the powers-that-be in football, there was no drug test. Why not? How should I know? That's something only Havelange, Blatter, Grondona can answer.

I celebrated my thirty-third birthday a day early in Sydney, because of the time difference. I was given a cake shaped like the World Cup and it was a real joy to share it with La Claudia,

Don Diego, with my friends. La Claudia woke me up early, gave me her present – a spectacular pair of Versace underpants – and my daughter's presents – two teddy bears, black and white. Then she played a recording of my daughters' voices singing to the tune of a football chant: *Vení, vení, cantá conmigo/ que un amigo vas a encontrar/ y de la mano, de Maradona/ todos la vuelta vamos a dar* (Come on come on, sing with me/ and a friend you're going to find/ held by the hand, of Maradona/ we will all run the victory lap). I couldn't hold back the tears. I remember Juan Pablo Varsky, of Channel 13, had a mobile TV unit at the door of the hotel, and he broadcast my party from there. I was happy. I was enjoying new things, things that some consider to be privileges but that to me are no more than a sign of recognition, recognition for my life's work. For example, my wife turned up at my hotel room. I remember stating publicly, so that it would be clear to everybody: 'Look boys, I'm thirty-three, and if after everything I've played and won I can't ask my wife to travel to the *concentración* with me, well . . . what can I say? I'm a grown-up now!' I think they understood me, and if anyone didn't, fuck them, they let the tortoise get away.

Everyone was very surprised by my physical appearance. I was really thin: I weighed seventy-two kilos. Richard Gere eat your heart out! Cerrini drove himself crazy but he managed to find the oats I needed for my breakfast every day.

The day after my birthday we drew with Australia 1–1. Balbo scored from my cross. It was good for me. I felt like the captain once more. I wore a new armband, blue with the faces of my two daughters on it. And I felt the group was beginning to bond. I ended up limping, but Coco asked me to stay on the pitch until the end: 'Stay on, stay on. Redondo can move up a few metres and you can drop back, but stay . . . stay on!' I felt important again. But I wasn't at all happy with the way the team was performing. I blamed it on the pain I was feeling, but the truth is I was disillusioned. I felt I should have created more chances for Balbo and Batistuta, that I should have lasted better. The draw tasted of nothing.

We suffered afterwards. Two weeks later, on 17 November, we drew 1–1 again at the Monumental. We had qualified, but only just. Still, that had been our aim, we now needed to wait and see how it would pan out.

For me, it didn't pan out so well. It was a nasty summer that one. I was injured in December playing for Newell's; there was the incident with journalists outside my house – the air rifle and that whole shitty story. After I left Newell's in February I took the holidays I deserved. I went back to Oriente, to the Marisol beach, near Tres Arroyos, and I concentrated on enjoying my family and shark-fishing. I needed this: the pleasure of a grilled fish; a clean shave under the sun just like in Villa Fiorito; living daily with humble people, with working people. I didn't go to Saint Tropez; my little house in Oriente had two rooms and a garage with a barbecue. It wasn't a palace. It was Oriente, where I knew I would be treated like one of the people. Where I was just going to be El Diego and nothing more.

I stayed there for a couple of weeks and when I went back to Buenos Aires I went to the stadium to watch Boca play Racing. I was asked by a journalist about the national squad and I said what I felt: 'I want to play in the World Cup.' The following day I was training with the rest of the squad in Ezeiza.

There was a friendly against Brazil, on 23 March. I knew I wouldn't be ready, but I really wanted to be there so I asked Coco to include me in the line-up. He persuaded me not to play, saying he preferred to have me fit for the World Cup rather than the warm-up friendlies. I travelled to Recife anyway, to hang out with the lads and spend time with them. I sat on the national first team's bench for only the second time in my whole life: the first had been my debut. This was courtesy of Coco, who didn't want to send me to the stands.

As soon as we got back I set myself an ultimatum: I told Basile that, within five days, I would tell him if I could continue in the national squad. I didn't want to lie to anybody. I wasn't going to go to the US if I wasn't up to it.

To those who say I'm irresponsible I'd like to point out that I met my deadline: exactly five days later, on Tuesday 5 April, along with Marcos Franchi, I started calling everyone I had to talk to. First, Basile: 'I'm going to try, Coco, but for a while I'm going to train on my own, to reach the standard of the rest of the lads.' Then, Fernando Signorini: 'I want you with me, let's develop one of your programmes.' And also Professor Antonio Dal Monte, who had prepared me for Mexico '86 and Italia '90, and Doctor Néstor Lentini who was to take his place at USA '94. Lentini was contacted by Signorini when he was director of CENARD, a centre of sports excellence, and to this day I am grateful for everything he ever did for me. He was always a model of discretion and he always gave me everything I needed.

In the end we also called Don Angel Rosa. I'd met Don Angel during my holidays in Oriente. A great guy, one of those true country men. During one of many hands of *truco*, an Argentinian card game that we played, he made me an offer: 'Diego, whenever you like you can come by my ranch, it's beyond Santa Rosa in La Pampa. You can hunt in peace there.' I hadn't forgotten and now I needed such a place, I needed calm. But when Franchi called him on my behalf, Don Angel didn't believe him.

'It's true, Don Angel. I'm calling on behalf of Diego Maradona. We want to accept your offer and spend a few days in your campo.'

'Yeah, sure, right.'

'Don Angel, don't you believe me? Remember, I beat you at *truco* with a hand of thirty-three . . .'

'Marcos!'

So off we went. Me, Fernando, Marcos, and German Perez

and Rodolfo Gonzalez, a little mute guy who is a friend of the family from Esquina. He'd been with us for years and was always ready to give my folks a hand with anything. We arrived on Sunday 10 April and stayed until Sunday the 17th. In one week I achieved so much: I did aerobic exercises with Signorini, I was running sixteen kilometres a day, I also boxed with Miguel Angel Campanino, an Argentinian ex-champion, and then I would go to the gym. Everything was under the control and guidance of Doctor Lentini from Buenos Aires.

The *campo*, which was called 'Marito', was sixty-one kilometres from Santa Rosa. It had a humble little house, like everything round there, but very comfortable: two storeys, tiled roof, six bedrooms, a black and white TV, its own generator and a fresh veranda, perfect for playing *truco*.

Coco Basile and Prof Echeverría came out there to chat with me and finalise details over a few *mates*. Coco had called me up to play against Morocco, in Salta in the north of Argentina, and he wanted to know how I was doing. I said I felt like 'a plane', I felt I could fly, and he understood me immediately because he's from the 'hood, like me. He said: 'The less time there is, the better. The closer the target, the better.' Fernando Signorini gave El Prof Echeverría a load of reports on my fitness and he took them under his arm patting me on the head with the warmth he always showed me. He knew that if they left me alone I'd make it without problems.

The match against Morocco was on 20 April, at the Gimnasia y Tiro stadium in Salta. We won 3–1 and I scored from a penalty. I hadn't found the net since 22 May 1990. Afterwards I read that I'd gone 1,255 minutes without scoring. That was really satisfying, I felt useful. I had fun during that match, I had so much fun I even played keepy-uppy with an orange someone threw from the terraces. I'd only intended to play for sixty minutes but when Coco Basile signalled me to come off I asked him to leave me on a little longer. I felt great. I couldn't believe it. Three months earlier I had been writhing on the ground, now I felt I could make a difference. And I knew something else, too: everything depended on me. With fifteen minutes to go El Coco made the substitution anyway. And he was right, because Ortega, Ariel Ortega, came on. I ran towards him, we slapped fives and I shouted: 'Give it to them!'

Everyone thinks 'El Burrito' Ortega is a little idiot but I think he is very intelligent. And this isn't because he speaks highly of me. We shared a room in the Argentina *concentración* for a while but he was moved out because executives from his club, River, thought I would fill his head with . . . whatever was in mine. Orteguita said to me: 'I want to stay sharing a room with you.' But I said to him: 'No, kid, no, no. Because I'm out of here tomorrow but you have to go on.' The guy who moved him out was that stutterer Alfredo Davicce, River's president, and I said to Basile not to worry, to move the kid to another room. El Burrito spoke to me like a man. He knew all about the drug problems of his native province, Jujuy; he spoke to me about how professional he was and also about how unprofessional he could be just because he fucking felt like it. Ortega was a phenomenon.

Then the Japanese wouldn't give me a visa because of my record of drug use and we had to cancel our tour over there. I felt pissed off because of the discrimination but also pleased because of the team's solidarity: my team-mates refused to travel and the AFA cancelled the tour. Another tour was set up at the last minute, to Ecuador, Israel (of course, for good luck) and Croatia. We lost the first match 1–0, thrashed Israel 3–0, and drew 0–0 with Croatia.

It wasn't the best of tours, truth be told. It reminded me of Bilardo's worst days, because of the team's performance and because of the difficulties in moving from one place to the other. I threatened to return to Argentina from Croatia. Perhaps it had been partly my fault because of the Japan fiasco which meant everything had been set up in a hurry. But eventually I stood firm and said: 'Either we improve this gig or I'm out.'

We didn't improve much but I didn't leave either. We went off to the US, to our new home in the outskirts of Boston. First at a Sheraton in Needham, on a motorway. Afterwards at Babson College, which was the place the AFA had organised for us. It was a spectacular place and I felt everything very intensely. I knew it was my last World Cup, maybe it would be the end of my career. After it was over, I might not play again. I didn't even have a club at that point.

I wanted Dalma and Gianinna to see their dad in a *concentración*, in a training camp, in a match. Everything felt like a goodbye. But I was full of enthusiasm, full of dreams – as always in a World Cup. I had three under my belt but I felt the same sense of responsibility as I had as a first-timer. Argentina weren't favourites and I liked that because that's how it had been in Mexico '86 and we ended up champions; because we'd been taken for dead in Italia '90 and we'd reached the final. I said what I had said four years earlier: 'If they want the cup, they'll have to rip it out of my hands.' Although this time I didn't actually have it.

I wanted to be fit for our first match, against Greece, seven points out of ten according to Doctor Lentini's plan, which was closely monitored by Fernando Signorini and Prof Echeverría. I worked three times as hard as my team-mates, because I trained with them and then did my own programme as well. Fernando used to say that I would be fitter against Greece than I had been against Cameroon in 1990.

I asked Daniel Cerrini to join the group once we were already in the States. He arrived on Thursday 9 June because I and only I asked for him. I wanted him to be there and I wouldn't take no for an answer. He had helped me get fit before, when I first went to Newell's and then when I rejoined the national squad against Australia, and now I wanted him again. I felt he could help me with my diet and my weight. I wanted to start at seventy-six kilos and not seventy-two, like I had at Newell's. Back then Signorini had said: 'He's too light, if anyone touches him, he flies away', and he was right. I knew Franchi and Signorini didn't much like the idea of Cerrini joining us but I was adamant. In my life, I make all the decisions. No entourage or clan makes them for me. If I make a mistake, *I* make it. And *I* called Cerrini to come to the States. And with him came another great friend who I wanted in my team: Salvatore Carmando. He had been the masseur at Napoli and he'd been with me in Mexico '86. He hadn't been with me in '90 because the Italian squad had pinched him.

When the competition kicked off we were the best team by far. We had promised ourselves to avenge everything we'd been through and we were managing it. We had the best forward, Batistuta, and he was in his prime. We had Caniggia, who was really motivated by me. Balbo had fitted phenomenally well into a new position.

We'd even solved the problem of the goalkeeper. Initially Basile had thought that he could alternate between Islas and Sergio Goycochea, that they could start one match each. But then Islas didn't want that and he and Basile couldn't come to an agreement. The problem then was, who would tell Goyco he wasn't going to play? Nobody wanted to. So I spoke to him and said: 'Look, Goyco, let's make things clear. Islas is going to be the number one goalie because of his merits on the pitch and in training.' I didn't want to lie to Goyco, because Goyco is an exceptional guy. So I had to show the balls, as captain, to tell my friend that he wasn't going to start. Even though I wanted him to. I had to tell him he was out of the World Cup when he had fought all the way with me, elbow to elbow. The decision had been Basile's, I never put anyone in nor took anyone out. I was the first, with Ruggeri, to support Goyco and make him feel a part of a team that was already playing like an orchestra.

We didn't need to defend. We defended with the ball. That was Basile's proposal. He'd said to us: 'Look, if we want to play the way I line you up, with Maradona, Caniggia, Balbo, Batistuta, Simeone and Redondo, we're going to lose 5–0. However, if we keep possession of the ball and we adapt to being each other's shadow, filling in for each other, taking turns, the thing is going to work.' We were a side full of attacking players, so to avoid weakness at the back we shadowed each other. That way, if one of us lost possession, someone was always there to get it back quickly. And how it worked! We all reached the area and that's how I scored against Greece: one touch, *tac, tac, tac*, like a machine gun, one-two, Redondo, me, *golazo, golazo*. But Diego 'El Cholo' Simeone would also reach the area, and José Chamot . . . we had a great team and that's how we thrashed Greece on 21 June, 2–1, and then turned the Nigerians over 25 June, 2–1. We were a great team and that's why I'm so bitter, it's a feeling I will carry with me my whole life.

Later, Bebeto and Romario of Brazil said to me: 'When we saw how you guys turned the game against Nigeria round, we thought, oops, this is teamwork, it's not just Maradona . . . it's a team with mental strength, with physical strength, with presence.' It wasn't just anybody saying that, it was Bebeto and Romario. They were trying to say that Brazil had realised, with just two matches played, that Argentina were the team to watch out for. For everyone, we were *the* team. We'd thrashed Greece, we'd come back against Nigeria . . . and then what happened happened.

I'll never forget the afternoon of 25 June 1994. Never. I felt I'd had an exceptional game against Nigeria, I was happy. The nurse came to get me at the side of the pitch, because I was still celebrating with the crowd, and I didn't suspect anything. Why would I, if I was clean, clean? The only thing I did, I remember, was look up at Claudia and pull a face, as if to say, 'Who's this girl, then?' But it was more a little gesture between us, because it was a woman, and not anything else. I was calm because I had done drugs tests before and during the World Cup, and the results were always OK. I hadn't taken anything. Nothing! Total abstinence, even from the other stuff, the evil stuff that holds you back. That's why I walked off with that plump little nurse, still celebrating. Why else would I have been laughing?

Any of the journalists who saw me after the test can tell you: I was happy, totally happy. Someone aware that they'd just fucked up that badly wouldn't have been as happy as I was.

Three days later, on Tuesday 28 June, I was drinking *mate* in the car park at Babson College, enjoying a couple of the free hours that El Coco Basile gave us now and again. It was hot, as it was every day during that tournament. But nothing bothered us. We were as happy as children. I was chatting about any old thing with La Claudia, Goycoechea and his wife, Ana Laura. My old man was also there. Suddenly, Marcos turned up, with a terrible look on his face. Who died? I thought to myself.

'Diego, I need to talk to you for a minute,' he said, and he moved me away from the rest of the group. He put his arm on my shoulder and broke the news. 'Look, Diego, your drug test against Nigeria has come up positive. But don't worry, the AFA directors are handling things really well.'

I hardly heard the last bit, I'd turned round looking for Claudia ... I could hardly make her out, my eyes were already full of tears. My voice broke when I said to her:

'We're leaving the World Cup.'

And then I started sobbing like a child.

We walked away together, with our arms round each other, towards my room, number 127, and once inside I exploded. I started punching the walls and shouting: 'I worked my arse off, you hear me? I busted my balls! I worked my arse off like never before and now this!'

None of the people with me dared say a word. Not Claudia, not Marcos, not my poor old masseur Carmando. I didn't believe in anyone or anything, I didn't believe the directors would handle it. I knew, I knew all too well the end had come.

Daniel Bolotnicoff travelled to Los Angeles with Cerrini and one of the AFA directors, David Pintado, where a control test would be done. Cerrini had no role there, really, because he wasn't even on the delegation's official list. Doctor Carlos Peidró, the squad's cardiologist and first assistant to the team doctor, that thermos-head Ugaldo, also travelled with them.

The world had caved in on top of me. I didn't know what to do, which way to turn. I had to show my face, sure, but I didn't want to destroy the rest of the lads. We were supposed to travel to Dallas for the match against Bulgaria and it broke my heart to know that . . . to know that I wasn't going to be there, on the pitch. I didn't dare say anything to anybody; those who knew, knew, and that was it. Maybe deep inside I held some hope that the directors would be able to do something, that they would believe me, that they would realise I'd worked my arse off, that I'd been training three times a day. They'd seen me, for fuck's sake!

On Wednesday the 29th we arrived in Dallas. As we walked into the hotel, I led the way. I was wearing the squad uniform, dark glasses and a little blue Mickey Mouse cap that my daughters had given me. The cameras pointed at me but for no special reason, that's just how it always was. Nobody knew anything yet and it was a weird and dreadful sensation. I could see the faces of journalists who were friends, smiling, full of hope. Many of them had gone out on a limb to defend me in the past and now they were enjoying this revenge as much as I was. I was in so much pain carrying what I knew inside.

That same afternoon we went to recce the stadium, the Cotton Bowl, the way you always do in a World Cup, the day before the game, stepping on the turf. I went along, but I was somewhere else. I knew very well I wouldn't be there the following day, I wouldn't be allowed to be there. Not all my team-mates knew the truth, which is why some wondered why I was being quieter than usual. I didn't even touch a ball, didn't bother to play keepy-uppy. I went up to the goal and stood there, holding on to the net, like a prisoner.

When we started leaving, I noticed a commotion among the journalists who were up in the stands. They'd heard. It was obvious. I saw Julio Grondona walk up to them from the pitch, and I hurried my steps. I heard them shouting: 'Diego, just one question! Maradona, over here, please!' I didn't look over, I just raised my arm and waved. I waved goodbye. That's what I did: I waved goodbye. Once I'd left the turf behind and was about to lose myself down the tunnel that led out of the stadium I turned my head and saw Grondona gesticulating with two hundred microphones and cameras focused on him. *The directors are handling things really well*, Franchi had said to me. I felt a shiver down my spine.

That night the hotel lobby was hell. Everyone had heard the news by then. First they thought it was El Negro Vázquez, Sergio Vázquez, who had also had a drug test with me and was injured, so he was taking medication. But afterwards everyone knew it was me.

The directors were still negotiating but at the end of the day, as I was trying to fall asleep, Marcos knocked on my door and brought me the news: 'Diego, it's all over. The control test is also positive.' The AFA decided to remove my name from the official list. I no longer belonged to the national squad.

I was alone, alone. I shouted out: 'Help me, please help me! I'm frightened of doing something stupid! Please help me!'

Some of the players came into my room but there was nothing they could do, nothing they could say. I just wanted to weep because I knew the following day I would have to show my face to the whole world and I really didn't want to cry then. I'd promised Claudia and I would keep my promise.

When daylight finally came I hadn't slept a wink. Franchi had spent the whole night with me, so had Signorini.

When the time came, the squad left for the stadium. I didn't. I stayed behind. I wanted to explain everything to the Argentinian people. Journalist Adrian Paenza was there, with a Channel 13 crew. We went to Franchi's room and I sat on a bed, the one nearest to the window, while Adrian and the cameraman, El Cordobes, got everything ready. I asked Franchi, Signorini and Carmando to sit behind me if they wanted to. I took a deep breath, cleared my throat, and told them I was ready. And what I said can be summarised in a phrase that I can easily repeat: I insist, today, they cut my legs off.

The truth? I didn't feel like fucking talking but I thought the people deserved at least an explanation. I thought if they heard me maybe they would understand. Also, I didn't want them to hear just one side of the story. I sat on the edge of the bed and decided to face the camera. I'd spoken to Claudia on the phone just before and I'd promised her again that I wouldn't cry, that I wouldn't give them the pleasure like in '90. But the truth is it was fucking difficult not to crack.

I started off by saying what I'd been telling Marcos as we walked down the hallway towards the interview: that I wanted to run, that I wanted to train, that I wanted to fly. I'd prepared so well for that World Cup, so well. I was like never before. And they were hitting me over the head just when I was beginning to emerge again. And I remember I also said, because it was the truth: 'The day I took drugs I went to the judge and said: "I took drugs. How much is the fine? What's the penalty?" and I paid it. And I had two very hard years of going every three or four months or whenever the judge called me to have a test under a microscope or have a piss. But I don't understand this. I don't understand because they have no case. I thought justice would be fair but in my case they've made a mistake.'

I swore and swore again that I hadn't taken any performance-enhancing substance. I hadn't taken drugs to play or run better.

I swore on my daughters' lives and I still do swear on my daughters' lives. If I had trained the way I had, why would I need to take drugs? I just wanted the fans to understand that I hadn't run because of the drugs, that I had run with my heart and for the jersey. Nothing more. And I remember that when I said that bit, I cracked, I crumbled. I may have promised Claudia that I wouldn't weep but I couldn't hold it in any longer.

At that moment I didn't even want revenge, my legs had been cut off, my soul had been destroyed. I was convinced I'd paid my dues with the Italy thing, with that penalty, with my defeat. But it seems FIFA wanted still more of my blood; my pain wasn't enough for them ... they wanted more.

I heard my interview was broadcast alongside the images of the players singing the anthem before our match against Bulgaria. I don't know, I didn't see it, and I would never dare watch it, ever, I don't think I could bear it. I bore enough at the time. I still don't know how I managed.

I went to watch the game in another room. I invited a small group of journalist friends who hadn't gone to the stadium, who'd stayed behind to see what I did. Signorini and Carmando were also there. Franchi was running around trying to see if something could be done. What the fuck could be done?! What the fuck could be done?!

I sat on the floor with my back against the bed. The TV was less than a metre away from me. The game kicked off, I didn't shout once, I never leapt to my feet, never moved. It wasn't me watching that game: my jersey was there on the pitch, that's where I should have been. My flag was also there, the one that my daughters had given me and that I passed on to Cani, with all my heart.

My lasting memories of that match against Bulgaria are the words that Redondo said to me. When I told Dalmita what he'd said – because she asked a lot of questions – we both started crying. After the match Redondo said to me, with tears in his eyes: 'I was looking for you, I was looking for you on the pitch, and I couldn't find you . . . I looked for you the whole match.' Of course, we'd become a team that knew each other by heart. By heart: pass it to Diego, he will pass it inch perfect back to you; to Balbo, to Bati, to Redondo, to Cholo. We all felt the same way about the game . . . we played as if it was a kickabout.

I only lasted twenty-five minutes, no more. I made my excuses and went off to my room. I stayed there on my own until Franchi returned, until the lads returned. I just wanted to get out of that place and I had a flight back to Boston, to meet Claudia and the girls at five in the morning. My daughters didn't understand anything at this stage. I rang Claudia and asked her how they were. She said they had already asked some questions and she told them I'd been given a medicine and that's why I hadn't been able to play. I got a lump in my throat and hung up. I wanted to hang myself . . . slit my veins. I felt more alone than ever.

Julio Grondona's attitude, face to face, was excellent. But later I felt he wasn't able to defend me the way I would have liked. Firstly because what had happened here was not a cocaine relapse. And secondly because it had been an innocent mistake by Cerrini. We had run out of the supplements I was taking in Argentina and they bought the same stuff right there, in the US; it was the same product but the US one contained a small percentage of ephedrine. Instead of Ripped Fast, which is what I had been taking and run out of, Cerrini bought Ripped Fuel, which could also be bought over the counter and was practically identical. Both were called Ripped, but the Fuel version had some herbs, some shit, that produced ephedrine. A tiny bit. Doctor Lentini carried out loads of tests in Buenos Aires and he established that that product could cause the appearance of the substances that were found in my system.

11

The Farewell

Boca '95/'96

When I came back from the USA World Cup, with my legs cut off and my heart in a worse condition, it crossed my mind that everything was over, that there was nothing more to do. The ban came into effect in August: it was another fifteen months.

I used to say to Claudia: I'd like to lie down, sleep, wake up and be a Boca player, ready to go on the pitch, without prohibitions, without sanctions, nothing. But it was a dream. Now I was living a nightmare. And it was time to fight. Against whoever crossed my path: Havelange, Grondona, Passarella.

After USA '94, I was Lucifer and Passarella was God. He was appointed manager of the national side. That's why I jumped – because no one else did – when he tried to play the saint and banned long hair, earrings. He ordered rhinoscopies for the whole squad: it was an outrage, a farce.

I had to do something during the fifteen-month sentence FIFA had thrown at me. Mandiyú of Corrientes was the first club that dared to offer me an opportunity: to be manager of a team. It was a marvellous experience, working alongside Carlitos Fren, but it wasn't without its problems. We had to be trainers, presidents, psychologists, and at the same time beg Adidas for balls. Everything. It was difficult, but it made me grow as a man and helped me earn the respect of all the players I managed. When I got there they had nothing. They didn't have a ball to train with, the goals didn't have nets.

My first match in charge of Mandiyú was against Central. I managed from the stands with my brother Lalo by my side. We were like any other couple of fans; I wasn't authorised to sit on the bench. We lost 2–1 and it tired me out more than playing an international game into extra time. The best result I got during my short stint as manager was a draw against River at the Monumental.

I didn't last long at Mandiyú, just two months, from 3 October to 6 December, twelve matches, one victory, six draws, five defeats. One day Osvaldo Cruz, who owned the club or something, turned up in our changing room and shouted, 'Lads, you've got to show more balls, alright?!'

I had my back to him and Fren was facing him. I looked at Carlitos and said, 'Do you want to hit him or shall I?'

I turned round, faced Cruz and shouted, 'You motherfucking fatso, what the fuck are you coming in here to talk to the players for? We talk to the players . . . get out!'

'No, it's just that . . .'

'Get out! Or I'll smash your face in with my bare hands!'

And that's when he said to me, 'And who are you?'

What! I laid into him until someone dragged him away. The dressing room is mine when I'm manager, mine! And I couldn't stand him coming to tell the players they weren't putting enough balls into it. After that I left, naturally.

Nineteen ninety-four was ending badly, but '95 seemed like it was getting off to a much better start. I got a call from France. I was being paid the tribute I had always wished would come from my own country. On 1 January 1995, in the middle of my ban, the French magazine *France Football* handed me the Balon d'Or in recognition of my footballing career. It was enormously emotional and it was a pivotal moment: Guillermo Cóppola came back into my life. I pleaded with him to come with me on that trip because he had a lot to do with the reasons why I had been given that award. I had lived the most successful years of my footballing career, the most important titles, with Guillermo, although nobody remembers that. Everyone prefers to dish the dirt on him. From that moment on he simply came on board; we never had a formal agreement for him to be my manager or anything like that. In the meantime, Daniel Bolotnicoff was still working as my lawyer. The Marcos Franchi era was over.

After Mandiyú came Racing – an experience that didn't turn out as well as the Mandiyú one, in all honesty. De Stéfano was the president, Juan De Stéfano. On a personal level he always behaved well with me but as a director he didn't stick to what we had agreed. I'd asked for a central marker and they didn't give me one: I'd spoken to Coyo Héctor Almandoz, for me at the time the best *líbero* in Argentina, who was playing for Vélez Sarsfield. Almandoz had personally spoken to Carlos Bianchi, the Vélez manager, and asked him to let him come to Racing. But because Bianchi and I had fallen out at the time, Vélez came out asking for $1.8 million, an absurd amount. Racing didn't even have money to buy strips; the players weren't getting paid their wages. We had a team struggling to avoid relegation; it was like Mandiyú, but with a history. A heavy history at that.

I had four months of struggle there, especially against the referees. As manager at Racing I had to fight against a real mafia and I couldn't stand it. To top it all off, De Stéfano lost the election. I'd said I'd leave with him and I did. Exactly four months later – eleven matches: two victories, six draws and three defeats. As clear as that.

I enjoyed being a manager. I became a lot more sentimental. The things that happened to my players hurt more than the ones that had actually happened to me when I was playing. At Racing, many a time I wanted to go on the pitch because of the referees, they drove me off my head: Juan Bava, Angel Sánchez, major hassles I had with them and I'm convinced that it was my fault that Racing lost. They had it in for me, it was personal. But I loved being in charge of a group, the training sessions, enjoying the relationship with the players. I would have loved to have been in charge of a powerful team. I still would.

I was offered that chance by the person I least expected, Pelé. He invited me to one of his homes, in Sao Paolo, and on Saturday 13 May I travelled over with Guillermo; Marcelo Simonián, a businessman who is a friend; and Daniel Bolotnicoff. Pelé wanted me to become player-manager at Santos, the Brazilian club he had played for and with whom he still had very strong ties. The idea didn't stop with football, there was also a possibility of doing things for the street kids of Argentina and Brazil.

I did want to be manager and player, but at Boca. Two things got in the way: one, Boca didn't have a penny and anyway getting any dough out of Carlos Heller, the vice-president, was harder than finding hot water in Villa Fiorito. On top of that Don Antonio Alegre, the president, didn't want to know about the idea of a player-manager. Silvio Marzolini was the manager, as he had been in 1981, and shifting him from the bench didn't cross the old man's head. Then the press started saying I was trying to pull the rug from under Marzolini's feet. I couldn't even go to the Bombonera without them shouting hysterically; they were really taking the cat's milk with that bullshit. I was going to watch Boca, *viejo*, like any other fan! People would cheer me, yeah, but I couldn't avoid that.

Then the best thing that could happen happened: Pelé Sports Marketing invited me on a tour of Europe. Leaving the scene worked wonders.

When I returned Heller called me. It was a Sunday morning and I was playing a *picado* in Tortuguitas, at Adidas's pitch, and Heller rang me on Cóppola's mobile. That same day, both of them went to have lunch together and I went to watch Boca–San Lorenzo on TV at the Olivos presidential residency together with

President Menem. That day Boca lost against San Lorenzo and I lived it like I was one of their players, although physically I was in such bad form that even biting my nails tired me out.

On Thursday there was a meeting, without me, between all the people who could resolve the situation one way or another: Heller and Spataro were representing Boca; Cóppola and Bolotnicoff were representing me; Carlos Avila was representing ... the money. At that meeting they agreed on the figures, mainly thanks to a classic money-spinner: friendlies, aiming at the Asian market, Japan, Korea, China ... any of those would pay a million for watching me play for ninety minutes. The thing is, when that meeting was over, Guillermo called me on the phone and said: 'Look Diego, these people seriously want you. Seriously. I could feel it in my bones. Everything else can be arranged, including Marzolini. We'll talk later.' That call was very good for me. I went to sleep with an enormous sense of peace, thinking about one phrase: *These people seriously want you.*

When I got up the next day I felt phenomenal. I grabbed Claudia's face with both my hands, I kissed her forehead and said: 'I'm happy, Clau ... for them to have demonstrated a serious interest makes me very, but very, happy.'

And I went off to train at the CENARD, where I had been working since my return from Europe. With Renegado Vilamitjiana, under Doctor Lentini's control, with the other guys, really fired up. I worked harder than any other day and when I finished, as always, I said too much. Or rather, I said what I had to say, in case anyone had any doubts still. Like *Crónica* in '81 but this time it was the programme *Las Voces del Fútbol*, on Radio Libertad. I shot from the hip: 'I'm very happy about the offer, I love it. I feel like a Boca player.' I had Carlos Heller listening to me on another mobile and I added, right there and then: 'Carlitos, I like your offer, let's go ahead.' And I didn't stop there. I rang Marzolini: 'Silvio, everything's OK. There are things I don't share with you along footballing lines, but I know we'll reach an agreement ... We've done it once before.' Of course, we'd done it in '81: he didn't want me and he'd had to accept me. Now I didn't want him but I had to put up with it.

I had no right to rush them, in all honesty, and the mere fact of wearing the Boca strip once again made me feel very, very happy. The money thing was guaranteed, because the businessman Eduardo Eurnakian, the boss of the América media group, had come on board. He'd bumped into Guillermo in a café and asked what I was up to. Guillermo told him and the old man said: 'I want to be in on that deal.' So they sorted it out with Torneos, who from then on would only be in charge of the production side of things, and that was it. There was no lack of people willing to put money into it: the figures resembled those of my '87–'93 contract with Naples when the deal had been for twenty million dollars over four years, around five million a year.

The only things left to do were to get fit, to reply to Pelé saying thanks but no thanks, and to beg for the days to pass quickly. Grondona had tried to get FIFA to reduce my ban but I don't think we can say they took much notice of him. So I got ready to wait.

I returned to the Bombonera. Boca was a grey team at that point, it lacked sparkle, and I suffered because of it, but to hear the old song, *Vale diez palos verdes/ se llama Maradona/ y todas las gallinas/ le chupan bien las bolas* (He's worth ten million, his name is Maradona, and all the hens suck his balls), got me into a good mood. I returned to that stadium, my home, wandered round the changing room, said hello to the lads, whom I considered my team-mates already, and sat in a box at the Bombonera, right by the centre of the pitch. And straightaway I had to swallow a defeat against Belgrano de Córdoba. That's where I read the fax Pelé had sent me, concerning the closure of our negotiations. Honestly? Pelé behaved well, very well, because the fax said:

Cóppola came on the plane, as always, and Gérman Pérez, who was like an assistant of mine – and someone who I knew would cause a scandal in Argentina: Daniel Cerrini. I knew he could help me better than anybody but also I knew that in Argentina, the land of hypocrites, where nobody gets given a second chance, I wanted to be different. He'd made a mistake in the World Cup, sure, but so had I. And we weren't about to trip over that same stone again. That had turned out to be a useful experience for everybody.

I took a few days to settle in. At 7.00 a.m. on that first Sunday in September I woke everyone up shouting: 'We came here to work didn't we? So, let's get to work!' That place was right for it too, Liberman's 'little' farm was a monster, with football pitches, ideal grounds for running in, everything you could ask for. I started a diet once again. And once again, Boca made me suffer: that Sunday they drew with Lanús. At that stage, I was behind Marzolini one hundred per cent. I stated that if he got the sack, I wouldn't return.

From Punta del Este I flew to Buenos Aires; from Buenos Aires – after resting for just a couple of days – to Madrid; from Madrid to Paris; and in Paris, on Monday 18 September, an old dream became reality: I founded the World Union of Footallers. I was supported by a gang, a serious gang, with Eric Cantona at the head of it. He was suspended at the time, like me, and was the first to add his voice to mine. Also there were George Weah, Abedi Pelé, Gianluca Vialli, Gianfranco Zola, Laurent Blanc, Rai, Thomas Brolin, Ciro Ferrara, and Michael Preud'homme ... a first-class team. Our aim was simple but impossible because of the attitude of the directors: we wanted to be heard. Footballers have a voice and a vote and we wanted them to listen once and for all.

From there I sprinted to Istanbul on a private plane, a crazy trip to attend a charity match for the children of Bosnia. I got there just as the match was about to end, did a bit of keepy-uppy,

people applauded me, and off I went again. The following day
I had to be in Korea to start getting ready. Boca were playing a
friendly there which was to mark my return to football. From
Istanbul to London and from London to Seoul. The time was
coming: at last I was going to put on the Boca strip for real.

I was on the other side of the world, but I felt very close to
Boca. I trained alone, but in my mind I was with all the others:
I crossed balls and shouted: 'Run, Cani!' I thought about the
team, where to put each player, Mac Allister, Carrizo, Giunta.
I didn't want to miss the match the lads were playing in Buenos
Aires, against Independiente. I would listen to the match any
way I could, and it was like stepping back in time. In Fiorito
my old man and I used to move the radio about because we kept
losing the signal and we'd end up hearing just a hum. In Barcelona,
I'd hang on the phone and my brothers would hold the radio
up to the other end, and I did the same in Seoul. I got given
one of those phones with speakers and we asked the people at
Radio Mitre to call us; we enjoyed it as if we were back home.
It was another Sunday without success so everyone started talking
about me as the saviour. Truth be told I didn't feel that, but I
knew I could bring some order, make everyone feel more opti-
mistic at least. I was as good as new.

I returned to the pitch, for real, on Saturday 30 September 1995,
at the Olympic stadium in Seoul.

Nothing and no one was missing. President Menem was
there; Bilardo; Menotti was there . . . Each one was doing their
own thing but they were there, with me! The President, who
happened to be in Korea on an official visit, had been the one
to ask me the key question a few months back, planting the
idea of returning to Boca inside me once and for all. El Narigón
and El Flaco, well, now they were both journalists, and it was
hard to expect them to agree on anything. But at least they
were both happy about my return. Boca beat the Korean

national team 2–1 and I played better, much better, than I dreamt I would.

It was the best of all my comebacks, for sure, because I was in better shape than in any of the others and because when I play well I have fun. That night I had so much fun.

I wasn't just happy for myself. I was happy for my daughters. I rang them as soon as we got back to the hotel and we wept like mad, all three of us. Because I was happy for my old girl, my old man, my people. And because a very, very hard year and a half was coming to a close. In Argentina people can be very kind when they want to be kind, but they can also be right motherfuckers. And I had responded there, on the pitch, where I talk. I had shown them that it had been an injustice to keep me from playing for fifteen months, that when I put my balls into something I can run more than anyone. Without drugs, without dope. Because all you need to play football is, always, the ball. Let's see if this is clear; I will repeat it until the blockheads learn it: cocaine is no good for playing football, cocaine pulls you back on the pitch, cocaine kills you.

Saturday 7 October 1995. From the *concentración* at the Hindu club we took the bus to the Bombonera. I was sitting on the front seat, alone. I watched the people waving at us. Suddenly I saw some kids pointing at the River strip on their chest. I thought: This lot are going to throw something at me! But no, far from it. The kids were moving their lips as if they were speaking to a deaf person: '*We love you anyway!*' That was it, that was my biggest triumph.

I forgot everything when I got on the pitch. It was an unbelievable party ... but it killed me when Dalma and Gianinna popped out of a box in the middle of the pitch. It killed me! My legs were shaking, once again. I thanked everyone for their good intentions but the idea of making the girls pop out with a sign that said: DAD, THANKS FOR COMING BACK, when I had my mind totally on the game and on nothing but the game, that killed me. They let the tortoise get away with that one.

Then I looked up, as if to find peace in the sky, and I saw a banner hanging from one of the terraces: CON LA DIEZ? DIOS – WHO IS WITH THE NUMBER TEN? GOD. It took me forty-five minutes to find my feet: I played the first half as if I were a beginner, a debutant, and I made all the same mistakes that up till then I'd been pointing out to the team. I was really hyped up.

All sorts of things happened during that match: I fought with Julio César Toresani, keen to make his name by going for Diego, and we ended up winning 1–0, only just, with a last-minute goal by Darío Scotto. I shouted like never before during a match, because I felt like the manager as well. That idea had never left my head, and because I couldn't turn it into reality I thought I would just go ahead and behave as manager on the pitch. I didn't even think Marzolini might get cross; on the contrary, it was good for him.

I enjoyed hitting long balls and making precision touches. But I also realised there were things I couldn't yet do. For example, I didn't dare shoot at goal from outside the area ... nor from inside. Of course, regardless of my actual performance I was picked for the drugs test. I don't believe it was a coincidence. Before I got there, Caniggia had been picked three times in a row.

At the end, after the match against Colón, at the press conference, someone asked me if I was living again. 'Am I living again? I've never been dead, maestro ...' We all went to a surprise party Cóppola had prepared for me, at the Soul Café, owned by Zorrito Von Quintiero, a great musician and a great friend. It was the opening night of the joint, in the Las Cañitas neighbourhood, but there weren't as many restaurants there then as there are now – we made it famous! I enjoyed it with all my soul: there was a giant screen, they showed the match again and I watched it all. It was like an old-fashioned wedding: my whole family was there, my wife, my daughters, my parents, my parents-in-law, my sisters, my friends, and also a whole bunch of famous guests.

But I was in a championship once again, and I had to get my head down, seven days later I had another game. Not just any game, this was Boca against Argentinos Juniors. Now my nephew Dany was playing there, the son of my sister Ana and my brother-in-law Carlos Lopez. The whole family settled down to watch at the Vélez stadium. My mum was smoking her Marlboro and mouthing off against a newspaper that had published a story saying that she preferred a draw because it was the first time her son and her grandson would face each other. And on Mother's Day!

Dany showed no respect and he fouled me, he nearly vaccinated us. But that night – maybe because of my age, or maybe out of respect – the night was mine. Even though I was playing against kids like Tomatito Pena who was three months old when I played my first game in the first division. I'd played against his dad! He fouled Scotto on the edge of the box; I placed the ball, shot . . . and nailed it in the corner. I swear, I swear I took a few seconds to think about what to do: should I celebrate or not? First I thought not, to be honest, for the sake of my brother-in-law Gabriel, who is fanatical about Argentinos. On that very pitch I'd scored four against Gatti, when we were fighting relegation! And those motherfuckers were whistling at me now, those imbeciles for hire. But then I thought about La Tota, on Mother's Day, her day, and I thanked the Beard who had once again given me the opportunity of giving her something . . . of giving her a goal.

Afterwards, when I went into the changing room and kissed my mum on the lips, I found out that my brother-in-law, El Morsa, had taken on all of the toughest gang of Argentinos fans singlehandedly. He couldn't stand them whistling at me, he couldn't stand it.

＊   ＊   ＊

I was almost thirty-five and I was preparing my birthday party, one of those I like, with all the trimmings. But before that I celebrated with a little bit of football. We had to travel to Córdoba, to play against Belgrano, who had vaccinated Boca the last four times they'd played, and I wanted revenge at all costs. But that week a huge scandal came out, a nasty one, that could only have been generated by Mariana Nannis, Caniggia's wife. Statements coming, statements going, she accused me of fucking up her husband's life when in fact Caniggia was someone I loved from the bottom of my heart. Once again, I was the rotten apple. I think that episode screwed me up more than Cani. It knocked me out, I got really depressed. And I didn't train all week. The only one who managed to pull me out of it, as on so many other occasions, was Cóppola. And that's how I got to Córdoba, in a right state but willing to do anything, as always.

The Cordobese were in a worse state than me, poor people. As in so many parts of the country, the economic situation was bad. For that reason I was pleased I travelled, because they welcomed me with a joy that went beyond football. I don't know if all the people who cheered for me when I landed there were Belgrano fans, but I was so motivated by them that when I went out on to the pitch I felt like I'd trained for a whole month non-stop. I'd also been told that Enrique Nieto, Belgrano's manager, had said to his players: 'Don't go getting your picture taken with Maradona, I don't want starfuckers in my team!' But as soon as they stepped on to the turf they all started coming up to me, slowly, shyly almost, afraid, and asked me for a picture. Every match I played felt like a testimonial. I took such a sense of pride away with me from every stadium. A lot of those players went in hard on me, didn't give me an easy time, and after the match they said to me: 'Diego, we wish you all the luck in the world.' That was priceless to me. Opponents would come up to me and dish out praise: 'You're a phenomenon, Diego', or: 'Diego, if I hack you I won't be allowed back into my home tonight.' But

one of the most prestigious universities in the world, dressed by them in a toga and awarded the title of *Master Inspirer of Dreams*, I was actually thinking of my daughters . . . and my folks, who gave me the education they could.

I returned to Buenos Aires feeling I could fly. Boca was once again a serious contender for the championship.

The 20th of October 1995 marked the nineteenth anniversary of my first game in the first division. After nineteen years I felt the same as I did back in 1976, I swear. The same desire to play, to go out there on the pitch, to win . . . the same.

I was doing too well, better than I thought possible. We played against San Lorenzo next. We drew, but I played well, very well. I had quite a few brushes with El Cabezón Ruggeri and I loved each one of them; it was great because I could take them and because we were two little old men still giving it all we had. That afternoon it wasn't just the Boca fans applauding me, the San Lorenzo fans gave me an ovation too.

And then what I knew might happen, happened. I knew from the start that if I didn't do well all the two-faced stiffs would jump up to say that I was too old, that I was shameful, that I should have retired. But I did do well, and they resorted to making up stuff about me. First, Fernando Miele, San Lorenzo's president, started whingeing, saying the championship had been 'arranged' in our favour. Grondona stopped him in his tracks immediately, but the issue was out on the streets. Then a journalist suggested there had been a positive drug test at Boca. Caniggia wasn't playing so of course all fingers pointed at me. They were like daggers. They knocked me out, they knocked me down once again. And I locked myself in again.

It seemed the more of myself I gave people the more they wanted to get inside my house (the journalists, I mean). 'Maradona reappears' they published, when I would just be walking out of my front door after a difficult week during which I had been unfairly accused over an issue that hurt me a lot, too much. I swear on my daughters' lives, that was in bad faith, bad taste. Even though I was quite thick-skinned by then, it still hurt. It was confirmation that I was always in the eye of the storm, and I no longer wanted to spend my life having to give explanations. I wanted some peace. Was it too much to ask? I know I'm not a saint but who is? It's always the same thing: everyone goes on about role models. Role models my arse! In Argentina we don't have a single living role model so stop breaking my balls about it.

I lived everything very intensely – every training session, every match – and I achieved what I wanted: to beat all the records for box-office takings. There wasn't a single match in which the house wasn't full to the brim. That was my objective and I'd achieved it. We still needed to see if we could crown it with the title; I was going to give my life for that. But in Argentina corruption exists on and off the pitch. And I wasn't going to be the one to knock it on the head.

There were – and possibly still are – managers who asked their players for money in order to play them. I was told by Insúa, Rubén Insúa, that he once didn't join a club because the manager asked him for money and he refused. 'Why don't you make that public?' I asked him. *It's the system*, was his answer. Fuck's sake, what system are we talking about?!

And then there was the issue of the referees, terrible. The clubs were putting enormous pressure on them, they made mistakes, and everybody thought badly of them. They said Boca had everything fixed in their favour. Bollocks! We were winning every game 1–0 and hanging on to the crossbar by the skin of our teeth. We were denied obvious penalties, while Vélez, our main rival, never had one given against them. What was I going to say? That everything was now fixed in their favour? That sort of nonsense meant the refs never knew where they stood. I was going through some difficult and ugly stuff, comparable to what I'd lived through when I left Sevilla and when I left Newell's. I loved – and love – playing football, but if football made my daughters cry I could easily send football to motherfucking hell. Grateful as I am for everything it's given me, which is every-thing I have, still, for me the smiles of Dalmita and Gianinna are way more important than making thirty million Argentinians smile. No comparison.

I still had two years left on my contract at Boca and I was still dreaming of playing in the Copa Libertadores in the second year. For that to become a reality we had to win the domestic championship, and I was more depressed than angry. That wasn't good, because *bronca* has always worked better as an incentive for me. Racing thrashed us 6–4 and knocked us down from the top of the table. The club leadership changed and a young busi-nessman, Mauricio Macri, won the elections and became the new president of Boca. Alegre and Heller had to leave.

It was a very strong blow, too strong. I felt groggy and I didn't recover. I didn't make it to the last match against Estudiantes where we had a minimal chance of winning the title. It was all over.

We started to talk about Marzolini's replacement. He was leaving at the end of the championship. It was when it came to suggesting names that I had my first clash with Macri. 'If Bilardo comes, I leave,' I told him. I was willing to show my face to those who deserved it: the fans. On the night of Tuesday 16 December I entered the coldest and quietest Bombonera I can ever remember. I was fuming; I'd said that would be my last match. I raised my eyes and my arms, as always, looking at our end of the terraces and I saw a load of empty yellow steps. It was hideous. I could read the banners. One said: WHEN WILL THE BUCK STOP? STOP PLAYING WITH THE FANS. STOP THE INTERNAL POLITICS. ENOUGH WITH FILLING YOUR POCKETS WITHOUT WINNING ANY CHAMPIONSHIPS. I felt terrible. I felt this time it was me who'd taken the cat's milk, who'd let them down, all those people who'd packed out the Bombonera every Sunday to see Maradona play, to watch El Diego. When the match was over, a very sad 2–2, those poor five thousand souls who'd put up with it started shouting: *Diego won't be leaving! Diego won't be leaving!* And I decided there and then that I would stay at Boca, with or without Bilardo. For the people, again. I got to the dressing room, I called Cóppola and I said: 'Go on, fix everything.'

In the meantime I'd decided to put some other things in their place. In January 1996 I kickstarted President Menem's campaign 'Sun without Drugs' and I confessed my addiction to cocaine. I did it for the kids, above all else. I said: 'I have been, am and always will be a drug addict', to confirm to everybody, in case they didn't know, that in our country there were – and still are – a lot of drugs. Unlike most people who think it will never affect them, I know that drugs exist everywhere and I didn't want, nor will I ever want, kids to get hold of them. I have two daughters, haven't I? So it seemed right to say all that. It was my duty as a father and it was my duty to myself. I'm not a hypocrite. I left myself exposed. The drugs trade is too big for Maradona to stop it. Let's make this clear: the powers-that-be don't want to stop the drugs trade, and today, on this subject, I am nothing more than a smokescreen, an escape route, a distraction.

I felt as if my head was split in two: on the one hand, the campaign took up a lot of my time and a lot of travelling; on the other, I was trying to concentrate on my return to working with Boca and my re-encounter with Bilardo. I was clear from the start: everything was going to be just fine with El Narigón because I put all my cards on the table and everyone understood the rules of the game. But I also wanted to make it clear that I had accepted Bilardo as manager only because of the fans. Once again, as with Marzolini, I'd given in because of the people. I did ask the fans to be alert, though, because I wasn't made of iron and if anything happened, *chau* . . . bye bye. When I said 'if anything happened' I meant: 'Don't take me off if you've just made me go on with painkilling jabs', which was what he'd done in Sevilla. But Bilardo was in good shape, crazier than ever but in good shape!

The problem now was coming from elsewhere. I'd never had a good relationship with Mauricio Macri, mainly because of the fact that he used to say we were workers and our job was the same, the same as selling cars. He had never in his fucking life been inside a changing room, unless his father had bought him one as a present.

I had already agreed that I would join pre-season training late, so I was in Punta del Este when a journalist friend called me to see how I was doing and to tell me about the trouble at Boca's training ground. A huge scrap had broken out over the prize money. Macri had already been round saying stupid things like: *If you like it fine and if not, fine too.* Or even worse: *We'll pull the blinds down and that's that.* I didn't hesitate for a minute. I hired a private plane at Punta del Este and flew off. An hour and a half later, there I was with the lads sorting everything out. And we sorted it. We sat down with the directors and we told them what we thought. They listened to Mono Navarro Montoya, to Carlos 'El Colarado' Mac Allister and, above all, to me. I was the squad's representative, the captain. I asked them for respect, I asked them to win the players over. I advised them to do things in such a way that we could trust them.

But things weren't that clear-cut. I started playing in the summer tournament against Racing, against Independiente, and after that we were due to fly out to Mendoza, to play against River, towards the end of January '96.

I had a prior commitment to the 'Sun without Drugs' campaign and I warned Bilardo that I might not make it to Mendoza and that he should start getting a possible replacement ready. He understood it better than anyone. He'd said to me: 'I need a solution for this team when you're not here, I have to find a way round this ... and I will.' At the time I was bothered by some stuff which had nothing to do with timing: I had a slight pull in a muscle which was bothersome and I also felt that the directors were lying to me. Yes, that they were lying to me. So I lost it: I hated it when they fucked with me.

After my Mendoza absence, I explained to Macri why I hadn't been there and put myself at his disposal, which was the right thing to do. We were both interviewed at the same time on a radio programme, and we were on air when the journalist asked me: 'Why didn't the fans hear earlier that you weren't going to play?'

'"Earlier" seems to me to be bullshit. I said I wasn't going to play the summer matches and I was there against Independiente and Racing nevertheless. It's not me who should matter here, what should matter is the jersey, otherwise, with all due respect, Argentinos, All Boys, Ferro would be playing. This tournament is for the biggest clubs in Argentine football . . .'

And that's when Macri intervened. On air. He said we shouldn't be too humble, this, that and the other. He asked me how much effort it would have been to let people know; and declared that if I was injured I could have said . . . What!? I got into position and went for him studs up: 'This isn't something to discuss on the radio. I think you're way out of line, Mauricio. This is something we should talk about among ourselves and now you're trying to turn the people against me. Because the one who decides who starts and who doesn't play with five minutes to go is Bilardo. And you can ask Bilardo and sack both of us if you like, otherwise we'll carry on doing things the way we like or the way Bilardo likes. I don't want to talk for fear of being out of order, but now you're out of order . . . goodbye.' And I put the phone down. I'd told him to go fuck himself! It wasn't a good climate.

In spite of everything I returned to working with the team. We played a friendly against Armenia, which was part of Caniggia's contract, and for the first time I felt that I was being whistled at, that the Boca fans were whistling me.

After that we went down south, to San Martín de los Andes, to do some sort of pre-season training, and it did all of us a lot of good to get a bit of distance from the madness. But all the same I told anyone who would listen that all the stuff about me and Macri having a really bad relationship wasn't a rumour, it was a reality. I defined it with very few words: he was born to very rich parents and I was born to very poor ones. Let people draw their own conclusions.

We had no choice but to carry on seeing each other. Once he turned up at Ezeiza, where we trained, dressed as a player. He wanted to indulge his whim, the bastard, he wanted to play with his employees. He was in my team, up front, paired with Caniggia. We won 1–0, I scored, and when I was asked for my opinion I was blunt: as a footballer . . . he's a good businessman.

When I stopped fighting I started playing. Although it was also a struggle on the pitch, truth be told. That team was more up for biting than for winning the championship. We were good enough only for fourth or fifth place.

For real – for points, I mean – the Bilardo–Maradona era kicked off with a goalfest: 8 March, Vélez stadium, we scored four against Gimnasia y Esgrima de Jujuy. I scored the first, from a penalty. Afterwards it was just a matter of getting the ball to Caniggia. Cani was in such good form he won matches singlehandedly. Against Platense, against Lanús. And still Passarella refused to call him up for the national squad. He wouldn't call Batistuta either. He was leaving out the best two forwards in Argentinian football.

We fought any way we could. If I had to define myself at that point I would say I was a talented little old man: I could play the ball long, I made some good passes, did a little dribbling, but I was finding it hard to finish in the box, very hard. Would we have gone further if I'd scored any of the five penalty kicks I missed in a row during those fatal six months? How can I know? The only thing I can think of is that those five curses ended up marking me during a forgettable era.

Everything started in Rosario, against Newell's, on 13 April 1996. We were unbeaten up to that point, and we hadn't conceded many. That night everything went wrong for me: the goalie saved my penalty, and on top of that I got another pull in my leg. I had to go off, I couldn't stand the pain. And some thermos-head in the crowd booed me. They didn't believe me! They didn't believe I was injured. How was that possible? I felt I had a tennis ball in my leg and some idiot doubted me.

I took a while to come back, partly because of the boos and partly for other reasons. I saw things differently from Bilardo, and not being out there on the pitch, I found it harder to bear. We had Kily Gonzalez, Juan Sebastian Verón, Caniggia. We needed balance at the back and who better for that than Pepe Basualdo? But Bilardo was stubborn, he wouldn't play him. I found it hard to come back.

When I did it was against Argentinos. We scored four, and started looking at the table from a different viewpoint. Or at least the rest of the team did because I pulled another muscle and had to stop again. Until we played against Belgrano at the Bombonera, on June the 9th, and, motherfuckers, upon my return came the curse of the penalty: Labarre saved it. What despair. I was walking back up to the middle of the pitch and heard *Maradooó, Maradooó* cool and quiet, as if to forgive me but not too much. What I could hear behind me, from the terraces, hurt. But not as much as what I knew was going on in the VIP box to my side. I knew Claudia and the girls would be weeping. In the end I saved the day, as the match was ending, just as we were going to have to settle for a useless draw. I got the ball right beneath the VIP boxes and ballooned it over all the players. It landed behind Labarre and went in at the far post. I vaccinated them, the lot of them. The Beard had given me a hand once again.

But I could see that I would not be able to enjoy my come-back in peace. I had the Beard on my side but the devil had crossed our path ... no, not the devil, worse still: a referee called Castrilli. That Sunday night, 16 June at the Vélez stadium, deter-mined how my story with Boca would end. We were playing against our main direct rivals in the struggle for the championship and we were beating them, really beating them. I played half an hour of the best football I had played since my comeback. Cani, a genius as ever, a saviour, headed the first goal, just fifteen minutes into the game. And I was moving the ball about, from here to there ... I even put a back-heeled flick past them! But whereas I stuck Vélez with a back-heeled flick that even their fans applauded, we had a hand stuck into our pockets. Vélez were awarded a goal, a free kick and a penalty, and none of them were valid. None of them!

After the penalty, two minutes before the end of the first half, I went mad. If it had been just up to me, I would've smashed Castrilli's mouth in, but, thinking of the others, I treated him with respect. I stood in front of him with my hands behind my back, and I asked him why he had sent me off. He wouldn't answer, so I begged: 'Please, we're human beings, tell me why!' But he still wouldn't answer, so I shouted at him: 'What's the matter with you? Are you dead?' And I had a fit, an actual fit, I nearly fainted. Of course, I was picked for the drug test. 'What about him? Why don't you test him for drugs?' I asked everyone, but nobody answered. They were probably afraid of being sent off. Once again we were looking at the title through a telescope. If we'd won that game, we would have gone on straight to the title. And that really would have been the retirement I deserved.

I was back to play against Central, on the night of Saturday 29 June, in the Gigante de Arroyito stadium in Rosario. We won, the team played quite well and so did I, but I missed another penalty. The third in a row. It was a disgrace, yeah, but a disgrace that was starting to break my balls.

The same thing happened against River two weeks later. Everything that night had a different flavour, though: my penalty hit the post, sure, but we scored four against the hens! One from Basualdo and a hat-trick from Cani, who was unstoppable. I still felt Vélez was the better team but we were improving every game ... El Narigón had found a team: Mono Navarro Montoya in goal; Gamboa as *líbero*; Fabbri and El Colorado

Mac Allister at the back; Basualdo and Kily Gonzalez in the midfield out wide; Fabi Carrizo in the centre; La Brujita Verón all over the place; Caniggia and Tchami – black and white – up front ... and me? I played where I could, supporting. I think at this stage I was mainly a presence. Our rivals respected me.

After that *super-clasico* we went to China to play a couple of friendlies which were going to contribute towards my transfer fee. It was an incredible trip to a place where I never imagined I would be so well known ... I couldn't even walk in peace around the Forbidden City! I thought that trip was good for the team but El Narigón was in a state, because our good run was coming to an end.

Then I received an incredible offer. Considering I was thirty-five it was probably the most important of my whole life: twenty million dollars to play in Japan for two years. Aside from the money, there were a lot of other factors that made the idea of leaving tempting. I didn't like the way Boca built its youth divisions by buying kids from other clubs in Argentina, for example. But love was stronger and I also knew I wouldn't swap running a victory lap at the Bombonera holding my daughters' hands for all the gold in the world. That had no price.

It had no price and I just gave it away. Fuck's sake! Again it was Racing who ruined our party. On the night of 7 August – a terrible night to be honest – Piojo López vaccinated us; I missed my fifth penalty in a row and everything came crashing down, again. In the dressing room I burst into tears. I knew I wouldn't have many opportunities left to turn my final dream into reality. The championship was over for us and I wanted to die. A week later, on 11 August, I went out on to the pitch to play against Estudiantes, certain it would be my last match wearing the Boca strip. Dalma and Gianinna had wept a lot after that match against Racing. They'd never seen me so sad. I felt the weight of everything that had happened to Boca that season, the good and the bad, on my shoulders.

It would be eleven months before I would wear the Boca strip again. Eleven months! Too long ... This time, maybe as a rebelliousness, I made the decision. Me myself alone. This time it wasn't the powerful men of football.

If there was a powerful man who ruined those days for me it was Judge Hernán Bernasconi – responsible for depriving my friend Guillermo Cóppola of his freedom,* and therefore me of my peace of mind. It was a terrible blow. The only thing that interested me, the most important, was that justice be carried out.

I spent almost a year doing all sorts of things and having all sorts of things happen to me, except playing football. It was so crazy that I can hardly remember them at all. It's like I've obliterated that whole period.

I went to Switzerland first. It was a trip organised by Cóppola, on a Sunday night, straight after that last game against Estudiantes. There was a clinic where they would be able to help me get off drugs, or that's what they'd told Cóppola. And the place seemed serious until, two days after I got there, the doctor who was treating me gave a press conference and revealed everything about me, right down to my blood group. Two-faced bastard! At least I had the peace of mind that the drug test taken after the match against Estudiantes had been negative.

My thirty-sixth birthday was one of the saddest in my life. I was back in Buenos Aires and chose to train with the Boca lads, to make it pass as quickly as possible.

I confess: I didn't know whether I was coming or going. One day I would say I wanted to play for Boca, the next that I wanted to retire for ever. Then I would say I wanted to leave the country. It sounded contradictory, I know, but I now realise why: I didn't know how to live without playing football. Even the exhibition games that kept coming up all over the world weren't enough. The last one of these, at the end of '96, was in Montevideo, at

---

* Guillermo Cópolla was arrested on cocaine charges in late 1996.

the Centenario stadium. And it opened the door for another comeback, but a comeback for real. Peñarol of Montevideo, no less, had taken the bait. Without meaning it to, it awakened my desire to wear the Boca strip once more. Even if it now belonged to Nike, even if it now had a little white line between the blue and the yellow, even though it looked more like a Michigan University sweatshirt. It was Boca's strip, and I loved it.

In the meantime I organised another meeting of the World Footballers' Union. Di Stéfano, Cruyff, Socrates, Zidane, Stoichkov, Klinsmann, Weah, each one of those babies was there! That was in February, when Boca was being managed by Héctor 'El Bambino' Veira. Bilardo had already left.

When I returned, the push and pull with Boca started. It was exhausting, awful. So much so that in early April, on a trip to Chile – I'd been invited by a TV programme over there – I had such a downer that I had to be wheeled out of the studio in a wheelchair. To me that was a warning, an alarm bell. On the 22nd I signed a new contract with Boca. I no longer gave a fuck if the strip had a little white tick or not, the team was in a state, the fans worse, and I wanted to lend a hand. I had a load of tests done on me; the machine was in working order in spite of everything, and I pushed forward. In June, I went to Canada and I hired Ben Johnson. Yes, Ben Johnson! The fastest man on earth, whatever anyone says. He was a phenomenon, and he helped me a lot.

On 9 July 1997, when I returned to play for Boca, in a match that was a party against Newell's, I weighed under seventy-five kilos. I was flying. That afternoon I scored from a free kick. The legend lived on. I played one of the last matches of the Clausura tournament, against Racing, and got seriously ready to kick off the Apertura. Seriously ready! And I started poking into what I know about, just like I had done at Napoli: who we should buy, who we needed to bring to Boca, who wasn't good enough. I'd like to state for the record that it was me who bought Martin Palermo to Boca. Nowadays, I would have made a percentage from the deal. I'd have given that money to the Boca fans, of course, but I regret that I didn't invest money of my own. If I had, Palermo would be a little mine.

My story with Boca ended with a new positive drug test, bang on the first fixture of the Apertura championship that was to be my last one, on 24th August, against Argentinos Juniors of all teams.

So I gave up, the truth is I gave up. I felt I was being handed a gun to kill myself. My addiction was enough of a cross to bear; this was too much. I knew about cocaine. How could I not know? It was a cancer I'd been dragging around with me for fifteen years. I was more careful about cocaine than about wetting my bed. I was going to take cocaine immediately before a match? Please! If that's what I was after I'd go to a nightclub.

But I returned, once more. The judiciary granted me an injunction. I was allowed to play again. I played against Newell's, scored from a penalty, we won. The derby against River was coming up, at the Monumental, and I wanted to be there. I wanted to be there! I played for forty-five minutes, but I played. We won Boca style, turned the game around, it ended 2–1. I enjoyed it a lot, such a lot. I never thought that would be my last match.

Five days later, on 30 October 1997, my thirty-seventh birthday, amid rumours about my drug test, about whether or not I'd been taking dope, someone had the bright idea of putting out the rumour that my father had died. I woke up, I went mad, looked for a phone, called my house, spoke to La Tota . . .

'Ma, ma, what's happened to Dad, what's happened?'

'Nothing, Pelu . . . He's here. Why?'

That was it. I said, 'Enough'. I had started with this, with this football thing, because of a dream I had. And I had continued, afterwards, for my family. I felt the time had come to stop making them suffer. And I said goodbye to football. For ever? I could never say that.

At a Glance

My Loved Ones; the Stars

They say that I can't keep quiet, that I talk about everything, and it's true. They say I fell out with the Pope. It's true. I'm expected not to have opinions, am I, just because I'm from Villa Fiorito? I am the voice of the voiceless, the representative of the people. I'm one of them, no different. It's just that I get microphones shoved in my face, and I get the chance to speak for them. No one's given those people a chance in their whole fucking lives. Let's see if we can get this point across once and for all: I am El Diego.

So yes, I fell out with the Pope. I went to the Vatican and I saw that the ceilings were made of gold. And I heard the Pope saying the church takes care of poor children, but if so, sell the ceiling, tiger. Do something! You've got nothing going for you. You were only a goalkeeper.

I met the Pope. It was disappointing. He gave a rosary to my mum, La Tota. He gave a rosary to Claudia. When it came to my turn he said to me, in Italian, 'This one's special, just for you.' I was very nervous. I said thank you. I couldn't get any other words out. As we walked around I asked my old girl to show me hers, and it was the same as mine. So I said to La Tota, 'No, mine is special, the Pope told me it was special.' I went back to him and asked him, 'Excuse me, Your Holiness, what is the difference between mine and my mother's?' He didn't answer. He just looked at me, gave me a little pat on the back, smiled dies, and she leaves for the funeral at four in the morning. So I don't like to compare her with anybody because she's unique! She's a jewel, she's my jewel.

She was the one who always kept calm. If at any given moment, with all that happened, she'd lost it, as could happen to any woman in the world . . . I don't know, I don't know what would have happened to me, how and where I would have ended up.

She stood by me, always did. When I arrived in Cuba I was dead, do you understand? And she put up with me, because she has a strong personality, a great temperament, otherwise I wouldn't have been able to make it, no one would have been able to cope. I want this understood: she's not some poor victim, pitiful, running after Maradona. She's not just some trophy wife. She's the dearest love of a man called Diego Armando Maradona, when times are good and when times are bad, in the glory and the agony. And she's always there, always. That's why, when so many ask how she stands me, how she stays with me in spite of everything, how she can put up with me going out all the time and all that, I say that, well, everyone goes out! Everyone goes out but nobody gets their picture taken like I do. I don't have to make up excuses, like so many blokes do in order to go out cheating. I let her know. I go out with her permission, you know? My life is like this, I chose her and she chose me.

There's a phrase of hers which prompted me to write her a song, back in the US, after the damned ephedrine fiasco. Some journalists came up to her and asked her what was she going to do from then on. She never gives interviews but she answered them: *Without him, I'd die.* And it seems to me that that is eternal love, total. *Without him, I'd die!* she said. Do you see?

She's the mother of my daughters. An earth mother who coped with travelling alone, alone, to Buenos Aires to give birth, because I wanted my daughters to be born in Argentina. And those who think they know everything about me, did they know why I wasn't present at the birth of either of my daughters? I wasn't out partying, OK? I was in Italy, playing football, keeping to my contracts, piling up so many matches that I had the most number of appearances of any foreign player in the league during those years. When Dalma was born, on 2 April 1987, I was training to play against Empoli. And when Gianinna came, on 16 May 1989, I had just been on the subs bench, on the subs bench!, against Roma and was about to go on the pitch against Torino. One detail which has to be acknowledged, they both came with bread under their arms: with Dalma came the first *scudetto* and with Gianinna the UEFA Cup. But the fact that I didn't meet my daughters until much later than most fathers do doesn't make me feel like a hero; on the contrary. If today, with everything I've lived through and everything that's happened to me, there's anyone with the right to reprimand me for anything, it would be my daughters.

People take the piss because I say I do everything for the girls? Fuck them! My daughters know who I am, they know all my virtues and all my defects.

And my folks have the right to reprimand me too. Don Diego and Doña Tota. Or my sisters ... but they don't do it, they don't and won't. And do you know why? Because they love me the way I am. Because my dad is the most straighforward guy in the world, and I wish there were more people like him; the world would be a better place, much better. Because for my old girl, I'm still her favourite, like when I was a boy. Once she was at our house when Claudia and I had a row, you know, like couples do, nothing serious. And Claudia said she was going to take my keys away from me, so I wouldn't be able to get in again. La Tota jumped down her throat: *You know in my house my boy's still got his room waiting for him!*

That's why I've said that I can't be as bad as people make out; I can see it in the eyes of my sisters, in the way they look at me. How they love me. Ana is fifty now and we still kiss each other on the lips, we need each other. I talk to them and ask how is La Ana, how is La Rita, how is La Mary, how is La Caly

... I bought a very big house because the Beard gave me the opportunity, because he said: 'You'll all be able to fit in here.' And more than once I've said it's probably because we all have the memory of a tiny room, a room smaller than the kitchen of my current apartment, a room where we all slept, all eight of us. So, what are they talking about now, what are they coming to say to me, what are they judging me for?

Today I have with me the people I love, the ones I want with me. I would only ask to recover two friendships, just that, two friends I've lost in my life. I'd like to get my brothers Lalo and El Turco back. I don't want to go into it, but I feel today that I no longer have them as friends. And that's something that makes me want to cry. Because I have them as brothers, sure, but I want them as friends. But, because of a number of things we disagreed about – and maybe I was wrong – I lost them ... I let them go. I'd love to get them back, even if we're little old men, so we can hang out again, be friends once again.

But back to football. If I was forced to pick my ideal squad, for example, from 1976 to 1997, when I retired, I'd be in a fine mess. But what the hell, I'll get myself into a mess, like I always do, even though nobody's forcing my hand. As always, you get it, don't you? *Ha, ha* ...

So, in my squad five would be in the starting line-up without question: Fillol, Passarella, Kempes, Caniggia, and ... me. I would play friends and I would play monsters. To play alongside those five names I'd add Juan Simón, for the part he played in that fantastic team in '79, in Japan. Tarantini because in my mind he was a phenomenon, he had balls. Valdano because he was and is as intelligent off the pitch as he was on it. Ruggeri because he always pressed forward, from when he was a kid; Burruchaga because he understood me like few others. Checho Batista because he didn't need to run to win possession. El Negro Enrique because as he says he initiated the move that resulted in my goal against the

English. Olarticoechea because he really played in every position and well ... I could include so many: Barbas, Pasculli, Giusti, Gallego. Pelado Díaz, why not? And I would play Bocha Bochini, my idol from those early years.

And of course many friends as well. Some names may not mean much to people, some will, but for me they were all important, very important, more than just as players. Negro Carrizo from Argentinos; Tabita García, also from El Bicho; Guaso Domenech, another one from La Paternal.

Friends, friends, friends. Like Caniggia, because I consider myself to be Cani's friend, although I don't know if he would say the same about me. And I have a lot of respect for El Colorado Mac Allister and great admiration for the Colombian Bermúdez. I said that if he ever returned to Boca he should be the captain and he eventually was; obviously Bianchi heard me.

I cannot forget one who encapsulates them all, Alfredo Di Stéfano. I had the honour of meeting him once, at some awards ceremony. I love him, he loves me, in spite of the age difference, we see things the same way. Once, in 1988, I invited him on to a TV show I had in Napoli. When the time came to introduce him I got really emotional: I was so moved. In Argentina, before I went to play in Spain, I'd heard a lot about Alfredo, but I hadn't quite grasped how immense a figure he is in world football. I only discovered that when I got to Spain, when I played at Barcelona. That's where I understood what an ambassador for Argentinian football he had been. For me he's the greatest in history and I'll put my name to that claim. I said that to him once and he answered in proper Buenos Aires tango slang: *Get away, kid, you're only saying that because you're a pal.* Just like Aníbal Troilo, our greatest accordion player, used to say.

But I was saying it because I was convinced it was true: he's the greatest. In Italy everyone was arguing about whether I was better or worse than Pelé; in Spain there's no room for

questions about Pelé or Di Stéfano, nobody dares discuss it even
– there's no contest. I agree with the Spanish.

The press once asked Alfredo what differences existed between
him and me. The Maestro said: 'Technically, individually, Diego
is superior to me. Everything he does with his feet, with his
head, with his body, I'd be incapable of doing. I didn't have as
much skill, but I played all over the pitch, across its entire length
and width. Diego could do that with the right training.' A
phenomenon, that old guy! He was standing next to me when
France Football gave me one of my favourite awards: a boot clad
in precious stones, as recognition of my career. They'd given
Alfredo one too, for best European player of all time. I feel . . .
I feel close to Alfredo, for many reasons. I used to dream of
being managed by him when he had a Boca team in his hands.
In the '69/'70 season he had some lovely boys playing for him!
Rojitas, whom I loved; I had a poster of him in my room in
Fiorito. Muñeco Madurga, Tano Novello, the Peruvian Meléndez
. . . I was a snotty kid, I wasn't even ten years old, but Dad used
to take me to the terraces. I'd fallen in love with Pocho Pianetti.
I'd fix my eyes on him from the moment he left the tunnel and
I followed his every move for ninety minutes. For me Pocho
Pianetti was a tremendous player, he kicked like an animal, but
he played like the best.

Many years later I clashed with Alfredo. He was manager and
I was player. It was the Nacional '81, at the Bombonera, in the
morning: River beat us 3–2 but I managed to put one past Fillol.
Perotti gave me the ball on the left, I dummied, made as though
I was going to cross it and I saw Fillol betting on the far post,
waiting for it to go that way. So I didn't hesitate: I hit it hard,
straight into the hole left between Pato and the near post. By
the time he reacted, the ball was already in. The funniest thing
was that later Pato said he slipped!

We continued to face each other in Spain when he was manager
of Real Madrid, although between us it was really just a football

matter. He had me marked in two ways: first he tried zonal marking, but they could never catch me out; then he got Sanchíz to stick himself to me like a clam, but I drove him mad. In '83, in a great final, we won the Copa del Rey. They also beat us, they did. But we both thought the same way, you can have all the tactics in the world, but the ones who really make the difference are the players.

There are players who have delighted me, who have, I confess, disappointed me too, and there are too many to try to create the perfect team. It seems easier just to throw out some names. Ping-pong is what they call it, right? Well, I'm actually going to hit the ball against the wall, first with my left, then with my right. Here it goes, *pic, pac, pic, pac* . . . One hundred shots. It's not a ranking, eh? I'm numbering them just to show that there are a hundred names, a hundred players, and a few words about each one. And it's only one hundred. There are so many more – I could have filled another book!

1. **Pelé:** as a player he was the best, but he didn't use his talent to glorify football. He thought politically. He thought he could be the president of Brazil. And I don't believe that a footballer, or an ex-footballer, should think about being president of a country. I would have liked him to propose that he preside over an organisation which defended players' rights, like I did. I would have liked him to look after Garrincha instead of letting him die broke. I would have liked him to fight against the actions of the powers-that-be which were damaging for us players. I've never compared myself to him, I've always maintained that, and I'll say it again here. And when I say that I don't compare myself to him, I'm not just talking about football matters. I've had the opportunity to meet him many times. The first, in 1979, was when *El Gráfico* took me to Rio to meet him. Later, we met

in testimonial matches, that kind of thing. The last time
we saw each other was in '95, when we had the opportunity to go into business together. We just never clicked,
we always rubbed each other up the wrong way; we would
see each other and sparks would fly.

2.   **Roberto Rivelinho:** I've always mentioned him in terms
of being one of the greatest and many people are
surprised. I don't know why. He performed on the pitch
with such elegance, such rebelliousness. The things I'm
told about Rivelinho are incredible. He also rebelled
against the powerful. I fell in love with the player and,
when I met him, the man seduced me, too. There's a
wonderful story that captures him from head to toe. It
turns out that he was in Brazil's *concentración* in Mexico
'70. Doing nothing, because those guys didn't need to
do anything to play. And so there he was, sitting around
with Gerson and Tostao . . . Then Pelé shows up. And
they thought: *This fucker, what can we say to him? He
does everything right, the son of a bitch.* So Rivelinho,
who always had an answer for everything, thought of
what to say. He looked Pelé straight in the eyes, he was
already the best in the world, and said: 'Tell me the
truth, you would have liked to be left-footed, right?'

3.   **Johann Cruyff:** I only got to see him in the twilight of
his career but I thought he was a fantastic player. He
was faster than everybody else, both physically and
mentally, and that's what he drew his advantage from.
He could accelerate like Caniggia, from 1 to 100 kilometres per hour, and then he'd slam on the brakes. And
his vision, the way he could see the whole pitch was
amazing. It's a shame he said some stupid things about
me without knowing me well at all.

4.   **Angel Clemente Rojas:** Rojitas! I had a picture of him
pinned to my wall in Fiorito. I loved how he moved his

waist, his dummies. Of course, at my house we were all Boca fans. Later on I caught the Bochini bug, but the first, the very first player I looked to, was Rojitas.

5. **Ubaldo Matildo Fillol:** simply the best goalkeeper I've ever seen in my life.

6. **Daniel Alberto Passarella:** the best defender I ever saw in my life, too. The best at heading the ball, and at both ends, something that Argentine football is missing these days. What goes on between us off the pitch has nothing to do with what I think of him as a footballer.

7. **Mario Alberto Kempes:** a phenomenon as a man, I love him, and as a player, too. We're all very grateful to El Flaco Menotti for the World Cup win of '78 and that's fine; but we've been very ungrateful to Mario. He was the top goalscorer, the soul of the team, everything . . . We've been unfair to him. He deserves a tribute in Argentina instead of having to run all over the world, coaching here and there. I love him.

8. **René Orlando Houseman:** *El Loco* was the greatest I ever saw in terms of skill, dribbling, inventiveness. René had fun with the ball and few do that today. One memory of him stands out in particular, and it's a story that fills me with pride, because it shows the trust there was when I was young, because he realised that I was like him; we shared the same background. In '78, whenever he got drunk, he would call me from wherever he was drinking and ask me to carry him on my back, piggyback, and I would haul him up to his room on the second floor. Bertoni and I would sit with him and he wouldn't let me leave the room until he was asleep: he wanted me to talk to him. For me, that's one of the unforgettable things that football has given me, the best people in football. I was willing to buy a ticket just to see El Loco's genius at work.

9. **Michel Platini:** great skill, a phenomenon. In Italy, he won everything, but it always seemed to me that he didn't have fun playing football. He was cold, too cold.

10. **Hristo Stoichkov:** he became a great player in Spain when he was at Barcelona. Before that he was just a goalscorer, but later he became a phenomenon. And he was a great guy, a great person.

11. **Antonio Cabrini:** I always liked him. He was a pretty son of a bitch. In Italy they called him 'Il Fidanzato d'Italia', Italy's fiancé. He could give you hell on the pitch, he could create havoc when he played, he played so well.

12. **Antonio Careca:** a phenomenon and a friend. One of the best partners I had in my career.

13. **Zico:** a director of games. They chucked Pelé's number 10 jersey at him and it fitted like a glove, no problem. He had the authority of a great leader. A sensational bloke and a fantastic player.

14. **Enzo Francescoli:** he didn't need to be World Champion to earn his place among the greatest in the world, with nothing and no one to envy. As a bloke, the best. I feel he is my friend.

15. **José Luis Chilavert:** I think he's a great goalkeeper, but I don't go with those who say one thing today and another tomorrow. When they sentenced him,* I actually called him because it seemed too harsh and I thought that an injustice was being committed in my country.

*On 3 April 1994, after a match between Gimnasia y Esgrima de la Plata and Vélez, a battle took place involving players and fans from both teams. Several players were sanctioned by AFA but only two were charged in a court of law. Chilavert, one of the two, received a harsher sentence. The prosecutor claimed as a foreigner he was more duty bound to obey the law of the land, which in turn led to a debate in Argentina about xenophobia, with several members of the judiciary arguing that the issue of nationality should not influence the harshness of the sentence.

But for him to come and tell me how I should live in my own country is too much. He's not my kind of person, but I have to admit that he's one hell of a goalie and when it comes to free kicks he counts as another forward, because he can really shoot. Although he's nothing new: Higuita was the first.

16. **Ronaldo:** the kid's a great player, but he got caught up in the whole fame bandwagon. And those advertising contracts drove it into his head that he had to be World Champion so badly that before the final in France '98 he had an attack of . . . asthma? I don't believe that. The kid didn't get a touch. He was eaten up by the anxiety of having to play well and it's not his fault, we can all play badly. But they demanded that he score and go out swinging his Nike boots like a lasso. They filled his head with so much stuff that they consumed him. But he got over it. I still don't think he has surpassed Romario or Rivaldo, though.

17. **Marco Van Basten:** a goal-scoring machine that broke down just when he was about to become the best of all time. He was brilliant, anyway, but he never made it to number one.

18. **Romario:** A great player, I'm very fond of him. I've never seen a finisher like him. I've seen him do incredible things inside the box: terribly quick. When he went for goal, he vaccinated. I've never had doubts about him. He's on my dream team.

19. **Edmundo:** He's mad, but his madness is nice, and he's a fantastic player. I didn't agree with Batistuta when he got angry because Edmundo went off to the carnival in Rio and missed a Fiorentina match. It was in his contract, and Brazilians are like that: when I played in Italy, they all disappeared at carnival time: Falçao, Toninho Cerezo. Only us Argentinians would be left, because we have less carnival than a Buddhist retreat.

20. **Paolo Maldini:** another great player who chose the wrong profession. He should have been an actor; he's too pretty to play football.
21. **Ruud Gullit:** a bull. He was brute strength rather than technical skill but he made up for everything with his power and physical preparation.
22. **Christian Vieri:** he's a gypsy. He moves from one team to another, getting richer every time. He's scored goals everywhere, but I can't say if he's one of the greats.
23. **Gabriel Omar Batistuta:** an animal. An animal who, thank God, is Argentinian. Our football doesn't know how to appreciate him, and if those of us who wanted him hadn't made the fuss we did, Passarella wouldn't have taken him to the World Cup in 1998.
24. **Roberto Baggio:** Il Divino (the divine one, that's what they call him in Italy) is a great player. Even though he never really took off fully.
25. **Paul Gascoigne:** He started out looking like he'd be a major player, and at his best, he was. But then he got stuck, he went off the rails.
26. **Gary Lineker:** a great goalscorer, but he didn't fulfil his potential.
27. **Zinedine Zidane:** I want to defend him, because he has such extraordinary vision, but he looks to me as if he feels less like playing every day that goes by. He's just like Platini: he doesn't have fun. They both lack joy when they play.
28. **Alessandro del Piero:** there you have it. This one's the opposite of Zidane: he likes to play, he feels it in his soul. Between him and the French guy, I choose this one.
29. **Michael Owen:** for me, the only good thing to come out of the '98 World Cup. Speed, cunning, balls. I hope injury doesn't destroy him.

30. **Lothar Matthäus:** the best rival I had in my whole career. I think that's probably enough to describe him.

31. **Jorge Alberto Valdano:** an extraordinary guy with whom I've always loved and always will love playing football and talking. For ever.

32. **Ricardo Enrique Bochini:** he was my idol. Watching him play drove me crazy with delight. When he came in against Belgium in the World Cup, the first thing I did was look for him and pass him the ball. I remember I said: 'It was like playing a one-two with God.'

33. **Claudio Paul Caniggia:** I love him like a brother. I felt the need to protect him as soon as I saw him. His change of gear is something I've never seen in anyone else. He replaced me in the heart of the people.

34. **Alemão:** I had wanted Checho Batista, not Alemão at Napoli. But then the Brazilian showed me what he was worth. A great player.

35. **Michel Laudrup:** he was one of the ones I liked the most Mexico '86. He had a one-touch game, made it look very easy.

36. **Hugo Sánchez:** he was a good player inside the box. But I couldn't get into all those pirouettes he did every time he scored. He played to the crowd too much.

37. **Emilio Butrageño:** a deadly midget, a guy I would have really liked to play with. He and Valdano picked holes in any defence they encountered. They were a terrific duo.

38. **Paolo Rossi:** a counter-attack artist. The Italian knew exactly what the score was and in Spain '82 he had a ball. But he was one of those who said they could never play for Napoli; he was too posh.

39. **Oscar Ruggeri:** El Cabezón is a winner. Ever since he was a kid he has always gone forward. He's really got the balls for it.

40. **Sergio Javier Goycochea:** a sensational guy. He saved us all in Italia '90. Argentinians love him.

41. **René Higuita:** a beautiful character, a madman, a *loco*. I've said it before: he was the one who invented the idea that goalies could take penalty kicks, free kicks and also score goals. So don't anybody try to steal his patent, understood?

42. **Juan Sebastian Verón:** one of the best players we have in Argentina. He plays a really open game and has a strong personality. He let the tortoise get away with some of the things he said about me, he let it get away badly, very badly. That's why it's now an issue with no solution.

43. and 44. **Javier Saviola and Pablo Aimar:** I love these two, shame they play for River. They're so fast. Poor Saviola – they tried to do his head in with the idea that he was the new Maradona. Saviola is Saviola; stop busting his balls.

45. **Juan Román Riquelme:** I like him a lot, he carried the load of the number 10 for Boca. It was hard for him at first because he has a special style, but he kept at it and kept at it ... and he was crucial. He doesn't have the speed I had, that short sprint with which I could tip the balance, so he has to take advantage of other things.

46. **George Best:** a great player, but crazier than me.

47. **Ciro Ferrara:** I told him once that he was the best defender in the world. I don't know if that's true, but I love him so much that's how I felt. He was the best friend Napoli gave me.

48. **Osvaldo Ardiles:** another one of the guys I love to listen to, like Valdano. He always worried more about the team than about himself. A phenomenon.

49. **Diego Simeone:** he ran for me at Sevilla. When we were together in the national squad he was willing to die for

the jersey just like me. We were friends and then ... I don't know what happened to him then. I get the impression Passarella brainwashed him, but the truth is he never called me again. Maybe he got scared, I don't know.

50. **Davor Suker:** a real character, he always fooled you. It always looked like he'd played better than he actually did.

51. **Fernando Redondo:** we're very different off the pitch, but at USA '94 we understood each other perfectly. I gave those long legs of his some room and he knew that I'd always return the ball straight to him; we were always looking for each other. He's got a lot of personality, even though I don't like many of the decisions he makes.

52. **Gianfranco Zola:** he was my successor at Napoli. He paid really close attention to the things I did during training sessions ... and some of it stayed with him. Also, a great guy.

53. **Kevin Keegan:** he was my idol for a long time. I loved to watch him play. He was short and stocky like me. He orchestrated matches on his own.

54. **Iván Zamorano:** they were always bringing players to replace him in each and every club he's played for and the Chilean fucked them all over, scoring one goal after another. He deserves it. He's one of the best guys in football.

55. **Carlos Valderrama:** he showed all Colombians how to play football. He reminds me of Bochini. He could still be playing at forty, even at fifty, because he doesn't need to run in order to play.

56. and 57. **Guillermo and Gustavo Barros Schelotto:** Guille is a real footballer. He has that cunning so characteristic of Argentinian football. When everyone else gets

nervous, he remains unfazed. Gustavo's also got something about him: he pushes forward. I always liked him. And I loved it when they played together.

58. **Hugo Orlando Gatti:** El Loco called me fatso once, and I replied by putting four goals past him. But later he turned out to be a great guy, always by my side. He had his style, he's done amazing things, but as a goalie I'd rather have Fillol on my team any time.

59. **Carlos Aguilera:** one of the greats in every sense! He left his mark at the clubs where he played in Italy . . . and his goals. People can't even begin to imagine what his game was like.

60. **Karl-Heinz Rummenigge:** German, German in every sense of the word. If you wanted to beat him you had to kill him.

61. **Obdulio Varela:** I didn't see him play of course, but he said a wonderful thing that helped me throughout my career. Before playing the 1950 final against Brazil in the Maracaná, he said, 'We will have accomplished something only if we become champions.' Give me team-mates like that Uruguayan.

62. **Eric Cantona:** a partner, a friend. Also, more importantly, crazy and a rebel just like me. They suspended him for being honest. And his game wreaked havoc. Ask the Manchester fans: they always chose him as number one.

63. **Raúl:** has class. Valdano gave him his first game as a young kid and he carried the whole team – Real Madrid, no less – on his shoulders.

64. **Gaetano Scirea:** a gentleman and a great rival. His death made me very sad, very sad.

65. **Ronald Koeman:** a good, good player. But he made a mistake with me: he treated me badly after a Footballers' Union meeting in Barcelona, but he didn't dare say it to my face.

66. **Franz Beckenbauer:** I met him when I was a kid – I was preparing for the '79 Youth World Cup – and he was already huge, playing for Cosmos. I was always impressed by his elegance playing football.

67. **Socrates:** aside from being a different kind of footballer, he also fought for players' rights, like me. Even though FIFA wouldn't let him, he wore headbands in protest.

68. **Ramón Ángel Díaz:** he ended up scoring a lot of goals, but he should admit that I taught him how to finish in '79. Before that, it seemed like he had to make a hole in the goalie's chest to get the ball in the net.

69. **Ricardo Daniel Bertoni:** no one in the history of football has ever done anything like the one-twos I saw him play with Bochini. He was my team-mate during those first years at Napoli, when we were fighting relegation, and he always scored important goals.

70. **Miguel Ángel Brindisi:** he was a great partner of mine at Boca in '81, when he understood that he didn't have to score all the goals himself ... I don't know, I guess he felt the pressure because he had scored so many from the word go. He had incredible vision and played like he was strolling.

71. **Bernd Schuster:** they tried to pass the German off as mad to kick him out of football. He was crazy, just like me: he was my partner in the struggle against Núñez and an extraordinary player all over the pitch.

72. **Jorge Luis Burruchaga:** and to think they questioned my judgment! Burru ended up being the best example of a modern footballer. People called him my lieutenant in Mexico '86. They were right. He helped me a lot. He took the weight off my shoulders.

73. **Sergio Daniel Batista:** first and foremost, a friend. On the pitch he had wonderful reach: he was like an octopus, it was as if he sucked his opponents in and they handed

him the ball. I wanted to take him to Napoli, but Ferlaino bought Alemão instead. He would have done well, really well, in Italian football.

74. **Martín Palermo:** I'll stick by him to the death. I think his injury hurt me more than him, when he had already been sold to Italian football. I liked him when everyone was badmouthing him, I made Boca buy him.

75. **Paul Breitner:** he was an idol to me. He invited me to play in his testimonial, the earth shattered and it was him who provoked, without meaning to, my first big fight with Núñez in Barcelona. The Barça President couldn't understand that sharing the pitch with the German would be a dream come true for me. It was difficult to tell what position he played, he was everywhere.

76. **El Lobo Carrasco:** he was knowledgeable with the ball. He was one of the people who helped me the most when I got to Barcelona.

77. **Marcelo Trobbiani:** ball skills, close control, and a marker too. A great team-mate as well, one of those who knew how to support you from the sidelines. He proved that to me when we won the cup at Boca in '81 and again at Mexico '86.

78. **Pedro Pablo Pasculli:** a brother on the pitch, a brilliant partner. People questioned him but he always found a way to score important goals, in the qualifiers for Mexico '86 and then in the World Cup itself too, against Uruguay.

79. **Massimo Mauro:** an Italian-style Valdano. Less powerful on the pitch, but with the same intelligence.

80. **Jürgen Klinsmann:** a different sort of German. Tall and blond, yeah, but he moved like a ballet dancer. When I saw him in Munich for Matthäus's testimonial, I couldn't believe it. He's thinner than he used to be!

81. **Hector Enrique:** he was crucial in the World Champion

team in '86. He was the balance. The bastard says he made me that goal against the English with his pass! A wonderful player.

82. **Alberto César Tarantini:** much more than just a left back. He oozed desire, tremendous will and guts.

83. **Roberto Ayala:** he makes too many mistakes to be the captain of the Argentine national team. Sometimes, his 'Passarellism' prevents him from seeing things. He took the cat's milk when he said the two captains he looked to, the ones he admired wearing the armband, were Passarella and Ruggeri.

84. **Américo Gallego:** he invented a position: the midfield stopper. The ball always seemed to be attracted to him. For me he was a great team-mate at the beginning, I always felt him close, supporting me. He came to my daughters' christenings. I haven't forgotten that, even if my fight with Passarella has distanced us. He was an unconditional friend.

85. **Oreste Omar Corbatta:** I would have liked to see him play. And have a chat with him, knock back some wine. I imagine him as our Garrincha. No mean feat.

86. **Roberto Perfumo:** he was the one who gave authority to the Argentinian defense. El Flaco Menotti would talk to me about Federico Sacchi, but I never saw Sacchi play. I was, however, lucky enough to see Roberto's marking; he was the truly great captain, never mind about Passarella. That's why I say: if you want to talk about captains, he's the second best.

87. **Alberto José Márcico:** a sweet little rascal who played in Caballito, La Bombonera or France as if he was just kicking about in the potrero. Unfortunately, he had to leave Boca because my arrival restricted his chances to play.

88. **Carlos Bianchi:** as a goalscorer he was amazing. I got

to play against him in '81. We drew 1–1 at the Bombonera; we scored one each. Then ... some say he takes the cat's milk, others that he's a terrific bloke, but I don't want to go on what other people say. I'd prefer to get to know him myself, and I shake his hand for what he's done with Boca as manager.

89. **Falçao:** a leader. If you see him off the pitch he looks like a doctor, but when he put his shorts on he knew exactly what to do with the ball. He made Roma champions, no mean feat.

90. **Francisco Varallo:** I envy the record he holds: the greatest goalscorer in Boca's history. I wish I'd played longer just to challenge that. I read some things he said and loved two of them: one was that he said he resembled Batistuta, and the other was he wasn't one of those people who goes around saying the past was always better.

91. **Juan Simón:** perfect timing, ideal for playing *líbero*. He was a monster in Japan '79.

92. **Julio Olarticoechea:** you could chuck any jersey at El Vasquito and he would play well in every position.

93. **Ricardo Giusti:** I'll never forget his face when he got booked in the semi-final against Italy in '90. He realised he was going to miss the final, which was to be the last of his career. A guy who loved the Argentina jersey. Really loved it.

94. **Peter Shilton:** the thermos-head got cross because of my hand-goal. What about the other one, Shilton, didn't you see that one? He didn't invite me to his testimonial ... oh, my heart bleeds! How many people go to a goalkeeper's testimonial anyway? A goalkeeper's!

95. **George Weah:** that guy is pure power. And a real fighter off the pitch, too. He was one of the first to add his voice to my Footballers' Union and he's always fighting for his country, for Liberia.

96. **Juan Alberto Barbas:** the dreams we shared in Japan! We shared a room during the Youth World Cup. And we were promoted together to Menotti's first team. A great guy and a player who read the game very well. He had to fight against the fact that he was Menotti's favourite, he got slagged off a lot. But when he played in Europe, in Spain and Italy, he showed his worth. An old-fashioned number 8.

97. **Thomas Brolin:** a Swede with South American skill. Pity he got injured: he couldn't give everything he had in him.

98. **Leandro Romagnoli:** I love that little one. He lacks speed, physique, muscles, everything. But he makes up for it with his smart dribbling. The rest you find at the gym.

99. **Nakata:** if all the Japanese start playing like him, the rest of the world have had it. He knows how to kick a ball, how to dribble . . . Luckily, the Japanese are busy doing other things, for now.

100. **David Beckham:** another one too pretty to go out on the pitch. Although he worries too much about his Spice Girl, now and again he finds the time to play and he can play well, really well – he's got a great touch. He won everything with Manchester United. And he had to eat the hen that El Cholo Simeone sold him in France '98. But he paid us back.

But of course, my life isn't just football; never has been. I've always been fascinated by characters, by the big players, and often, on account of being Maradona, I've had the chance to meet them. That's how I was able to bring Ricky Martin round, for my daughters, for a barbecue and a bit of singing, if he fancied it. Sometimes, also on account of being Maradona, my idols couldn't believe that I admired them . . . you get all sorts in that group.

For example, I used to love watching Michael Jordan, Sergei

Bubka, Carl Lewis, and also all the Johnsons: Magic, Ben, Michael.

I loved Michael Jordan's joy when he played, the happiness with which he celebrated each and every point. He's the only star I would give anything to have my picture taken with. That would be my dream, to give him a hug. I say he's the only one because I've already got my picture with El Comandante, with Fidel Castro. I follow the NBA on TV and I'm also fascinated by the twin towers of San Antonio Spurs, Tim Duncan and David Robinson, or that monster Shaquille O'Neal.

Once I was watching TV and I almost died: Shaquille was walking around a corridor inside the stadium and someone threw a football at him. He passed it from foot to foot, with those boats he wears for shoes, tried to play keepy-uppy and looked at the camera and said: '*Diegou Maradouna*'. I nearly died! I was frozen in front of the TV. I love Shaquille!

In Formula 1 the person I liked the most was Ayrton Senna. If I ever have a son he will be called Ayrton, as a homage to him. I promised him that at his graveside, when I visited it in Sao Paolo. He was the greatest because he never held back: in the rain, when everyone else lifted their foot off, he would accelerate to the full. You need balls to do that.

Another thing: the best boxer I ever saw in my life was Sugar Ray Leonard. My old man, who knows a thing or two about boxing, says Ali was the best, but I never saw him. For a long time now boxing has been part of my training: my old man and my uncle Cirilo taught me a lot about boxing. And it's been handy, you know? These legs I have I owe to that . . . and the forbidden hand too. I love it, I love boxing. The only time I travelled to Vegas I saw Sugar Ray beat Tommy Hearns and it was some fight: it left its mark on me for ever. But no one compares to Carlos Monzón: if I hadn't been around, if I hadn't been awarded it, the trophy for the sportsman of the century would have gone to him, I'm sure. To Carlos Monzón.

And I say this because I'm very familiar with the debate that took place about that. Some thought the award should have gone to Juan Manuel Fangio and not to me. I respect the fact that in Italy people talk about Fandjio, as they pronounce it, but I have no fucking respect for those who go out on a limb to defend him and never saw a single race. They have no idea who he beat even. Fangio also took the cat's milk alright? Otherwise why didn't they name the Buenos Aires autodrome after him? Has anyone complained about that? No, nobody said a word. So, I repeat, if they wanted to give the sports personality of the century award to a dead man, they should have handed the award to Monzón's daughter! Fortunately they chose someone alive, very alive. Me.

I've also had the opportunity to meet many celebrities, many important people, who are not from the world of sport. Of all of them, I choose one. The one who most impressed me, and I can't see anyone surpassing him, is without doubt Fidel Castro. Every time I see him I still get nervous, I'm moved, emotional. I remember our first meeting very well: it was Tuesday 28 July 1987, nearly midnight. El Comandante greeted us in his own office, in front of the Plaza de la Revolución. I was so nervous I couldn't speak. Thank goodness Claudia, with Dalmita a babe in arms, my old girl, and Fernando Signorini were with me. And we started chatting about any old thing, like did we need somewhere for Dalma to cat. I said: 'No, don't worry, Comandante, she's self-sufficient.' She was sucking away at the breast. We understood each other immediately. He said: 'Tell me, does it hurt when you kick or head the ball?'

'No.'

'But, *coño*, why did it hurt me so much when I played as a boy?'

'Because back then they used a different kind of ball, much heavier.'

'Ah. And tell me, what does a goalkeeper have to do to save a penalty?'

'He must stand in the centre of the goal and try to guess which way the other guy's going to shoot.'

'But that's difficult, comrade.'

'Very difficult. That's why we say a penalty is a goal.'

'Ah. And tell me, how do you take penalties?'

'I take a two-metre run-up and I only look up when I step down on my right foot and have my left ready to shoot. That's when I choose my corner.'

'But what are you saying? You shoot without looking at the ball?'

'Yes.'

'Comrade, what the human mind can do has no limit. I always ask myself how far it will go together with the body. That's one of the great challenges of sport. It's incredible. And tell me, is it true you rarely miss a penalty?'

'I've missed so many.'

At one point he got up, enormous as he is, excused himself and disappeared into the kitchen. He returned with some spectacular oysters. I knocked back five and he started talking about cookery with La Tota. They even exchanged recipes ... We returned to football and he surprised me: he told me when he played he was a right wing! So I teased him: 'Whaaaat!? You, on the right? You should have been a left wing!'

He asked me if I might one day be able to do something for Cuban football and I answered yes, it could grow, the Cubans have everything necessary. 'The only thing that might complicate matters is the heat, but otherwise you have everything: ability, flexibility, rhythm, feel, physical strength and desire.'

When we were leaving I looked up at his beret, raised my eyebrows, and he immediately knew what I meant, he practically didn't need to hear me say it.

'Comandante, excuse me, will you give it to me?'

He took it off and was going to put it on my head but stopped short.

'Wait, let me sign it first, otherwise it could be anybody's.'

It couldn't have been anybody's! It was El Comandante's beret.

I put it on, and he said goodbye to all my family, one by one, we hugged each other and I left. I felt like I'd been talking to an encyclopaedia. Seeing him was like touching the sky with my hands. He's a beast who knows about everything and his presence allows you to understand, just by looking at him, how he did what he did with ten soldiers and three rifles ... I've been saying this since that day: one can disagree with him but please, let the man work in peace! I'd like to see Cuba without the sanctions, see what happens then.

We met again in Christmas '94. This time I wandered into the Consejo de Estado, the government offices, as if it was my home, he was waiting for me. Gianinnita was with us by now. It was a really lovely meeting, very intimate. He gave me another beret but this time I gave him an Argentina shirt with the number 10 on the back. A few months later I got a letter at home, on Cuban Government headed paper. It was Fidel, asking permission, in his own handwriting, to put my strip in the Cuban museum of sport. A phenomenon!

And, well, what he's done for me during recent times is indescribable. I like to say that for this whole being alive thing I can only thank the two Beards: God and Fidel.

If El Comandante was the one who impressed me the most, Prince Alberto of Monaco was the one who impressed me the least. In Monte Carlo, the son of a bitch made me pay the bill for a meal to which he had invited us. He left before us, saying he had to get up early. When Cóppola asked for the bill, it came to five grand! I'd gone to Monaco hoping to meet Princess Stephanie or Caroline and I had to pay a fortune for meeting the boy Alberto.

Dr Carlos Menem, while he was President, helped me a lot in exchange for nothing, for nothing. I approached him when his son's tragedy happened.* I thought I could give him something. I don't know what, support. When the Peronists lost to

* President Menem's son Carlos was killed in a helicopter crash on 15th March 1995.

De La Rúa, in '99, I went to visit him, because I felt I should
be close to him during the bad times too and show everyone
that I wasn't just interested in his power. I went to see him
when he wasn't up to running a victory lap ... the victory lap
is run by the idiots who jump on the bandwagon of the winners.
I'm not one of those.

And obviously I would have loved to meet Che Guevara. I
don't think anybody can be surprised by this. Dear old Ernesto
Che Guevara de la Serna, to give him his full name. I carry him
on my arm – I have a tattoo which is a work of art – but in
truth I carry him in my heart. I fell in love with him in Italy,
yes in Italy. I think the fact that it didn't start in Argentina is
significant, because when I was in Argentina El Che to me was
the same as for most of my fellow countrymen – an assassin, a
terrorist, a baddie, a revolutionary who put bombs in schools.
That was the version of history I'd been taught. But when I got
to Italy, to the world's leader in *scioperi*, strikes, powerful
workers, I started to see that in every one of their gatherings
and demonstrations they rolled out a flag with a picture of this
man, his face in black over a red background ... and I started
to read about him. And I started to ask myself: why don't we
speak the truth about Che Guevara in Argentina? Why don't
we reclaim his remains? And because I couldn't find any answers
I decided to pay tribute to him my own way. And I got the
tattoo, just below my shoulder, so I would have him with me
for ever. I learnt to love him, I read about his story: I think I
know the truth about him. About other figures from Argentinian
history, with all due respect, I couldn't say the same.

I would love it if kids were taught true history at school but
I would be satisfied if, in the schools of my country, mentioning
the name Che Guevara wasn't tantamount to swearing.

I am so grateful to football for everything it gave me, and to
God, too, because this whole extraordinary thing happened on
account of him: the possibility of helping my family, of sharing

my life with incredible team-mates and of meeting people that I would never in a million years have imagined I would ever meet.

How could I have ever imagined it in my tiny leaky room in Fiorito?

I Am El Diego

A Message

Always, always, my pride and joy has been playing for the national team. Always, no matter how many millions of dollars I was paid at whatever club. Nothing compared to it, nothing. Because the value of the national squad can't be measured in money, it can only be measured in glory. And I would love it if today's kids, and tomorrow's kids, could get this into their heads: there's a special quality, a mystique, to the Argentinian footballer and the blue and white jersey; we can't afford to lose that.

Although unfortunately we are losing it. And just as I can feel hurt, I'm sure the same could be said for all the Ruggeris, the Pumpidos, the Olarticoecheas, the Giustis, the Goycocheas. In the past, we would meet up to fight for the national squad, and if one of us said he was injured or something we would call him and say: 'Come anyway, come anyway!' I'm not saying we were or are an example: we were just aware that the squad needed us. There's no room for tiredness, there is no room for tiredness! You're representing your country, that's the biggest pride you can have! That's what we said: 'You've pulled a muscle? Come anyway!' We'd call whoever it was, and we'd make him come along anyway, even if he wasn't playing.

That's why I loved being captain. Because it gave me the power to confront those who wanted to impose things on us, things that went against footballers. And I don't think there is a single player, team-mate of mine, who could say to me: *You didn't do right by me, you didn't defend me well.* And I confronted Grondona, Blatter, Havelange, Macri . . . maybe with a footballing vocabulary rather than a political one, and that cost me a lot of things. But the result was worth it, it was worth it. I think if I stood on the Eiffel Tower today and shouted out I would get all the players in the world around me. Because Cantona said it to me, Weah said it to me, Stoichkov said it to me: 'We are members of the World Footballers' Association and you are the president.' I'm proud of that.

To me it represents twenty-five years of struggle, and not just on the pitch: twenty-five years of thinking that the football player is the most important thing in this business, by a long way. And this is a great truth that nobody can refute: us players make the managers, make the club directors.

And for saying things like this, the powers-that-be never forgave me. What they never managed to do was change my life. I may have done it right or I may have done it wrong, but I did it. I am not just a figure on Menotti's tactical drawings, or Bilardo's. I wasn't sketched out by Havelange, I wasn't sketched out by Blatter, I wasn't sketched out by Menem, I wasn't sketched out by any other politician. Nobody gave me the money as a gift, I earned it, running after the ball on the pitch. A lot, too much? They gave it to me for a reason. The powers-that-be made a lot more thanks to me. That's why they depend on us: if us footballers really united, we would kill!

Football directors don't know anything about the game and they have displaced us players from a very important position. They're well advised, they've studied, and they get the best sponsors. They think more about Coca-Cola and Hyundai than about the true heroes. I had to suffer that when I started the Footballers' Union. The World Cups make a huge amount of money and those of us who make the show get a few dog ends, 1 per cent. This is a factory which is doing better all the time, because its workers will put up with anything.

Because today, footballers make a lot of money without much effort. They don't care as much. They make twenty million dollars for nothing. Christian Vieri, for example, hops from one team to another for more and more millions, and he doesn't have a single title to celebrate. So, of course, what are they going to think about their national squads for? Why? They don't need to . . . and there's nobody going up to them and saying: *Look, kid, if you don't play for your country and then you don't do well for your club, you become a disaster, you'll be worth shit.*

It all changed when us oldies left. It wasn't as if we were more intelligent or anything like that, but we did understand that we had to represent the people. That meant we, the representatives, went out to play thinking about our old man, our old girl, our mates, the workers . . . everyone. And we enjoyed it as much as they did when we heard they were celebrating our triumphs at the Obelisco.*

Today, many matches are decided by men behind desks. And that works against the players. I paid a very high price for defending them, for demanding that matches not be played at lunchtime in Mexico, and for denouncing corruption, as in '90, where the final had to be Germany–Italy. I don't have any problem with continuing to pay that price. United, players would be able to fight against the bad things in football. For example, the matches ruined by bad refereeing: in 1990 they wouldn't stop going on about Fair Play, Fair Play, and in the first match Cameroon kicked the shit out of us. And then in the final came Codesal, the referee . . . As far as I was concerned, it was never a penalty.

And in Argentina, arrogance killed refereeing. Arrogance! In '95 Javier Castrilli sent me off when all I'd done was go up to him to say: 'Respect the people!' And that's what they're all like, they never let you talk. They excuse themselves with all

* The Obelisco is one of Buenos Aires' main landmarks, a rough equivalent of Trafalgar Square.

that about not earning what they should. Why don't they become professionals for real, then! And stop allowing themselves to be influenced, even by the stars. But don't go against the people, against the show. Because people go to watch Maradona, to watch Francescoli, to watch Gallardo, and if they send them off, that goes against the people. But they become famous and then they work on TV. Thanks to whom? Thanks to the players, of course.

I regret not having played more in Argentina. I'm sorry my country was unable to keep me so I could have been able to break records on my soil, play more matches with my national squad instead of listening to them over the phone from Italy. I don't think it's my fault. I had to go and earn money abroad.

From Italy I observed a very special phenomenon: in Argentina, the great coaches of the youth teams have always been great players from the past. Players like Pedernera, Grillo, Griffa, Gandulla, Pando, Sacchi. In my humble opinion, to great masters, great pupils. Well, that didn't happen in Italy. Ex-champions became senators, *onorevoles* (Italian members of parliament), football directors, TV and radio journalists, presidential advisers. But putting the jersey on and getting dirty in the mud like Adolfo Perdernera did until he was eighty years old? No way. Well, my fear is that in these times we live in we've lost that mystique.

It pisses me off that there are still footballers who don't dare denounce, for example, managers who ask them for money to include them in the starting line-up. That's corruption. As much corruption as when a national squad manager includes a player in the team, even if he's injured, because he wants to sell him to Europe. And I know that's happened too, sadly.

If I was to live again I would ask God to give me the same – because he gave me too much, really – and also the possibility of making every move, scoring every goal that the Neapolitans enjoyed so much, but I would score them in my country, live, for all the Argentinian people.

I'm proud of having always been faithful to my convictions, my virtues and my defects. I can look everybody in the face. I haven't fucked anyone over except myself. I don't owe anybody anything except my family. I fight for my life, every day, and I have my folks by my side, friends by my side, I have my wife, unconditional love, I have two daughters who are more amazing than I could ever have dreamt and I have, on top of all that, the respect of the country I love ... Yes, in spite of everything, I have and enjoy the respect of the Argentinian people.

I've tried to be as honest as possible about everything. I've told things, probably forgotten many others, but there is only one message: I will continue to speak the truth until the end. I will not compromise, because I can't stand to, I can't stand injustice.

To me it felt like I, El Diego, had been taken out of Villa Fiorito and given a kick in the arse that landed me on top of the world, like I was in Paris, on top of the Eiffel Tower. But I was still wearing the same pair of trousers as always, my only ones, the ones I wore in winter and in summer, that corduroy pair. That's where I landed and they asked me, they demanded of me, to say what I had to say, to behave like I had to behave, to do as they wanted me to do.

And I did.

I ... I did what I could. I don't think I did so badly.

I know I'm not one to change the world but I'm not going to let anybody into my world to tell me what to do. To dictate how my match is going to go, to dictate my life. Nobody will ever make me believe that my mistakes with drugs or in business have changed my feelings. Nothing. I am the same as always. I'm me, Maradona. I am El Diego.

Titles, Prizes and Awards

The most important ones, the prizes life gave me:
Dalma, Gianinna, Claudia and Guillermo

1978

Top goal scorer of the Metropolitano Championship, with Argentinos Juniors. Scored 22 goals.

1979

World Champion with Argentina Youth National Squad, in the Youth World Cup, Japan 1979.

Golden Ball for Footballer of the Year, awarded by the AFA's Centre of Accredited Journalists (Centro de Periodistas Acreditados de la AFA [CEPA]).

Top goal scorer of the Metropolitano Championship, with Argentinos Juniors. Scored 14 goals.

Silver Olimpia, best Argentinian footballer, Sports Journalists' Circle (Círculo de Periodistas Deportivos [CPD]).

Gold Olimpia, best Argentinian sportsman, Sports Journalists' Circle (CPD).

Best footballer in the Americas, according to a poll held by *El Mundo* newspaper, Caracas, Venezuela.

1980

Golden Ball for Footballer of the Year, awarded by the AFA's Centre of Accredited Journalists (CEPA).

Top goal scorer of the Metropolitano Championship, with Argentinos Juniors. Scored 25 goals.

Top goal scorer of the Nacional Championship, with Argentinos Juniors. Scored 18 goals.

Silver Olimpia, best Argentinian footballer, Sports Journalists' Circle (CPD).

Best footballer in the Americas, according to a poll held by *El Mundo* newspaper, Caracas, Venezuela.

1981

Champion, Metropolitano, with Boca Juniors.

Silver Olimpia, best Argentinian footballer, Sports Journalists' Circle (CPD).

Golden Ball for Footballer of the Year, awarded by the AFA's Centre of Accredited Journalists (CEPA).

1986

World Champion, with Argentina National Squad, Mexico '86 World Cup.

Golden Ball, best footballer of the Mexico '86 World Cup, awarded by FIFA.

Golden Ball, European Footballer of the Year, awarded by *France Football* magazine.

Silver Olimpia, best Argentinian footballer, Sports Journalists' Circle (CPD).

Gold Olimpia, best Argentinian sportsman, Sports Journalists' Circle (CPD).

Best footballer in the Americas, according to a poll held by *El Mundo* newspaper, Caracas, Venezuela.

Golden Onze, best footballer in the world, according to French magazine *Onze*.

1987

Champion, Italy's Serie A *scudetto* '86/'87, with Napoli.

Top goal scorer in Serie A, with Napoli. Scored 15 goals.

Winner of the Copa Italia, with Napoli.

Golden Onze, best footballer in the world, according to French magazine *Onze*.

1988

Top goal scorer in the Copa Italia, with Napoli. Scored 6 goals.

Winner UEFA Cup '87/'88, with Napoli.

1989

Best footballer in the Americas, according to a poll held by *El Mundo* newspaper, Caracas, Venezuela.

1990

Champion, Serie A *scudetto* '89/'90, with Napoli.

Finalist with Argentina National Squad, Italia '90 World Cup.

Best footballer in the Americas, according to a poll held by *El Mundo* newspaper, Caracas, Venezuela.

1992

Best footballer in the Americas, according to a poll held by *El Mundo* newspaper, Caracas, Venezuela.

1993

Winner, Artemio Franchi Cup, with Argentina National Squad. In this clash between the European Champions and the Champions of America, Argentina beat Denmark on penalties.

1996

Special Balon D'Or for lifetime achievement, awarded by *France Football*.

1999

Platinum Olimpia, best Argentinian sportsman of the twentieth century, awarded by the Sports Journalists' Circle (CPD).

Index